W9-BVF-013

Strategic Customer Service

Strategic Customer Service

Managing the Customer Experience to Increase Positive Word of Mouth, Build Loyalty, and Maximize Profits

John A. Goodman

AMACOM
American Management Association
New York • Atlanta • Brussels • Chicago • Mexico City • San Francisco
Shanghai • Tokyo • Toronto • Washington, D.C.

*Special discounts on bulk quantities of AMACOM books are available to corporations, professional associations, and other organizations. For details, contact Special Sales Department, AMACOM, a division of American Management Association, 1601 Broadway, New York, NY 10019.
Tel: 212-903-8316. Fax: 212-903-8083.
E-mail: specialsls@amanet.org
Website: www.amacombooks.org/go/specialsales
To view all AMACOM titles go to: www.amacombooks.org*

Library of Congress Cataloging-in-Publication Data

Goodman, John A.
Strategic customer service : managing the customer experience to increase positive word of mouth, build loyalty, and maximize profits / John A. Goodman.—1st ed.
p. cm.
Includes index.
ISBN-13: 978-0-8144-1333-3
ISBN-10: 0-8144-1333-1
1. Customer services. 2. Customer relations—Management. I. Title.
HF5415.5.G672 2009
658.8'12—dc22

2008055729

Printing number

10 9 8 7 6 5

Contents

PART 3: RESPONDING TO CUSTOMERS' QUESTIONS AND PROBLEMS

Foreword

IN THE INTEREST of full disclosure, you should know that John's colleagues do not like this book. Those of us working at TARP—the company John founded over 35 years ago—do not like seeing such wisdom (aka "intellectual property") shared with everyone. The principles, ideas, and advice shared in ***Strategic Customer Service*** are valuable and actionable. This book provides guidance from the nation's leading authority on measuring and improving the customer experience. No one knows more about this subject than John. And now he shares it directly with you for the price of this book. That's why we don't like it.

On the other hand, we are career professionals committed to helping companies improve their customer service. Like doctors, we cannot hoard what we know will cure various ills. In fact, we have an obligation to celebrate this book. We are proud of the material and the author. We know the content will help business leaders see the power of strategic customer service. We know the case studies and proven approaches will help you realize the bottom line impact of taking care of the customer. Moreover, publishing the thinking that made TARP the leading expert in this field is inspiring. This is what we do—and that's why we actually do like this book.

There has never been a better time for John's work. As I write this the worldwide economy plunges into the most perilous period in our lifetime. The level of uncertainty is matched only by the stress everyone feels as consumers, citizens, and managers. So much is unknown about the road ahead—and people are entering a time of hair trigger sensitivity to how they are being treated. Woe to any service that takes even one interaction for granted. Woe to any leader who fails to see the opportunities and risks in the customer experience. Following the guiding principles in this book will strengthen any firm during a tough period—providing the comfort and confidence to do the right thing. This book directly challenges small-minded managers who think it is wise to reduce expenses by under-serving customers. ***Strategic Customer Service*** is a port in this economic storm—an intellectual reminder that nothing in one's bag of tricks is more powerful than a positive customer experience.

Since I first met John Goodman in the 1980s, I have admired his work and thought leadership. John is a very popular speaker and sought after consultant. Since founding TARP Worldwide in 1971, John has helped improve the customer service practices of hundreds of companies—including many widely respected firms like GE, USAA, Chick-fil-A, American Express, Marriott, Harley Davidson, and Neiman Marcus. John has "seen it all" as they say and some of his best experiences and lessons are shared in these pages. It is an honor to introduce this book—to tell you that I am confident you will be totally satisfied by the unique blend of experience, analysis, and common sense in John Goodman's *Strategic Customer Service*.

Dennis E. Gonier, CEO, TARP Worldwide

Strategic Customer Service

INTRODUCTION

Why *Strategic* Customer Service?

EVERY ORGANIZATION'S SUCCESS depends on its keeping customers satisfied with the goods or services that it offers, yet most executives tend to view the customer service function of their business as little more than a necessary nuisance. That strikes me as paradoxical. Companies that spare no expense to build their brands, improve their operations, and leverage their technologies often skimp on investments that preserve and strengthen this final, vital link in their revenue chain. Indeed, leaving aside the investment aspect, many of these same companies simply don't have a customer service strategy to manage the end-to-end customer experience, from sales to billing.

That is why I have aimed this book at all senior management, with an emphasis on finance and aspiring chief customer officers. The book will not focus on answering the phone, but rather on the revenue and word-of-mouth implications of having or not having a strategic approach for all customer touches and managing an end-to-end experience.

As we all know from being customers ourselves, poor service can undermine all of a company's efforts to retain and expand its customer base. As customers, we know how we respond to poor service: We go elsewhere, and we often tell our friends and colleagues to do the same. But as businesspeople, we undergo a kind of amnesia that prevents us from seeing how that same mechanism applies to *our* customers. Not long ago, I was speaking with the CFO of a leading electronics firm who suffered from this amnesia. As an engineer, he felt that the superiority of his company's electronic products ensured their superior market position. I then asked him what brand of car he drove and how he liked the dealership. He scowled and said, "I hate them! They're just terrible." When I pointed out, "You have customers who feel the same about your company," he immediately saw my point.

Some executive teams, blessed with extraordinary empathy or insight (or perhaps competitiveness), do understand the role of customer service in the growth of their revenue, profits, and business. My work with organizations that consistently excel at this responsibility has led me to conclude that they have one thing in common: a strategic view of, and approach to, customer service.

A strategic view perceives customer service as vital to the end-to-end customer experience, and thus to the customer relationship. This view also considers customer service to be a full-fledged member of the marketing-sales-service triumvirate. Such a view starts with setting expectations, moves on to selling and delivering the product in ways that suit the customer, and extends through superb support and clear, accurate billing. A strategic approach also recognizes that the service function produces a wellspring of data on customer attitudes, needs, and behavior. These data, when combined with available operational and survey data, can be used as input in virtually every effort to shape the customer experience, from product development to marketing and sales messages, and from handling of customer complaints to the overall management of the entire customer relationship. In these ways, customer service acts as a strategic catalyst for every organizational function and process that touches the customer.

Why a strategic catalyst?

Strategic customer service stands at the point where all organizational strategies come to fruition in a great customer experience—or do not. Product development, operations, marketing, sales, finance, accounting, human resources, and risk management all affect the customer in myriad ways, for better or worse. But when something goes wrong, customers don't call the director of product development, the manager of operations, or the vice president of marketing (and they probably shouldn't be calling salespeople—about which more in Chapter 3). They call customer service. When they do, customer service must preserve the relationship, gather information, and improve the process, wherever the problem originated.

As a catalyst, strategic customer service can, like any catalyst, transform the entities and functions it touches, making the organization more proactive, accelerating its responsiveness, and boosting its effectiveness. Service can help marketing, for instance, move from sales messaging to capitalizing on customer intelligence and improving products and services. For example, Allstate is now contacting the parents of young motorists as they turn 16, before they pass their driver's tests. The company suggests a parent-teen contract, explains how the impending rate increase will be calculated, and provides guidance on coaching new drivers (including an extremely popular Web video whose music has moved into the mainstream). This program results in calmer parents who feel more in control and who exhibit significantly greater loyalty to Allstate. Likewise, strategic customer service can accelerate product development and uncover new distribution channels. It can relieve salespeople and channel partners of troubleshooting duties so that they can focus on selling. It can transform finance from a countinghouse into a funding source that is supportive of new processes and services that increase customer retention, positive word of mouth, and market share.

Moreover, strategic customer service is applicable in any market, from consumer packaged goods and financial services to health care, from business-to-business environments such as chemicals and pharmaceuticals to government agencies and nonprofits. TARP has helped organizations in all of these arenas to benefit from a strategic approach to service, beyond the tactical service functions of responding to customer inquiries and problems.

BEYOND THE COMPLAINT DEPARTMENT

Customer service has come a long way from the days when "complaint departments" received letters from irate customers and decided whether to "make good" on some explicit or implied promise. Today's tactical service function is often outsourced, offshored, and global, supported by state-of-the-art technology, aligned with the brand strategy, and integrated with the customer experience. It is now a support, sales, and relationship management function. It's a means of tracking the value of every customer and, on that basis, satisfying customers, delighting them, explaining why you'll have to charge them more, or gently showing them the door. Service interactions are also the prime generator of the single most powerful marketing mechanism: positive word of mouth and word of mouse.[1] Companies with great word of mouth incur almost no marketing expense because they let their customers do their selling for them.

None of this happens by accident or only at the tactical level. It happens when senior management grasps the pivotal role of service in the customer relationship and recasts this outcast stepchild of marketing, sales, and operations as a guide, problem solver, communicator, reporter, and breadwinner. Often, the executive committee anoints one of its number as the chief customer experience officer. Where such a position doesn't exist, the head of customer service often performs that role.

The evolution begins with an examination of the current customer experience, all current customer service and customer-touching activities, and your current sources of information on those activities. Take market research. Recently a telecom executive told me, "We're spending $12 million a year on surveys, and we have almost no actionable information." Once the company recognized this, it used customer contact data to supplement the surveys and produced a real-time picture of the customer experience. This, along with data on product performance and problems and on customer attitudes and preferences, enabled the company to identify massive savings while improving the customer experience. Some companies know the value of customer contact data, yet even I was surprised to hear Powell Taylor, the General Electric executive who established the GE Answer Center, say, "The average GE customer service rep can provide the input of data equal to about 10,000 completed market research surveys, because that is how many customers they've talked with." That makes a strong case for compiling *and* analyzing data from customer service interactions. That's also why the GE Answer Center reports to the Appliance Division's senior management.

So, in both purpose and functionality, customer service has evolved far beyond the complaint departments of 30 or more years ago to become pivotal in building and sustaining customer relationships.

WHY BOTHER WITH STRATEGIC CUSTOMER SERVICE?

The payoff from a strategic approach to customer service is simple: more revenue, higher margins, lower costs, and positive word of mouth producing more customers at a lower marketing cost. An organization can establish and sustain a *long-term* market advantage in very few ways. Leadership via technological and product innovation is fleeting, as innovations can be copied, and the same is true of most other growth strategies. It's no coincidence that market leaders in their industries have typically committed themselves to strategic customer service, implicitly or explicitly. Companies like 3M, Allstate, American Express, Bath & Body Works, Chick-fil-A, Coca-Cola, FedEx, GE, Harley-Davidson, Hewlett-Packard, IBM, Johnson & Johnson, Marriott, Neiman Marcus, Panasonic, Procter & Gamble, Sears, Starbucks, and Toyota go beyond the intermittent efforts and lip service that characterize nonstrategic approaches. These companies know how much revenue can be lost as a result of a less than perfect customer experience and intend to retain as much of that money as possible. They invest in aligning all functions to support their brand promise and then reap substantial rewards, including:

- Happy customers who willingly pay premium prices or go out of their way to patronize the company.
- Solid information on which to base decisions that affect customers and provide greater value.
- More selling time—and less aggravation—for salespeople.
- Fewer problems because they fix root causes, educate customers, and set realistic expectations.
- Intense emotional bonds with customers that block competitors and boost brand loyalty. (Harley-Davidson customers sport tattoos of the company logo—now *that's* loyalty.)
- Lower employee turnover as a result of a sense of mission, belonging, excellence, teamwork, and job satisfaction.

- Positive word of mouth such that companies like Chick-fil-A, Cheesecake Factory, and USAA have their customers doing their selling for them.
- A sustainable market advantage because competitors cannot copy or adopt the management and cultural elements of strategic customer service. (American Express retains its "members" despite repeated competitive assaults.)

Companies that use strategic customer service can make rational financial decisions about where to invest in people, processes, and platforms. They can easily differentiate among things that are nice to have, squeaky wheels that may not deserve grease, and critical, often unstated needs. They proactively establish and fulfill customer expectations. They understand how a decrease in inventory can save money but also disappoint shoppers, leading them not to come back.

Do these organizations make mistakes? Of course. Even the best companies make mistakes and occasionally cause problems for customers that go way beyond inconvenience. Yet companies with a strategic approach respond to these errors differently from those without one. While I was editing this chapter at a Marriot Hotel restaurant, the waitress spilled water all over the manuscript. She and the manager took four separate actions to make things better, including ironing the pages. By the end I was feeling sorry they had gone to so much effort.

Great companies also identify the systemic points of pain that their customers experience in transactions, then do something to relieve that pain. Avis equipped its return-lot attendants with handheld computers to speed the rental return process after the company learned that waiting in lines at airport return stations was *the* major point of pain for customers. This action revolutionized the industry. But beware! The strategic response is not always to "fix" things in the usual sense of the term. You need to decide between overengineering the product so that the problem will never happen, on the one hand, and tolerating the occasional occurance (such as aircraft mechanical delays) on the other, warning the customer, letting the problem happen, and then implementing recovery. Which you select will depend upon which has the lower cost/benefit ratio. Sometimes you can just make the problem go away. When a leading auto company learned that customers found the wear-and-tear charge assessed when returning leased vehicles to be a huge, unpleasant surprise, the company factored an allowance for wear and tear into the lease payments, reducing or eliminating the surprise.

A strategic approach precludes knee-jerk reactions to customer complaints. Instead, it views each problem that customers present in a larger context. For instance, most companies prioritize problems for remediation on the basis of woefully unscientific criteria. They fix the problems that occur most frequently or those that come to the CEO's attention (when customers' screams reach the executive suite). However, a few simple calculations can often identify less frequent problems unknown to management that are cheaper—and more profitable—to fix. For instance, a TARP study conducted for Motorola found that not returning customers' phone calls reduces customer satisfaction by 20 to 30 percent. People seldom complain about unreturned phone calls, especially if they involve salespeople, whom customers don't want to get in trouble, but they damage satisfaction and can prompt customers to call another vendor.

So the reasons to focus on customer service are numerous and varied, with the result that virtually everyone in the organization has a stake in the function's performance.

EVERYONE HAS A STAKE IN SERVICE

When you accept the strategic importance of customer service, you realize that you have a stake in it regardless of your function in the organization. I don't mean this in some idealistic or remote sense. Rather, I mean that, regardless of where in the company you work—information technology, risk management, or human resources—as an executive, you can identify ways of directly improving your customers' experience and thus your organization's market position and future revenues. You can also help your organization avoid, rather than ignore, the blowback of additional costs resulting from hassles with customers.

Of course, the potential payoff is highest for managers and professionals in sales and marketing, particularly in certain industries. More than 50 percent of all new customers for investment, retail, and health-care products come from word-of-mouth referrals. For business-to-business companies, references and referrals are as important as, or even more important than, the sales rep's offering. Service is also critical for franchisees, distributors, and other channel partners. The stakes are also high for businesses that are out to deliver high value. Executives at John Deere, Lexus, and American Express have all said, "We don't want to have to compete on price," and they don't have to because of their service and their quality. More broadly, strategic customer service applies in every venue across all industries, and also in nonprofits and government agencies.[2] All ultimately depend on satisfied customers for their continued existence.

In addition, certain ongoing developments demand a strategic approach to customer service, including the following:

- The Internet now provides most of the information that salespeople used to supply, plus competitive data and user reviews; this has changed the mission of sales, marketing, and service in fundamental ways.
- Almost half of all customer complaints, questions, and comments are submitted on the Web or via e-mail, but many companies still focus on their toll-free numbers, to the neglect of their Web-based capabilities.
- Global markets and the outsourcing of service activities have created angst for customers and raised cultural, financial, and risk management issues for companies.
- The emerging middle classes in China, India, and elsewhere will demand customer experiences on a par with those delivered to their Western counterparts, driving large investments in service.
- Turnover and labor shortages in customer service continually increase the cost of delivering superior service and squeeze tight margins even tighter.
- Gains from increased productivity as a result of technology, outsourcing, and industry consolidation have largely been realized, leaving service, broadly defined, as one of the few remaining targets for cost saving and profit growth.

Most executives and managers care about their customers and aim to provide them with superior service, or at least the right level of service given economic realities. Yet most of them also hold outdated or erroneous views of customer service. Perhaps the most prevalent of these views is that customer service in all its forms—call centers, retail salespeople, field service personnel, and technology-based systems—is an organizational backwater and a cost center, rather than the ultimate word-of-mouth-management mechanism and *the* differentiator in today's marketplace.

This book presents a view of and an approach to customer service that can generate outsized returns and sustainable advantages for any company that depends on repeat customers, positive word of mouth, or both.

THE ORIGINS OF THIS BOOK

This book grew out of the work that TARP began in the early 1970s, after I founded the company in 1971 with two other entrepreneurs, Marc Grainer and Joe Falkson, in the basement of a building at Harvard Law School, and that has continued ever since. The firm's service work began in earnest with an original, landmark study of consumer complaint behavior and customer service for the White House Office of Consumer Affairs, under the sponsorship of Virginia Knauer and Esther Peterson, both Assistants to the President for Consumer Affairs. In the ensuing more than 30 years, TARP has studied, analyzed, and reported on customer behavior in every major industry and in nonprofit and government agencies in North America and, later, globally.

Starting in 1971, TARP has pioneered many concepts, principles, and practices that have become standard in customer service in an array of industries. It was the first organization to:

- Analyze the cost of keeping a current customer compared to that of winning a new one
- Recommend calculating the lifetime value of a customer and considering that value in decisions that affect loyalty and retention
- Quantify the positive impacts of customer education
- Recommend the concept of using toll-free numbers to make complaining easier and to manage customer complaints and feedback
- Develop the functional framework of today's customer relationship management systems

- Quantify word of mouth with Coca-Cola in 1980 and in 1998 coin the phrase "word of mouse" for online word-of-mouth complaints and referrals

Oh, and about our company name. We were originally called Citizen Research Assistance Programs. However, when we were hired for our first study for then Secretary of Health, Education, and Welfare, Elliott Richardson, it was politely pointed out to us that the federal government simply could not do business with an outfit whose name was C.R.A.P. So we changed the name to TARP, Technical Assistance Research Programs, and, more recently and officially, to TARP Worldwide.

THE STRUCTURE OF THIS BOOK

This book contains twelve chapters grouped into five parts, with the following titles and general content:

Part 1, "The Importance of Customer Service," describes strategic customer service and its behavioral context in detail and introduces the financial rationale for investments in improvements to your customer service.

Part 2, "Identifying Immediate Revenue and Profit Opportunities," reveals things you can do right now to enhance the basic customer experience and produce more useful data and tangible payoffs.

Part 3, "Responding to Customers' Questions and Problems," shows how you can create an efficient, cost-effective system for handling and, when appropriate, preventing unnecessary customer contacts.

Part 4, "Moving to the Next Level," reveals ways in which you can create an aggressive customer service system, a brand-aligned service strategy, cost-effective delight, and an enduring emotional bond with customers.

Part 5, "Into the Future," demonstrates how you can deal with ongoing trends and emerging issues, such as labor shortages, outsourcing, product complexity, and environmental concerns; it also shows you how to build strategic customer service (and possibly a chief customer officer) into your organizational culture.

Each chapter within each part examines customer and organizational behavior in a specific context and suggests approaches to measurement and analysis, the decisions each party makes, and the impact of those decisions on each party. Each chapter also shows what to do and how and why to do it, based on decades of research across dozens of industries, and ends with several specific takeaway lessons.

STARTING STRATEGICALLY

As you might imagine, adopting strategic customer service typically requires several mental and managerial shifts. Specifically, the organization—whether profit, nonprofit, or government entity—must:

- View ongoing customer relationships as essential to the organization's financial health
- Map the end-to-end customer experience and align the company to it (and not vice versa), and appoint someone to at least monitor it, if not manage it
- Use customer service not just to respond to problems and collect data, but to measure and inform the impact of management decisions on loyalty and revenue
- Structure customer service and the product development, marketing, sales, and operations areas so that they work together to deliver the right level of service to various customers, and to delight customers when it makes economic sense
- Enlist the finance area to help you view every customer touch in terms of the revenue, loyalty, word of mouth, and risk that it creates or dissipates
- Organize service employees, the resources that support them, and the functions that affect service for maximum speed and flexibility, with few specific rules beyond doing what is best for the customer

Customer service has become too important to leave to business-as-usual tactical methods. It now demands a strategic approach and what Sue Cook, formerly of Apple University, calls "bold goals," backed with proper funding and rigorous execution. The stakes couldn't be higher. Companies with strong customer loyalty and retention consistently rank among the revenue, margin, and earnings leaders in their categories. Companies with strong positive word of mouth can spend little to nothing on marketing. Any brand equity that a company possesses depends completely on satisfied customers. Every strategy for developing and selling a product or service, or for winning and keeping a market, ultimately depends on satisfied customers. TARP has even helped regulated companies reduce regulatory complaints by as much as 40 percent through better service systems.

This is an exciting time to be working in customer service in any capacity. So many products and services have been reduced to commodity status that superior service stands as the chief differentiator in many, if not most, categories. Meanwhile, the worldwide consumer market is crashing down, and sensitivity to price and value is increasing. The key to survival, growth, and profitability the world over is, and will continue to be, satisfied customers. This book will show you how market leaders go about producing and keeping them.

I would like to thank my editors, Tom Gorman, Bob Nirkind, and Jim Bessent; my wife, Alice; current and past TARP team members who helped execute the research and contributed to this body of knowledge, Cindy Grimm, Dianne Ward, Patty David, Steve Newman, Crystal Collier, Ann Peters, Adelina Avidu, and TARP's CEO, Dennis Gonier; as well as many of TARP's clients, who contributed suggestions and stories.

NOTES

1. The term "word of mouse" was coined by TARP in 1999 in its first e-care study.
2. Most nonprofits and government agencies incur either revenue loss or extra cost when they give poor service. We'll address the quantification of this in Chapter 4.

PART I

The Importance of Customer Service

CHAPTER 1

Seeing Customer Service Strategically

Understanding the True Role of Customer Service in Your Business

A FEW MONTHS AGO, I bought two eggplants at my local grocery. Upon getting home, I peeled and sliced into them, and I found that both were brown and yucky in the middle. I took one large unsliced half of each back to the store's service desk, casually said, "I got two eggplants and they were bad; can I get two more?" and started for the produce area. The service counter rep stopped me and said, "Sir, I see only one eggplant." I asked if she were questioning my honesty, and she said, "I'm only saying that I see only one eggplant!" I had to return all the pieces of both eggplants in order to get replacements. Compare this to the New York Richard Rodgers Theater, where my family and I mistakenly arrived on a Saturday with Friday night tickets; Tim, the house manager, placed chairs at the end of a row so that we could see the play and be forever indebted to the Richard Rodgers Theater. Memorably bad service over

$2 worth of eggplant and memorably great service when the customer made a $750 mistake: How do you avoid the former and achieve the latter? That's what this book is about.

A strategic view of customer service requires thinking of the function not as a cost center to be minimized, but as a competitive differentiator, revenue retention and generation machine, and word-of-mouth management process. This begins when you see the true role that the service experience plays in your business and the broad impact of customer service on your financial performance.

This chapter will help you see your customer service function in strategic terms and grasp its true potential. The chapter begins by examining several ways in which customer service and customer reactions to service can affect an organization for better or worse. It then looks at how financial decisions about customer service and the overall customer experience are currently made, and how they could be made strategically. After pausing briefly to clearly define several key terms that will arise in most discussions of customer service, the chapter turns to presenting a model for a customer service function that can play a strategic role in your organization. It finally is brought to a close with six first steps you can take to establish strategic customer service in your organization and, as you'll see at the end of each chapter, key takeaway points.

HOW CUSTOMER SERVICE AFFECTS A BUSINESS

The idea that poor customer service harms a business is intuitively correct, but it cannot be incorporated into decision making unless it can be quantified. What follows here are some of the basic quantified findings of TARP's research from over the past three decades. First, I will give you the bad news, and then the good news.

The Bad News

Most customers do not complain, and noncomplaining customers hurt your business. With consumer packaged goods and other small-ticket items, only 5 to 10 percent of dissatisfied customers complain, and most of them complain only to the retailer. For serious problems with big-ticket items, the complaint rate rises to 20 to 50 percent reporting to a front-line rep, but only 1 out of 10 of these customers (or 2 to 5 percent of all complainers) escalates to the local manager or the corporate office. This means that at the manufacturer or headquarters level, for each complaint you hear, there are approximately 20 to 50 other customers with problems.

Customers' reasons for not complaining are usually that they believe it will do no good—what we term "trained hopelessness;" they do not know where to complain; and they fear retribution from the person they are complaining about. (To put this in its proper context, think of your trepidation about complaining to the manager of a restaurant about your waitress before she brings your entrée to the table.) When dissatisfied customers don't tell the company about their dissatisfaction, their problems can't be resolved. We see the same behaviors and even worse ratios of problems to complaints in nonprofits like museums, health clinics, and government agencies.

Customers who don't complain about problems are 20 to 40 percent less loyal than those who have no problem or those who complain and are satisfied. This means that for each five customers who have a problem but don't complain, you are losing at least one.

Problems result in lost customers and revenue. In some 1,000 studies in every industry in a score of countries in the Americas, Europe, Asia, and the Middle East, we have found that when a customer encounters a problem, there is, on average, a 20 percent drop in loyalty compared with customers who have had no problem. This means that for every five customers with problems, one will switch brands the next time he buys a specific good or service. This doesn't even include the effects of bad word of mouth, which, as you will see, can be quite significant.

Bad news travels far. TARP's landmark 1980 study for Coca-Cola revealed that, through word of mouth, an average of 5 people will hear about someone's good experience, but 10 will hear about a bad experience. A later TARP study for an automaker indicated that while 8 people will be told about a good auto-repair experience, 16 will be told about a bad one. Bad word of *mouse* travels even further: On the Web, four times as many people hear about a negative experience as hear about a positive experience. In addition, a 2008 TARP study found that 12 percent of dissatisfied online customers told their buddy lists, which averaged more than 60 persons. However, recent TARP research finds that positive experiences can also have great impact. In one packaged goods study, 40 percent of consumers who were told of a positive experience by another customer tried the product. Positive word of mouth can indeed be a powerful marketing tool.

The Good News

Now, as promised, here's the good news.

Employees are not the cause of most customer dissatisfaction. Contrary to the conventional wisdom, employee attitudes and errors are responsible for only about 20 percent of overall customer dissatisfaction. TARP research reveals that in most industries, employees come to work desperately wanting to do a good job. It's what they are told to do and say to customers that causes most dissatisfaction. About 60 percent of overall customer dissatisfaction is caused by products, processes, and marketing messages that are delivered as intended, but that contain unpleasant surprises. About 20 to 30 percent of problems are caused by customers' errors, erroneous expectations, or product misuse. (Every year, a leading liquid bleach manufacturer gets several calls from people asking whether it can make the product taste better for when they brush their teeth with it to whiten them.) However, regardless of the cause, customers tend to blame the organization, so it is to the organization's advantage to prevent or fix the problem.

Keeping customers is cheaper than winning them. We originated this widely accepted rule of thumb in 1978 during an analysis of marketing costs versus customer service costs for a U.S. automaker. In this study, TARP compared the expense of dealer advertising (only one part of the cost of acquiring new customers) with the average amount spent to retain a customer via effective complaint handling. The ads cost five times as much. In similar analyses in more than two dozen other industries, depending on the specific industry and organization, the cost of winning a new customer can be two to *twenty* times that of retaining an unhappy one by resolving her problem and restoring the relationship. In a business-to-business environment, a company can easily spend $10,000 to $100,000 to win a new client, but then undermine the relationship and future sales by skimping on installation, training, documentation, parts, or service.

Proper handling of complaints retains customers. In almost all business sectors, a customer who complains and is satisfied by the resolution of his complaint is actually 30 percent more loyal than a noncomplainer and 50 percent more loyal than a complainer who remains dissatisfied. Getting three noncomplaining customers to complain and satisfying them produces the same revenue as winning one new customer. Clearly, then, it's incumbent upon you to find effective ways of resolving problems and of encouraging customers to complain. Several TARP client companies have found it useful to imprint invoices or post signs with the statement: "We can solve only problems we know about!"

The economic imperative for service improvements is clear. When the right financial data are combined with the right data on customer behavior, CFOs and CEOs can readily recognize the returns on investments in customer service. Ironically, these data (with the exception of the noncomplaint rate and word-of-mouth data) already exist in most organizations or can be developed with existing resources. The missing element is typically a sound methodology for modeling the impact of service on revenue and word of mouth in a way that senior executives understand—a methodology I'll cover in detail in Chapter 4.

However, to be motivated to even consider such a methodology, management must understand the broad effects noted earlier, and then consider the business case for improvements in customer service.

MAKING THE BUSINESS CASE FOR IMPROVEMENTS IN SERVICE

An organization can implement full-scale strategic customer service or simply improve specific aspects of its service. Either way, the organization is making improvements in customer service, and, although there are some low-cost and even no-cost ways of doing that (such as trusting known customers, 98 percent of whom are honest), most improvements will cost money. Thus, you'll need to convince the finance function in your organization that there will be a tangible payoff from investments in an improved customer experience.

Unfortunately, investments in improvements in customer service are rarely presented to finance as true investments; instead, they are presented as costs on a budget line. That's why most companies just fix the problems that produce the most frequent or the loudest complaints. That's also why they add service reps and call stations when sales rise, and lay off reps and reduce resources when sales sag. There is no real understanding of the linkage between service and future revenue.

These approaches not only are shortsighted, but also shortchange customers, employees, and the organization itself. Strategic customer service focuses on the business case, that is, on the revenue benefits of improvements in service, which are usually 10 to 20 times the cost implications. That focus recognizes the links among customer service, customer behavior, and financial results. These links will be a theme throughout this book because I have found—as have scores of leading companies—that investments in customer service provide some of the largest returns on investment that a company can make, usually a multiple of the return on other investments, and some of the fastest. When you implement a change that improves your service, the benefits of increased loyalty, positive word of mouth, and reduced risk begin accruing on that very next phone call.

To bring the business case into sharper focus, let's look more closely at the revenue impact of problem prevention and resolution. In the previous section, I noted that when a customer encounters a problem, there is, on average, a 20 percent drop in loyalty. Thus, for every five customers with problems, the probabilities say that you will lose one of them (5 customers × 0.2 loyalty decrease = 1 customer lost). To make a strong business case—that is, a financial case—you must quantify the impact on revenue. So, let's say a customer is worth $1,000. That implies that for every five customers with problems, the company will lose one customer worth $1,000 in revenue. We have now linked problem occurrence to revenue implications—the most critical linkage we address in this book. You can then reverse the analysis and say that if you can prevent or fix five problems, you will retain one customer who otherwise would have been lost and thus save $1,000 in lost revenue. Moreover, that $1,000 in revenue can be attributed directly to the service process, because that process involves identifying, preventing, and resolving the problems. (You'll see how shortly.) That sort of calculation makes the basic case for this type of investment in customer service. If you can get the finance staff to accept the above linkage, you are more than halfway to gaining their support.

Analyzing investments to improve customer service requires you to know what a customer is worth to your organization. If you don't know how much the customer is worth, how can you decide how much to spend to keep him happy? This number can be calculated in various ways, such as the lifetime value of the average customer (the amount a typical customer will spend during his tenure as a customer), the average or median annual revenue per customer, or the averages or medians for specific customer segments or product lines. I find it disconcerting that most senior executives—even in sales and marketing—don't know the average value of their customers. Marketing should know, and if it doesn't, finance must know because loyal customers should be considered the company's most important asset. To think strategically about customer service, you *must* know the average revenue per customer for your organization.

CFOs quite rightly want to see the business case for customer service investments, as they would for any investment. Making that business case—the economic imperative, as I call it—goes to the heart of strategic customer service, which actually *requires* an economic rationale for every improvement in service. In this way, you don't end up fixing squeaky wheels that barely warrant a drop of oil.

The business case for strategic service depends on the relationship between revenue and several concepts, which in my experience usually warrant clarification.

CLARIFYING KEY CONCEPTS

Precisely defined terms enable you to collect, measure, compare, and track the right data and thus analyze potential investments and the resulting improvements over time. The most useful concepts relative to customer service are problems, complaints, satisfaction, loyalty, delight, and word of mouth. Broadly, we define these terms as follows:

Problems are any unpleasant surprises or questions that arise in dealing with a product or service, whether or not the customer complains about them. (A *complaint* is a situation in which a customer brings the problem to the company's attention via telephone, e-mail, or letter, or in person.) Problems can originate in product performance, design, packaging, delivery, installation, instructions, or safety; in employee performance; or in customer error or expectations. As you'll see, the total number of occurrences of specific problems often differs from the number of complaints by orders of magnitude. This ratio of problems to complaints, or what TARP calls the *multiplier*, can range from 10 to 1 to 2,000 to 1. Knowing this multiplier or ratio for your particular organization makes it possible for you to accurately analyze investments in improvements that prevent or resolve problems.

Satisfaction can be tough to define because it is often mitigated by expectations. When your expectations are low, you may be satisfied if your flight is "only" 60 minutes late or your lunch at the greasy spoon is edible. By the same token, a first-rate movie can seem like a dud if your best friend told you it was the best flick she's ever seen. Expectations therefore represent either a potential liability or a huge opportunity, and you can affect satisfaction by setting customers' expectations precisely. I had a US Airways pilot proactively set my expectations for a 45-minute flight when he announced, "We give same-day service."

Loyalty is measured by expressed intentions to repurchase, actual purchasing behavior, or both. Continued actual purchases are generally the most accurate measure of actual loyalty, but we have found a high correlation between expressed purchase intentions (especially negative ones) and future purchase behavior. For instance, at a major U.S. airline, we confirmed that about 60 percent of frequent flyers who said that they were going to stop flying the airline actually did reduce their number of miles flown dramatically the following year. However, organizations must define loyalty correctly and not confuse captive customers, or those who are merely doing what's convenient for them at the moment, with loyalists. Therefore, one of the best ways of measuring loyalty is to use word of mouth recommendation as a surrogate—would the customer recommend the product or service?

Delight occurs when an organization surprises a customer by exceeding her high or reasonable (as opposed to low) expectations. But not all delight leads to increased loyalty, so always exceeding expectations may be a major waste of money. More on that in Chapter 9.

Word of mouth (WOM), either positive or negative, is almost always the most important factor in most customers' purchase of a new product. WOM occurs because people have a social and psychological need to tell one another about good and bad experiences. Word of mouth and its cousin, word of mouse (which includes e-mails and comments about your organization on blogs and bulletin boards), have become increasingly important to customers. Certain products, such as consumer electronics, autos, and financial services, have become so sophisticated that consumers rely heavily on friends who have done research, made purchases, and experienced the product or acquired expertise. In one recent TARP study of consumer electronics, 12 percent of unhappy customers told a median of 67 persons on their blog or buddy list. In most product areas, at least a third, and in high-end financial products well over 50 percent, of all customers select products based on WOM referrals. Chick-fil-A, probably the most successful fast-food chain (based on profitability and sales growth), has found that a very high percentage of its new customers come from current customers dragging new ones in and saying, "You've got to try it!" Sophisticated companies now develop programs aimed at generating positive word of mouth as part of their marketing and service strategy and include actions that delight customers.

These terms enable organizations to think about customer attitudes and behavior in ways that can be quantified. Knowing that a customer is happy or didn't come back won't help you improve the customer experience in the future. By managing on the basis of problems, complaints, satisfaction, loyalty, delight, and word of mouth, you will be able to build the granular business case for specific improvments to the customer experience and create the economic imperative for actions to meet their needs more effectively. We now examine the operational model for the strategic service approach to managing your customers' experience.

A MODEL FOR MAXIMIZING CUSTOMER SATISFACTION AND LOYALTY

Our model for strategically managing the customer experience and maximizing customer satisfaction and loyalty, and thus revenue, boils down to a simple mnemonic: DIRFT. The acronym DIRFT means "Do It Right the First Time." This is usually the stated goal of every organization.

But despite the best intentions and training and resources, organizations often fail to do it right the first time. Thereon hangs the role of tactical service in the customer experience, which consists of two parts:

setting expectations and preparing the customer for the use of the product and, if the customer's experience is not perfect, *orchestrating the customer's interactions with the service process*. Setting expectations and helping customers get the most from the product are intrinsic to strategic customer service.

As the findings presented earlier indicate, customers' interactions with service represent opportunities to prevent and solve problems, increase loyalty, and generate good word of mouth—or to do the opposite. Figure 1-1 illustrates the dynamics of DIRFT and thus presents a framework for customer satisfaction systems.

Figure 1-1 also illustrates the three things an organization must do to maximize customer satisfaction cost-effectively, to which I'll add a fourth, more advanced, task:

1. Minimize the number of problems that customers experience by doing the right job right the first time.
2. Respond effectively to questions and problems that do arise.
3. Feed data about questions and problems to the right parties so that they can prevent or proactively deal with the problems.

Figure 1-1. TARP's Formula for Maximizing Customer Satisfaction and Loyalty

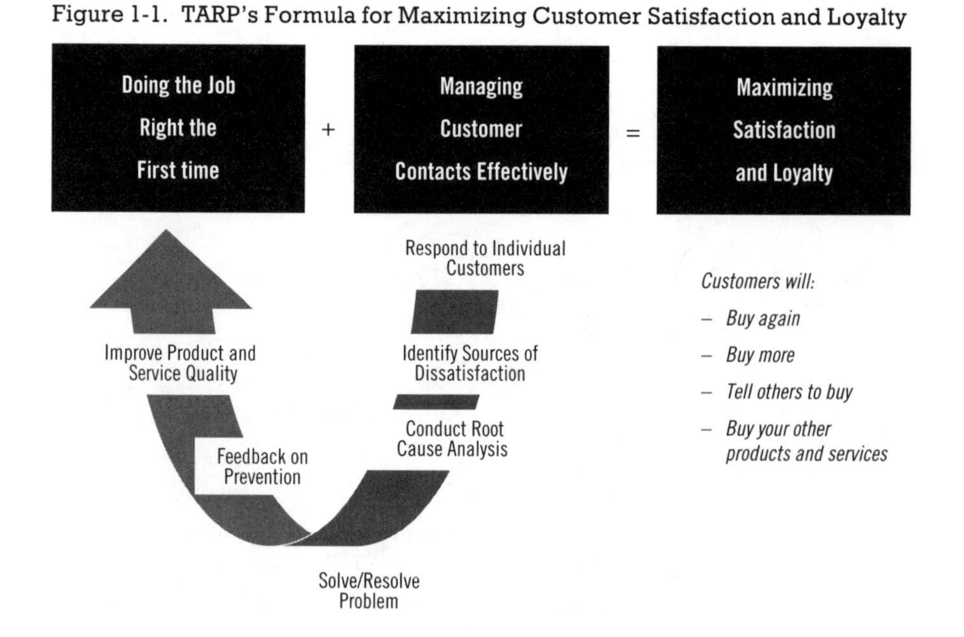

4. Capitalize on opportunities to sell ancillary or upgraded products, or higher levels of service as well as create connection and delight.

Here are these steps in greater detail.

Do It Right the First Time

First, the company must commit to doing the right job right the first time.[1] It must *consistently* provide products and services that *consistently* meet customers' needs and expectations. Consistency is much harder to deliver than the occasional "wow" experience, but one of the greatest delighters is "no unpleasant surprises" (see Chapter 9). This means understanding customers' true needs, setting proper expectations via marketing, selling honestly, and then meeting the expectations completely. The expectations constitute the brand promise, whether you are selling Kias or BMWs. Meeting those expectations—the first time or quickly after a failure to do so—builds brand equity.

To do the job right the first time, the company must develop and employ policies and procedures that prevent problems while generating customer satisfaction. Responsibility for no unpleasant surprises lies with everyone: product developers and production line workers, dispatchers and delivery people, marketing and sales professionals, installers and service technicians, billing and collection personnel—everyone who directly or indirectly touches the customer. This prevention effort is continuously improved based on the feedback loop depicted in Figure 1-1 and described here. A key factor in doing it right the first time and setting expectations is proactively educating customers about product uses, limitations, quirks, and requirements.

Respond Effectively to Questions and Problems That Arise

Second, problems or questions that can become problems will inevitably occur, and customers may become dissatisfied. Therefore, the company needs an effective system for handling questions and resolving problems (hereafter I will use the shorthand *issues* to mean both), and for alerting customers to ways of accessing that system. The service system itself must also be easy for customers to use, as explained in Part 3 (see chapters 6 through 8). Customer service reps (CSRs) must have the knowledge, skill, and authority to address most issues on the first call. When they cannot do so, they must assume ownership of the issue by finding a resolution and halting or mitigating any inconvenience or loss to the customer—or, if those solutions are impossible, routing the customer *directly* to someone who can assume that responsibility.

The middle box of the DIRFT formula, managing contacts, used to be labeled "managing complaints," but we found that the word *complaint* has negative connotations. Many managers concluded that if a customer complains, they should find the employee who's responsible and punish her for causing the dissatisfaction. This resulted in employees not wanting to hear or recognize complaints. AT&T, among other clients, jettisoned the term *complaint* and adopted the more useful term *request for assistance*, which shifts the focus away from blame and toward the customer's need for a solution. It was a smart move.

Feed Data About Issues to the Right Parties

Third, the service system must collect and compile customer contact data and other data describing the customer experience so that the right internal people can identify and remedy the root causes of customer problems. As the DIRFT formula shows, this feedback loop supports doing it right the first time, which includes doing the *right* job right. For instance, your web site may allow people to effeciently log on but if you force everyone to sign in using a password when they just want to browse your product list, you are creating unnecessary frustration. Therefore, to better meet customer needs, you may need to modify the the website to give access without signing on. DIRFT involves enhancing the delivery of all aspects of the offering from the sales message and service to the usage instructions or the product itself. You need to know which step is the right one.

Failure to address the root causes allows problems to continue, which increases customer dissatisfaction and service costs, decreases loyalty, and reduces future revenue. Remember that many customers do not complain; they just take their business elsewhere. In addition, some of them will spread bad word of mouth, further decreasing your future revenue. It's essential that clear descriptions of problems—such as incorrect expectations set by sales messages, misfires in product design or performance, snafus in delivery or installation, unclear directions for assembly or use, or systemic failure to resolve problems—be routed to people who can act on the information received.

Capitalize on Opportunities to Sell Ancillary or Upgraded Products or Service and Create Connection

Fourth, customers with questions or complaints often present sales opportunities to service reps. A complaint about a bounced check can turn into a sale of overdraft protection. Of course, not every customer with a question or problem is a sales prospect. However, some customers, particularly price-sensitive ones, tend to buy a grade of product or level of service that fails to meet their needs. They need more capacity, speed, power, durability, maintenance services, expertise, premium channels, or financial flexibility than they signed up for, and when they realize this, they call the company they're doing business with to find out how they can get it. This is especially true for companies that are dedicated to doing it right the first time. Individuals may not come right out and say that they want to make a purchase—they would have gone to sales for that—but a well-trained CSR, armed with the right customer data and a few targeted questions, can recognize potential customers in those situations. Moreover, many customers will take advice about future purchases from a service rep more readily than from a salesperson. TARP's experience at three different copier companies revealed that if the service tech attributes a breakdown to an overtaxed machine, customers will believe him when he says, "You need a bigger machine to handle this volume" more often than they will believe a sales rep, who is typically viewed as "just trying to make a sale."

Finally, if the queue is not backed up, the CSR can take the time to humanize the transaction and create an emotional connection, which can raise loyalty by as much at 25 percent (see Chapter 9).

So, at this point, we've examined some good and bad effects of customer service, noted the importance of the economic imperative for investments to improve customer service, and defined our terms. We've also introduced a model for customer service that addresses situations in which the organization has failed to do it right the first time and that feeds essential information back to the organization. We now conclude this discussion by turning to the first steps you can take toward establishing strategic customer service in your organization.

FIRST STEPS TO STRATEGIC CUSTOMER SERVICE: ECONOMIC IMPERATIVE AND VOC

Many, if not most, organizations already have the resources required to boost the performance of their tactical customer service functions and to move toward a strategic customer service process. Key components include customer service functions, customer relationship management (CRM) systems, and, most importantly, Voice of the Customer (VOC) capabilities. The VOC is the mechanism that describes the overall customer experience using all inputs—not just market research surveys, but also sources of customer data, such as warranty claims, customer complaints, and employee input. True VOC extends beyond the traditional issues of product features and price to gathering data on all dimensions of the customer experience, such as sales tactics and messaging, warranty provisions, dealer service, and preferred methods of selling and financing. Unfortunately, in most organizations, VOC tends to be fragmented. In one auto company, I asked the head of service who owned the VOC process. He told me that about seven different people owned various parts of it. That's unfortunate, since a fragmented VOC effort is actually more damaging than none at all because it generates erroneous findings, contradictions, confusion, and paralysis.

The first step toward establishing strategic customer service in your organization is to start viewing customer service strategically. That means thinking about it in terms of how your organization's service processes are currently affecting your customers and how they could affect your customers if they were improved. It also means thinking in terms of the financial impact of problems (especially the problems that you're not hearing about) and complaints, and about the way your service function handles them. And it means thinking about how to get your resources organized and focused at the tactical level, as well as at the strategic level. Although I'll discuss how to organize the service function in detail in Chapter 6, here are six basic guidelines for the design of customer service systems for you to consider—and perhaps start implementing—in the meantime:

1. **Endeavor to do it right the first time.** Prevent the need for service.
2. **Make it easy for customers to complain and make information easy to find.** Have a clear site map on your web site, and print the phone tree menu wherever you post the toll-free number.
3. **Empower CSRs to be successful at least 90 percent of the time.** If they're not, you increase costs by 50 percent and reduce loyalty by 10 to 30 percent.
4. **Use your service system to tap the full potential value of each customer.** Position your service reps to capitalize on cross-selling and up-selling opportunities. Recognize gold, silver, and lead customers (if only internally); treat them all with respect, but expend resources based on their profitability.
5. **View service as a word-of-mouth (WOM) management function.** Every transaction has potential positive or negative WOM impact, and you must measure both. Then you can design explicit tactics and incentives for cost effectively delighting customers and generating positive WOM.
6. **Make the economic imperative the basis for decisions about customer service.** When you identify the links between your customers' problems, complaints, points of pain, service, and delight and your financial performance, you can manage the customer experience for maximum revenue and profitability.

These guidelines all point toward a customer service system that achieves strategic goals. Such a system does not just deliver the right level of service quickly, efficiently, and cost-effectively. It also plays an explicit role in revenue retention and generation. The economic imperative for strategic customer service emerges when you quantify the benefits of preventing, fixing, and resolving problems; of creating delight and positive word of mouth; and of cross-selling and up-selling. Of course, all of this relates to the customer, whom we examine more closely in Chapter 2.

KEY TAKEAWAYS[2]

1. On average, problems damage loyalty by 20 percent; that is, for every five customers who experience a problem, one will stop buying the product or service.

2. Customers with problems often do not complain, but their loyalty is 20 to 40 percent lower than that of customers without problems.
3. When customers do complain, they are often left either mollified (that is, partially satisfied) or dissatisfied—with resulting 20 to 60 percent lower levels of loyalty.
4. When complaining customers are converted from dissatisfied to satisfied, their loyalty increases by at least 25 percent and possibly as much as 60 percent.
5. Customers who are delighted by proactive education or superior service are 10 to 30 percent more loyal than customers who have not been delighted.

NOTES

1. A good friend, Jon Theuerkauf, formerly with GE Capital and HSBC and now with Credit Suisse, pointed out that most companies assume that the right job is what they think the customer wants, as opposed to ensuring that they know what the customer really wants. Jon correctly says that you must "do the right job right the first time."
2. These findings, and virtually all of the findings in this book (unless otherwise noted), are quoted from client surveys conducted for consumer and B2B customers by TARP. Most of these surveys must remain confidential, although we can quote them in aggregate terms. The findings on these measures for your organization might differ from these ranges, but experience has shown that they will probably vary by no more than plus or minus 10 percent from the range limits quoted in these takeaways.

CHAPTER 2

What Do Customers Want (and What Should We Deliver)?

Understanding Customer Expectations and Setting Goals Strategically

FOR SEVERAL YEARS in the 1970s, Holiday Inn used the slogan "the best surprise is no surprise" in print and television advertisements that showed a family entering a motel room and finding it less than satisfactory. Like most successful campaigns, this one reflected the company's competitive advantage: standardization. Kemmons Wilson founded the motel chain in the 1950s on the principle of standardization after he experienced depressingly unpredictable accommodations on a drive he made from Tennessee to Washington, D.C. In contrast to the No Tell Motels and mom-and-pop rest stops for truckers, salespeople, and other road warriors, Holiday Inn promised a friendly atmosphere and clean rooms with crisply made-up beds and air conditioning that actually worked. Holiday Inn's campaign and the chain's success exemplified a general formula that's still foolproof today: Set realistic expectations for customers, and then meet them.

This chapter will, as its title indicates, explore customer expectations and how the organization can set strategic and tactical goals that will meet those expectations. First, however, I'll summarize some reasons for unmet expectations that counter conventional wisdom. Then I'll cover major trends in customer expectations, and then examine customer expectations for the tactical service system. With that background, the chapter will look at ways of setting goals for service at the strategic and tactical levels that will meet customer expectations.

UNEXPECTED REASONS FOR UNMET CUSTOMER EXPECTATIONS

Most executives assume that if you have an unhappy customer, a front-line employee is most likely the cause. *This is usually not true!* The hapless front-line employee didn't cause the airline mechanical delay or reject your health insurance claim—in most cases they are the messengers bearing the bad news. In most cases, the cause goes far beyond the front-line employee. Customers essentially approach each purchase or transaction with the expectation that they will receive exactly what they intended to buy, with no unpleasant surprises. Expectations are set by your company's image, brand, reputation, pricing, advertising, and sales and marketing messages. That promise of what you will deliver combines with your customers' previous experiences with your organization and other companies in your market and those of other customers, conveyed via word of mouth.

The basic formula for meeting customer expectations is the DIRFT model introduced in Chapter 1. The organization must be structured and given the resources to do it right the first time, and service must be positioned to address situations in which the organization fails in this endeavor. When customers' expectations are not met or when customers are disappointed, one or more of three factors—listed in the order of their importance—are almost always at work:

1. **Defective products, misleading marketing messages, ineffective policies, or broken internal processes.** This factor causes the

majority of problems—50 to 60 percent in most organizations. That's actually good news because the causes of those problems can be discovered and, usually, eliminated. In cases in which it is impossible or impractical to eliminate the problem, at least the effects on customers can be mitigated.

2. **Employee mistakes or bad attitudes.** Surprisingly, this factor usually causes only 20 to 30 percent of problems. Although almost all bad service is blamed on employees, very few people come to work intending to disappoint customers. Often they, along with customers, are victims of the primary cause of unmet expectations, in that they are given defective products, tools, policies, and response rules to work with.
3. **Customer errors or unreasonable expectations.** Customers can also misuse or abuse products or develop unrealistic expectations, either on their own or through erroneous word of mouth. This factor causes the remaining 20 to 30 percent of problems. I might add dishonest customers here as well, but they represent less than 2 percent of all complaints.

These three factors account for virtually all the problems that lead to customers' unmet expectations and disappointments. While the causes of these problems are usually to be found outside the service department, customer service can be instrumental in preventing or solving the problems. As indicated by the feedback loop portrayed in the DIRFT model, customer service feeds information on problems and their causes back to the organization. (Such data, combined with satisfaction surveys and operational data on quality, create the "Voice of the Customer," (VOC) which is covered in Chapter 5.)

TRENDS IN CUSTOMER EXPECTATIONS ABOUT SERVICE

Over the past two decades, TARP's research has identified a number of broad trends in customer expectations, as well as several operational expectations for tactical customer service.

Broad Trends in Customer Expectations

The following are five broad, sometimes contradictory trends in overall expectations that customers bring to interactions with organizations and particularly with the service function:

1. Clear brand promises and consistent delivery
2. Low expectations and reluctance to complain
3. Immediate resolution of problems
4. Genuine empathy when things go wrong
5. Recognition and knowledge of the customer

Clear Brand Promises and Consistent Delivery. Holiday Inn capitalized on this expectation at the product level, as did McDonald's. Today, the customer experience is defined more broadly, and delivering consistency has become more complex. The cheese expert at Whole Foods, the service writer at Lexus, and the barista at Starbucks all contribute to—or detract from—the experience. Thus, all employees in an organization must understand customers' expectations and their role in delivering the customer experience.

Low Expectations and Reluctance to Complain. In industries such as air travel and in some insurance, utility, and government organizations, customers have developed "trained hopelessness." They've learned that complaining fixes nothing and may have negative consequences or lead to retribution (as when Elaine in *Seinfeld* was labeled a troublemaker at the doctor's office). Low complaint rates in some industries create the myth that "Complaints are down, so things are improving!" Not true!

Immediate Resolution of Problems. The Web and mobile communications have contributed to customers expecting instant gratification from service. Yet 20 years ago in the *Harvard Business Review*, Japanese quality improvement pioneer Genichi Taguchi counseled, "Be efficient first, friendly second." Not all customers expect or want "warm fuzzies" in service interactions. Nor do many want "a relationship" or canned cordiality of the have-a-nice-day variety, especially when it's 9:00 p.m. in their time zone. Nor do they want repeated use of their name, especially not their first name (although respectful one-time use of their last name may make a good impression). And, perhaps most of all, they don't want to hear an answer that on its face is absurd or nonsense.

My favorite example of the latter comes from a PC manufacturer. When customers called to report failure of the motherboard at 110 days and found the warranty was 90 days rather than the more customary one year—the service reps were instructed to tell them, "The motherboards are so good that you need only a 90-day warranty," even when the product had just failed at 110 days. Every customer who was given that reply indicated that she would *never* buy that brand again, because on its face the rationale was nonsensical. Such an answer was also demoralizing for staff members to give because they knew that it would evoke both anger and challenges to which there were no logical responses.

Genuine Empathy When Things Go Wrong. I recently had a flight diverted at midnight to an airport I had not planned to visit. The first thing the ground staff said as we got off the plane was, "We are not responsible for hotels or anything else!" What a great welcome. A customer's desire for empathy, sympathy, or at least concern when an unpleasant surprise occurs has little to do with who caused the problem. When your flight is canceled as a result of bad weather, the airline is technically not responsible, but you're still stuck, perhaps until the next day. You want the employee to acknowledge your pain, which we call "apologizing without accepting blame" ("I'm sorry you're stuck here; I'd be upset if it were me"). Yet even in those situations, most customers value efficiency and effectiveness more than they value excessive warmth. Also, as Janelle Barlow advises in her book *A Complaint Is a Gift*, never apologize for the customer's "inconvenience." A canceled flight is not an inconvenience; it is a major hassle and a potential personal or business disaster. Eliminate the word *inconvenience* from your vocabulary.

Recognition and Knowledge of the Customer. Over the past ten years or so, the definition of "good service" has evolved. What was once personalized service delivered by someone who actually knew you is now usually service from someone who simply knows your value to and history with the organization. In most cases, the long term personal relationship is nice but not necessary. Customers simply want someone who can answer their questions and act immediately on his knowledge of the customer's world. They do not want to have to establish their value as a customer and recount their previous interactions.

The foregoing trends form the backdrop against which customers develop their expectations of service at the tactical level.

Operational Expectations for Tactical Customer Service

Having established these global expectations, there are five sets of operational expectations for tactical customer service, some elements of which are counterintuitive or belie the conventional wisdom:

1. Excellent accessibility
2. Accurate, clear, complete responses
3. Reliable follow-through
4. Customer education and problem prevention
5. Cross-selling and creating delight.

Excellent Accessibility. Decades ago, nine-to-five was the accepted norm, and postal mail was the usual contact medium. In the early 1980s, TARP's research, as highlighted in *BusinessWeek*,[1] helped companies to recognize that easy, free, instantaneous, anytime contact from customers was worth encouraging because it allowed the customers to get their problems solved; this resulted in toll-free numbers replacing mail. Within this context, customers now hold five general expectations regarding accessibility:

1. **Open hours.** Customers want accessibility to your customer service system (at least in some form) whenever they are using your product or service, reviewing your invoices, or considering a purchase. This includes daytime, evenings, weekends, and perhaps even the dead of night on a holiday. (Christmas Eve and Christmas Day are among the busiest periods of the year for customer service at toy and consumer electronics companies.)
2. **Human contact.** Despite their acceptance of Internet and telephone access to bank balances, flight departures and arrivals, and similar information, customers still want the option of talking to a live person if they have a problem with the self-service process.

3. **User-friendliness.** Customers using an automated phone system will tolerate up to three choices ("Press 1 if . . . , 2 if . . . " and so on). More menu choices or a second tier of menus will cause frustration *unless* the customer has been educated in advance with a printed menu (wherever the 800 number is given) of what she will encounter and is a frequent user. Customers also want no more than 15 seconds of introductory statements, such as "Welcome to the XYZ Company automated service center; if you're calling from a touch-tone phone, please press 1," and so on.
4. **Minimal transfers.** TARP's research reveals that a customer will tolerate *one* warm transfer during an initial call to customer service *if* he then reaches someone who can solve his problem. This should not be confused with a transfer to another queue or to a decision tree. In general, multiple transfers cause 10 percent to 25 percent of customer dissatisfaction with service interactions.
5. **A tolerable waiting period.** Our research has found that waiting time in a phone queue is less important than the service delivered once customers are connected. A 60-second wait is usually acceptable if callers then reach someone who can resolve their issue on that contact. For high-tech products, waiting times of up to two minutes are usually acceptable, although new research suggests that customers expect to have to wait up to ten minutes—a potential opportunity for technology companies that are able to answer in two or three minutes. This research implies that in most cases, spending the resources needed to answer all incoming calls within, say, 30 seconds is not cost-effective. Incidentally, perceived waiting time decreases if the customer is reading something useful on the screen or hearing some useful information (not an ad for flights when you're on the lost baggage line) while waiting on the phone.

Today, customers want instant access to answers and solutions. This has important implications for organizations that use voicemail or Internet contact in their service delivery systems or whose CSRs' phones are answered by voicemail. Voicemail automatically delays access to service and erodes satisfaction by 15 to 20 percent if a customer has an issue that requires an immediate response. Based on this information, IBM has required that sales reps' voice mails allow callers to "0" out to a "must answer" phone with a live person.

Customers have also come to think of the Internet as they do the telephone: They expect immediate automatic acknowledgement and a substantive answer within two to eight hours, depending upon the industry. An approach on a web site by a CSR offering to chat and provide immediate assistance can raise first contact resolution by 30 percent.

Accurate, Clear, Complete Responses. Ideally, the service system should resolve the issue on the customer's initial contact. As noted, failing to do so decreases satisfaction by 10 to 20 percent. For example, TARP conducted research using matched sets of calls in which half of the requests for service were completely resolved on the first contact and the other half were resolved with callbacks within 24 hours giving exactly the same answers. The set that achieved complete resolution on the first call received a 10 percent higher satisfaction rating. Resolution on the first contact satisfies customers and precludes their having to call service again—and service having to call customers. On that latter point, first-call resolution typically cuts costs by up to 50 percent by eliminating the need for the callback. The cost of calling customers back becomes significant indeed when you consider that only 30 to 40 percent of the calls placed reach their intended party, which means that one callback commitment can require your employees to make two to four (or more) calls.

First-call resolution does, however, require the following four components:

1. **Competence.** CSRs must have the requisite knowledge, skill, experience, and temperament to address customers' problems.
2. **Support.** CSRs should have the information and authority required to resolve problems, as well as confidence that the organization will deliver as promised.
3. **Empathy.** CSRs must listen well, thank the customer for presenting the opportunity, and, when necessary, apologize, even if the company is not at fault. Empathy defuses the customer's anger and generates more efficient resolution.

4. **Clarity and fair treatment.** CSRs must be able to clearly explain what has happened, present the rationale for company policies, parry customers' logical arguments, and leave customers knowing what will happen and feeling that they have been treated fairly.

A key goal in all problem resolution is to leave the customer feeling that she has been treated fairly, especially when the answer is not the one that she would have preferred. For instance, health insurance companies can maintain customer satisfaction and loyalty almost completely even if the claim is denied, as long as customers feel that the explanation regarding the reason for the denial of the claim is clear and fair.

Reliable Follow-Through. When CSRs cannot resolve the customer's issue on the spot, they or someone else must follow through to deliver the promised next step or resolution. That promise—even if the word *promise* is never used—sets an expectation that must be met or dissatisfaction will ensue. Thus, promises made by CSRs must be realistic, convincing, satisfying, and deliverable. Customers particularly dislike situations in which the rep treats them nicely but makes promises that go unfulfilled. In such cases, the immediate postcall survey says that the rep was great, but then the broken promise destroys long-term loyalty. This is a common problem with immediate postcall surveys—they don't detect the organization's failure to follow through.

CSRs who know that follow-through will occur project confidence to the customer, rather than vague hopes or, worse yet, cynicism. Reps who can rely on the back-end system (and they know when they can and when they cannot) will assure customers of a resolution, thus restoring their faith in the organization. That, in turn, translates into fewer follow-up calls from the customer and lower costs to the organization. On the other hand, we saw a mutual fund company where the reps protected themselves with weasel words ("It usually happens"); the company got 100,000 "confirmation calls" per month from customers making sure that their transactions had occurred as specified. One popular tactic, which can actually create delight, is proactive confirmation, as when Amazon.com communicates the progress of your request as it moves through the company's system.

Customer Education and Problem Prevention. Customer education represents another important, underexploited opportunity for many customer service functions. Customers expect to be proactively apprised of product quirks, common difficulties, and potential glitches. Doing so also increases customer safety and reduces risk to the organization. When customers find a new initiative confusing, as often occurs with a new product or promotion, service can clarify matters for those who call and ask sales and marketing to proactively educate those who might not call with a mailing, e-mail, or web site alert.

Customer education through service reps boosts revenue by informing customers about the availability of products, add-ons, and higher levels of service that can solve their problem or enhance their experience. Even customers who are not ready to buy at that moment will often return in the future. Service can also educate customers about other, less costly methods of accessing the service system, such as via the company's web site. A web site is among the most economical and effective tools for customer education ever created, as a visit to the site of any major high-technology, financial services, or pharmaceutical company will demonstrate.

Cross-Selling and Creating Delight. Although this is an advanced topic that we cover in detail in Chapter 9, many companies have increased revenue and profit per customer—and satisfaction and loyalty—through well-designed cross-selling and up-selling programs. For example, Compaq developed a cross-selling process that converted calls from customers who were with Web self service into sales of enhanced support contracts. Other examples include a bank selling overdraft protection when fielding complaints about bounced checks, and a cable company converting complaints about download times into sales of greater bandwidth.

The CSRs must focus primarily on solving the customer's actual problem rather than on making the sale. However, if the problem can be solved or prevented or the customer experience improved with an enhanced product, add-on, or higher level of service, the CSR can actually delight the customer while making a sale.

These five factors are the basic expectations for service. However, there is another factor that complicates things: Customers also derive their expectations of your service function from the last *good* experience they have had with the service function of another organization. TARP's research indicates that customers compare their service experiences across industries, not only within industries. So if, for example, a customer receives exceptional service in an interaction with an overnight delivery company, that customer will expect similar performance from the next credit card company or retail store that he deals with.

SETTING SERVICE GOALS STRATEGICALLY

The role of customer service can be anything from a complaint department and cleanup crew to a value enhancer and competitive differentiator. Companies that are committed to service as a value enhancer and competitive differentiator staff, manage, and fund the service function as such. In addition, they communicate to customers the role that service plays in ensuring a great experience in their marketing and sales messages at the front end, and they make sure that operations can deliver at the back end.

Strategic customer service demands that you set customer experience goals and then work down to tactical objectives. Although many companies work hard to deliver superior service, senior executives have typically not thought through the fit between customer service and the business, marketing, and overall customer experience strategies. Thus, they set only process-level goals along tactical dimensions such as time spent in the queue and calls handled per service rep. To set goals strategically, management must first define the overall strategic and tactical role and goals of the service function, then translate them into targets that the CFO and finance can buy into and fund.

In general, strategic service and customer experience goals should include:

- **Loyalty,** driven by problem prevention, positive word of mouth, and cross-selling, that is measured in surveys and, ultimately, the financial accounts
- **Value,** driven by a reputation for excellent service and quality, that is measured by operating metrics and surveys of customers
- **Word of mouth**, represented by the percentage of new customers resulting from positive word of mouth
- **Effective Voice of the Customer,** including identifying points of pain and revenue damage per month (as explained in Chapter

4), and the largest opportunities to add value and recommended action on those opportunities (no action means no payoff)

- **Reduced risk and associated costs,** driven by doing it right the first time, providing customer education, and preventing problems, and measured by insurance and product liability claims and regulatory complaints and interventions
- **High employee satisfaction**, represented by at least 80 percent of employees feeling very successful at their jobs and proud of the brand, and by low turnover

While these goals are logical, the second goal, "value," may seem counterintuitive given the success of Wal-Mart, Southwest Airlines, and other companies that successfully compete mainly on price. Even as an evangelist for superb customer service, I understand that some companies pursue a low-cost provider strategy and deemphasize the role of service in the customer experience. Yet customers bring expectations even to companies that succeed via low service and high volume delivering high value for price paid. Those companies communicate a specific value proposition—a mix of selection, location, quality, pricing, and, yes, service—on which they must deliver.

Thus in any market segment, management must translate customer expectations into specific, measurable, reachable experience goals. Then these goals must be firmly linked to one another and to operational measures of performance on the dimensions of access, response content, follow-through, and data capture. Management must then define target levels for these measures and identify the most economical, highest-return ways to bring performance to the target levels. The final step is to translate the customer experience goals related to satisfaction, loyalty, reduced risk, and positive word of mouth into goals for revenue and profitability.

In general, it's best to develop a mix that includes *process* measures, such as average and range for the amount of time that customers spend in the phone queue; experience or *outcome* measures, such as customer satisfaction and loyalty and service employee satisfaction; and *financial* measures, such as revenue attributable to service in the form of problems prevented or money saved through improved service efficiency. Figure 2-1 shows how process, outcome, and financial goals are linked.

Figure 2-1. Objectives and Measures for Customer Service

Process Goals ➡	*Outcome Goals* ➡	*Financial Goals*
Accessibility	Loyalty	
Response	Value for Price Paid	Revenue
Follow-Through	Word of Mouth	
Education &	Problem Rate	
Problem Prevention	Reduced Risk	Margin
Cross-Selling	VOC	
	Employee Satisfaction	

Other potentially useful measures would include the percentage of customers who encounter problems (problem rate), the complaint rate per 100 problems encountered, the number of problems resolved, and the time frame for resolution. Here's how the linkage among the goals occurs:

- Process goals measure accessibility and response, as well as suggest targets for problem prevention, education, and cross-selling.
- Outcome goals are the result of performance on those process goals, which determines customer attitudes and behavior, such as satisfaction, loyalty, and word of mouth, and also overall problem rate, employee satisfaction, and service efficiency.
- Performance on the outcome goals leads to performance on the financial goals of increased revenue and margin.
- Financial goals measure the contribution to higher revenue, higher margins, and reduced costs.

In the following sections, we show how service can set specific performance goals within each of these categories.

Operationalizing the Process Goals

The most common process goals are those that are easiest to quantify, which may be why they also foster so many customer service problems. We've all seen the cartoon where Dilbert gets the lowest talk time award after hanging up on customers. Certain process measures, particularly those that measure service reps' performance, can twist behavior in ways that reduce customer satisfaction. For instance, a call-center manager I know established a standard of 80 calls per shift and a limit of three minutes per call. This prompted reps to rush customers through calls and some to even hang up on callers in order to increase their call count. The result was decreased customer satisfaction and no education of customers on self-service.

So, bearing in mind the need to set and implement process goals carefully, examples of useful ones might include:

Accessibility:

- Access to web site 24/7 with at least 99.5 percent uptime.
- The option of always being able to speak with a live service rep from 6:00 a.m. to midnight, perhaps with shorter Saturday and Sunday hours. Think about when the customer primarily is using your product and be available at those times.
- A queue waiting time average of one minute with a two-and-a-half-minute maximum, and an abandoned call rate of 3 percent or less.
- Clear guidance (via "contact us" and web site map) on the company's web site and in literature regarding whom to contact for which needs, including a phone number for a satisfaction advocate or escalated complaint contact (about which more in Chapter 6).

Responses:

- CSRs handling ongoing customer accounts should be able to answer 95 percent of questions and inquiries on first contact.
- CSRs in durable goods markets should be able to resolve at least 85 percent of problems on the first call or assure the customer that it will be handled without a callback.

Follow-Through:

- Cycle time of 24 hours or less for at least 80 percent of referred problems.

- A system that enables CSRs to communicate with problem solvers in real time.
- A problem logging system that updates the CSRs (and customers by e-mail) at least twice daily, if not continually, on the status of the problem's resolution.
- No callbacks from 98 percent of customers regarding solutions in process, because they are satisfied or are contacted proactively about any change.

Education and Problem Prevention:

- Increases or decreases in the number of routine inquiries on a specific issue.
- Increases or decreases in the number of inquiries that can be handled via automatic response mechanisms.
- The number of inquiries regarding specific product or service enhancements (if there are many, this implies that the message was not clear).
- Fewer problems requiring warranty expense as a result of reduced customer misuse, fewer incorrect expectations, and improved product performance.

Cross-Selling:

- Appropriate offers presented by the CSR (including transfers to sales staff) as a percentage of calls handled.
- The value of sales as a percentage of offers presented.
- Sales cancelled as inappropriate.

Measures of CSR performance on process goals should balance efficiency (speed of call handling and number of calls handled) and effectiveness (satisfactory problem resolution, effective education on self-service, and successful cross-selling). In all performance measurement, anticipating unintended consequences is as important as designing useful goals and incentives. Some of the challenge involves establishing the right culture. For instance, having CSRs use a hard-sell approach when up-selling may work in the short term, but it will rarely maximize long-term customer value. CSRs must be trained in soft-sell techniques *and* given incentives to build relationships rather than sell aggressively.

In light of the importance of problem resolution to customer satisfaction, service must measure customers' actual satisfaction with the solutions provided. Brief follow-up surveys can establish that measure as well as future purchase intentions and the potential for positive or negative word of mouth. Inevitably, some portion of customers with problems will be dissatisfied or mollified rather than satisfied. As will be shown in Chapter 4, measuring the lost revenue caused by problems—and thus establishing the economic imperative for fixing or preventing them—requires accurate measures of customers' satisfaction and loyalty when they encounter these problems and receive a solution.

As we saw in Chapter 1, not all customers who experience problems take the trouble to complain. That makes the complainers incredibly useful and makes satisfying them incredibly important. When you satisfy a complainer, you retain a customer who might otherwise be lost. Similarly, when you prevent a problem from recurring—either by fixing the design, performance, or product flaw or by educating customers—you retain not only those who would have encountered the problem and complained, but also the much larger number of customers who would have encountered it and not complained.

Financial Goals

We will examine the financial impact of solving and preventing problems, and of increasing satisfaction, loyalty, and positive word of mouth, at various points in this book, particularly in Chapter 4, where we introduce TARP's Market Damage Model and Market-at-Risk calculation. These models quantify the impact of specific problems and of the overall experience on outcome measures, and thus quantify the revenue gained by fixing and preventing those problems.

The cost of fixing or preventing a specific problem must be considered as well. I grant you that this is not a new concept. Cost is the reason that organizations do not fix most of the problems they do know about. What's new is quantifying the revenue that is potentially lost each month that a specific problem goes unaddressed. Only with both values—the revenue at risk because of a problem and the cost of fixing or preventing that problem—can a company make the economic case for addressing or not addressing the problem.

I strongly recommend understanding the revenue impact of strategic customer service. Specific revenue goals would initially consider mainly incremental revenue from reducing customer attrition rather than revenue from cross-selling and up-selling. Once good resolution capabilities are in place, service can then adopt what I call "aggressive customer service," covered in Part 4. Aggressive customer service includes cross-selling and up-selling and actively delighting customers, which also increases revenue.

In addition to credit for revenue from selling, customer service should receive credit in some form for revenue saved because of problems fixed or prevented as a result of its efforts, which have led to the retention of some percentage of customers. Not only is that fair, but it's also the way to calculate the return on investments to improve service and fix or prevent problems. That calculation itself begins to transform management's view of service from cost center to revenue source.

Bound up in revenue and margin goals are the contributions of customer service to lowering risk, heightening innovation, increasing brand equity, and maintaining and increasing employee satisfaction. The impact of customer service on these areas is real and in many cases measurable, and thus they constitute valid strategic objectives.

When the right roles and goals are strategically defined, you can meet customer expectations in ways that mesh with the organization's business, marketing, pricing, and other strategies. Most importantly, you can link process goals to outcome goals and link outcome goals to revenue and margin goals. A strategic approach also calls for setting and pursuing goals in a logical order. For instance, you must link process goals to outcome goals or you may twist CSRs' behavior in ways that hurt customer satisfaction and loyalty. Similarly, you must develop a service process that handles customer contacts effectively and captures useful data on customers before you attempt to cross-sell and create delight.

Unfortunately, even in companies that go beyond process measures and set outcome goals, few executives broaden the focus beyond satisfaction and loyalty to include word-of-mouth measures, let alone the impact on revenue and risk. Fewer still employ customer service to produce a voice of the customer (VOC) that enhances revenue and margin by increasing innovation, reducing risk, and lowering service costs and employee turnover. At Procter & Gamble, one aspect of its VOC process is a file of digital recordings of customer calls titled "Listen to the Boss," meaning the customer. Any product manager can hear what customers think of his product at any time.

All of these process and outcome goals can be logically rolled up into the financial goals of increased revenue via higher volume (and lower customer attrition) and increased margins via higher prices and lower costs. Therefore, it behooves management to set goals in each of these areas—a task we'll return to from time to time and cover in greater depth in Chapter 4.

KEY TAKEAWAYS

1. Executing DIRFT means properly setting and consistently meeting expectations and eliminating unpleasant surprises as well as delivering traditional quality.
2. Poor product design, misleading marketing messages, and broken business processes are the root cause of much more customer dissatisfaction than employees with bad attitudes.
3. What CSRs deliver after they answer the phone—responsive actions; clear, believable answers; and fair treatment—is much more important than how fast the phone is answered.
4. Word of mouth and reduced risk are two major contributors to the bottom line that few companies set goals for and then measure.
5. Achieving the proper mix and linkage of process, outcome, and financial goals increases both the effectiveness and the efficiency of customer service and assures buy-in from finance.

NOTES

1. "Making Service a Potent Marketing Tool," *BusinessWeek*, June 11, 1984.

PART 2

Identifying Immediate Revenue and Profit Opportunities

CHAPTER 3

Tactical Responses and Strategic Solutions

Dealing with Customers' Problems and Addressing Their Causes

I RECENTLY HAD two interactions with credit card companies, one good and one not so good. In the first, I called American Express when I saw a charge on my bill that was not mine. The first person I talked to quickly removed it and said that he would get back to me if there was any indication of an ongoing problem. The second interaction was with United Mileage Plus Visa after my card was declined in a restaurant while I was traveling, although I had called the issuing bank and told it that I would be traveling to that city. When my wife called to inquire, she was told that this still happened occasionally; it was for our protection, and it could easily happen again while we were traveling. When she then appealed to a supervisor, reiterating that the bank was aware of our travel itinerary, the supervisor said, "The Risk Department does not look at the customer service record of your travel plans, and the disconnect between the two parts of our organization cannot be fixed." Needless to say, I used my American Express card for the rest of the trip.

As you'll recall from Chapter 1, when an organization fails to do it right the first time, customer service should stand ready to help customers who have experienced those failures. Responding to those customers at the tactical level means providing explanations, replacements, coupons, and, in the above Visa situation, assurance of an immediate resolution. The strategic element involves locating the causes of problems, learning how to prevent or solve them, and deciding which ones to prevent or solve. Consequently, when a customer contacts the service function, the twin goals of the system are to (1) *respond consistently to individual customers' questions, problems, and needs in a cost-effective manner*, and (2) *gather and distribute data from customer contacts in order to identify and remedy the causes of customers' problems.*

The second goal constitutes the feedback loop described in the DIRFT model in Chapter 1. From the strategic standpoint, the feedback loop supports the organization's efforts to do the job right the first time. Strategic customer service distinguishes between solving the problems of individual customers and addressing the systemic causes of those problems. The former is a tactical response; the second, a strategic decision. This strategic role is critical, because a failure to address the causes of problems allows those problems to continue and leads to decreased customer satisfaction, increased operating expenses, and reduced employee morale. Do not underestimate the corrosive effects of the latter; when service reps see the same problems recurring despite repeated reports, without an explanation, they conclude that management doesn't care about the customer or, perhaps, about them. Conversely, eliminating the causes of problems enables the organization to do it right the first time and encourages employees to pursue continuous improvement.

In this chapter, we first examine the actions that CSRs must take at the tactical level to solve customers' problems. We then suggest some strategic steps that the organization can take to prevent or eliminate those problems. Finally, we suggest several unconventional actions to enhance the overall interface between the tactical and strategic elements.

TACTICAL VERSUS STRATEGIC PROBLEM SOLVING

While every customer who complains about a problem should be satisfied, the ideal solution is to eliminate the cause of the problem so that both the complainers and the noncomplainers are satisfied. However, it's not always economically feasible to eliminate the root cause of a problem. Satisfying customers who complain is a tactical task, while locating causes and prioritizing problems for elimination are strategic issues.

As a case in point, one of the most highly rated auto firms had three staffers who telephoned any consumer who sent in a poor rating on their dealer visit. Their goal was to do whatever was necessary to win these customers back. I suggested that the firm reallocate those three people to consulting with key dealers to see how the firm could systematically eliminate the root causes of problems rather than repeatedly refighting the same battle. This reallocation of resources from the tactical to the strategic level can have a twentyfold effect because in the auto industry only about 5 percent of customers ever appeal to headquarters.

However, in cases where economics preclude the elimination of the root cause of a problem, customer service must solve the problem satisfactorily for each customer who encounters it. Depending upon the industry, this remedy can include replacement or return of the product, full or partial refund or credit, or other forms of added value and compensation. Solving the customer's problem—as opposed to eliminating the underlying cause—is often the logical option for satisfying customers and retaining (or increasing) loyalty. The course that you choose depends on the frequency as well as the revenue and profit impacts of the problem, which is a subject we address in Chapter 4.

Solving the problem only for customers who complain can be a dangerous option, though. Remember that many customers do not complain. Therefore, if you leave the root cause of a problem unaddressed, you virtually guarantee that the noncomplainers—usually 50 to 95 percent of the customers who encounter the problem—will remain dissatisfied and less loyal and will spread bad word of mouth.

In addition, any problem that creates significant safety issues, liability exposure, or risk to brand reputation must be addressed. An example is the rash of lawsuits against the Ford Motor Company in the 1970s and

1980s regarding the Pinto. These suits arose after it was alleged that the company continued to sell the model after it had learned that the fuel tank could explode during a rear-end collision. It was also alleged that Ford chose to risk the liability suits rather than redesign parts of the vehicle. Years later, a law review article maintained that the Pinto was no more unsafe than similar cars in this regard, but the damage to the brand had long since been done.

Deciding not to prevent or eliminate a particular problem can, under the right circumstances, be a valid decision, and, again, it's a strategic decision. But the damage it will do to revenue must be understood. The rationale for such a decision must also be understood by the members of the customer contact staff, as they will sometimes be asked, "How could this happen?" and must be able to explain that it is a conscious choice, rather than management ignorance or neglect. Customers will accept a logical rationale, but they won't accept what appears to be disdain for the customer.

This need for tactical problem solving linked to strategic problem prevention is yet another reason to take a strategic approach to customer service. When a customer contacts your service function, the company has both a second chance to produce a satisfied customer *and* an opportunity to diagnose the problem and prevent it from recurring. Tactical customer service is not only the eyes and ears of the organization, but also its microscope and stethoscope. The strategic approach is to invest in the diagnostic instruments, not just in an immediate response. The balance of this chapter describes the high-level tactical functions of customer service and then the high-level strategic functions, setting the stage for the rest of the book.

FIVE STEPS TO TACTICAL PROBLEM SOLVING

Effective front-line tactical problem solving usually results from strategic decisions. Recall the three main reasons that companies fail to do it right the first time: management policies and procedures, employee behavior and attitudes, and customer error and expectations. Each of these reasons can often be traced to management decisions in areas such as product design, quality, marketing and sales messages, staffing levels and training, and delivery and installation procedures. But, as I've noted, no matter how well management does its job, problems will occur, customers will ideally complain about them, and service must satisfy those customers who do complain.

The difficulty of solving individual customers' problems at the tactical level depends partly on management's decisions regarding such areas as those mentioned previously and partly on the nature of the business and the distribution system. For instance, a commercial bank dealing with electronic transfers and accounts faces a different set of challenges than a tire manufacturer that depends on a dealer network to fix a product with a hole in it while explaining the exclusions of the road hazard warranty. The bank has far more control over front-line, tactical-level solutions than the tire company. Essentially, the bank's customers will complain to the branch manager or call the bank's service function. Most of the tire company's customers will complain to the salesperson or service manager at the dealership, and the tire company cannot fix a tire over the phone or the Web. Worse, the tire company may not even be made aware of problems. A tire dealer we worked with logged fewer than 10 complaints per store each month, yet we knew from research that some 20 percent of its 900 customers per month—about 180—experienced problems. The tire company was, in essence, driving blind.

Fortunately, the model for sound tactical problem solving at the front line comprises the same five steps for most organizations, albeit with some customization:

1. Solicit and welcome complaints.
2. Identify key issues.
3. Assess the customer's problem and the potential causes.
4. Negotiate an agreement.
5. Take action to follow through and follow up.

Broadly, here is how to go about implementing these steps.

Step 1: Solicit and Welcome Complaints

You can solve only problems that you're aware of. Customers can be made to understand this if you follow the example of the companies mentioned in Chapter 1, which printed the phrase "We can solve only problems we know about" on their invoices. Given that few customers complain relative to the number who experience a problem, you want to encourage complaining via stickers, banner ads on the web site, and face to face via eye contact and a mix of phrases, such as "What else I can help you with today?" "What other concerns do you have?" and "Did we get that completely right?"

Soliciting complaints works only if you also welcome them when they are brought to you. Your service rep should thank the customer for going to the trouble of pointing out the problem and giving the company an opportunity to make things right.

Service reps must also, of course, be trained to deal with irritated or angry customers. Until you defuse the customer's anger, the blood does not return to his brain, and you are dealing with an irrational person. Do not make the mistake of believing that hiring people with "the right personality" can substitute for rigorous training and role playing in skillful listening, demonstrating empathy, acknowledging the customer's viewpoint, and avoiding loaded language.

Step 2: Identify Key Issues

While a call to customer service may begin with, or move quickly to, the substance of a complaint, identifying a customer's issues will often require getting beyond his feelings and directly to the facts of the situation. This step may involve letting the customer talk—or vent—for a bit while your rep clarifies what he has said and expresses empathy.

Open-ended questions such as "What can I do to help you?" should be used to get the customer started. This can be followed by "What can I do to make this right?" These questions will not only evoke specific desires but will help the customer move from using the emotional part of his brain to using the intellectual part. Such questions also allow the CSR to identify the customer's short-term issues, such as his car not being ready when the kids must be picked up at day care at 4:00 p.m. Once the customer is assured that your organization will provide transportation, he will calm down and the issue of getting the car repaired and back to him the next day can be addressed.

Finally, the rep should assume that the customer is honest until proven otherwise. Nothing will turn an honest customer off faster than insinuating that she is not. They may be mistaken but not dishonest.

Step 3: Assess the Customer's Problem and the Potential Causes

Assessing the problem will position your CSR to understand what the customer wants, where the responsibility lies, and the customer's history with and value to the company. The customer cannot be blamed for causing the problem; instead, the facts of the situation must be ascertained. Usually the cause of the problem lies with the company, the customer, a third party, or an act of God. With sufficient information to understand the nature of the problem, the rep can move on to establish its severity—Was anyone hurt? Are there potential safety or liability issues? Is the customer losing time, money, or his own customers?—and its cause. As will be explained in Chapter 5, a well-designed problem classification scheme is a critical component that will help your CSR and your organization to effectively classify and report problems and their causes.

Ideally, the CSR should have access to the information needed to establish the customer's value to and history with the organization. While many customers willingly, and sometimes even aggressively, inform the rep about their tenure as customers or their monthly volume, not all will do so. A sophisticated information system will enable the rep to know whom she is dealing with and to more effectively negotiate a win-win for both the customer and the company in the next step.

Step 4: Negotiate an Agreement

Given the cost of replacing a good customer, it's *always* best to err on the side of giving the customer what she feels is fair in order to retain her business. Service-oriented retailers like Neiman Marcus, Whole Foods, and Eddie Bauer have policies of full and unconditional refunds if a customer is not completely satisfied, because those polices make economic sense for those companies.

That said, no organization can afford to give away the store, and full, unconditional refunds are not practical or needed in every industry. Because issue circumstances and customers vary, there is seldom a single appropriate solution. As a result, it's often necessary to negotiate a resolution with the goal of the customer feeling he was treated fairly. A negotiated settlement occurs when what your company is willing to offer and what the customer considers a fair remedy overlap. There are often two parts to the remedy: what the customer needs right now and what he would like as compensation for his inconvenience. The best way to facilitate negotiated settlements is to give CSRs what TARP terms a Flexible Solution Space.™ This "space" is bounded by parameters that give them the latitude needed to negotiate resolution in a high percentage of cases (the organization's targeted percentage for front-line, full-resolution interactions), along with directives to refer the case to a second-level subject matter expert in the 2 to 5 percent of cases that might go beyond those parameters. This flexibility enables your reps to function when there is not a single set solution for common customer problems, which is the situation in most organizations.

Ideally, solutions—and the parameters of the Flexible Solution Space—should consider the source of the problem (the company, the distributor, the customer, the weather, or fate), the customer's history with the company, and the economics of the situation (the customer's value to the company, the damage to the customer, the cost to the company, and the risk because of bad word of mouth or legal or regulatory exposure). For a particular issue, there should usually be between two and four standard solutions from which CSRs can choose, using their common sense and experience combined with general guidance.

For instance, I recently arrived at the airport for the final leg of a four-city trip to find that my flight was running at least three hours late, as was the next flight. The US Airways employee noted I was a silver (that is, flying more than 30 times a year at business rates) customer on the airline and therefore offered, without my even asking, to put me on a competitor's flight that was leaving within the next hour. While the airline lost a little revenue on that one flight, I felt very good about it, and it got four times as much back on my next trip, which was to a more costly destination.

Solutions for similar problems and customers should be consistent, while recognizing the unique characteristics of certain customers and problems. The best way to train staff on the range of flexibility is through storytelling. If you describe a problem area and state that there are three perfectly acceptable approaches to this issue depending upon the circumstances, you can then describe three situations and tell the story about how each was handled. This puts stakes in the ground for guidance. The key is then to let your staff members use their judgment. In many cases, rather than throwing money at the issue, a clear explanation of the rationale behind a particular policy will move a customer from dissatisfied to at least mollified. The policy should also recognize that sometimes the answer to the customer must be no, and that when it is, it's better to deliver that negative answer—and the clear believeable reasons for it—than to string the customer along. However, the "no" has to be delivered with both empathy and a credible explanation of why this constitutes fair and reasonable treatment.

Step 5: Take Action to Follow Through and Follow Up

The first step after the negotiation of a solution is to confirm the action that will be taken, both verbally and in writing if at all possible, and to specify any steps that the customer must take and a time frame for the solution or for the steps to be taken. CSRs should proactively confirm their names and contact information, and should be sure that they have the customers' current contact data in case there's a need to get in touch as the solution is being sought or implemented. In emotional situations, customers often fail to take down a name, and providing it proactively shows confidence and good will. It's also good form to thank the customer again for bringing the problem to the organization's attention.

It is essential that information on a problem be captured and routed to the right parties in the organization. This allows the cause of that problem to be analyzed so that the strategic decision concerning how and whether to prevent or eliminate it can be made. *If you don't log it you can't analyze it.* This brings us to the feedback loop that links customer service's problem-solving efforts to the rest of the organization.

SIX TASKS CONNECTING THE TACTICAL RESPONSE TO THE STRATEGIC FEEDBACK LOOP

Figure 3-1, which reprises the second part of Figure 1-1 depicting the DIRFT model, illustrates the six tasks that customer service must execute when customers contact the organization with problems. (Note that these apply whether the contact occurs via phone, e-mail, Internet site, or any other mechanism.) These six tasks are to respond to the individual

Figure 3-1. Customer Service's Responses to Problems

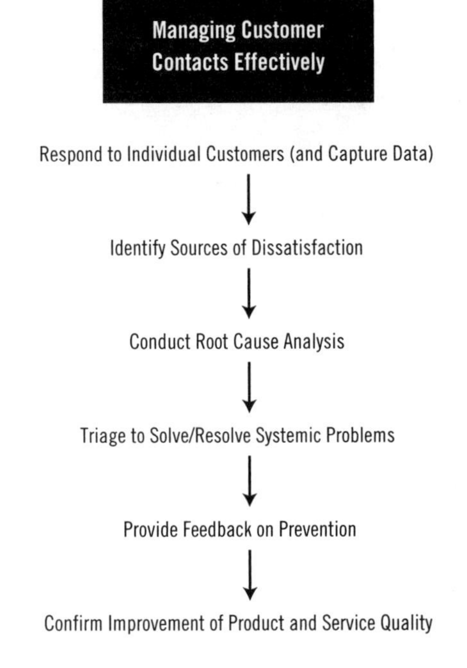

customer appropriately, which we've discussed previously, and then to identify the source of the customer's dissatisfaction, conduct a general causal analysis, solve or resolve the problem (again, discussed previously), provide feedback to the organization on prevention, and then help to permanently improve the product or service.

Let's examine each of these tasks.

Task 1: Respond to Individual Customers (and Capture Data)

When a customer presents your service representative with a problem or question, the rep must treat the customer as a person rather than as a problem. At the same time, the rep must collect enough information on the factors relating to the problem, the product, and the environment to allow immediate or subsequent diagnosis of how the situation arose. The resolution process must feed enough data into the system to facilitate future analysis. We examine the detailed components and design of such a system in Chapter 6.

Task 2: Identify Sources of Dissatisfaction

The CSR must manage the tension that may arise between the goals of resolving the customer's problem in the initial contact, maintaining productivity, and finding the root cause of the problem. The company needs to learn enough to understand the nature, origin, and potential ramifications of the problem, yet the customer mainly wants the problem solved. The customer may therefore see questions regarding usage, storage, maintenance, and expectations as irrelevant or even as attempts to shift the blame onto her. Thus, it's essential that the CSR phrase questions that are designed to identify causes in a nonaccusatory manner and to pose them with sensitivity and proper timing.

For instance, it often makes sense to first determine the cause of the customer's general problem or reason for dissatisfaction, then ask questions to get at the details. If dissatisfaction is expressed in general terms ("I'm really disappointed!"), the task is to help the customer be more specific. Why is the customer disappointed? Does the vacuum cleaner not pick up lint or embedded sand? Is it too loud? Is it difficult to operate? If the last, in what ways? The CSR can then resolve the problem to the customer's satisfaction with a remedy. *After* the customer is satisfied, the CSR can pose questions to determine the source of inaccurate expectations or the cause of the problem "so that we can spare other customers this trouble." Particularly with problems caused by customer error, expectations, or misuse, there's often a better chance of learning the details after satisfying the customer.

The goal should be to first satisfy the customer while gathering boilerplate data, such as model number, place and date of purchase, and the salesperson's name (if applicable), and then ask questions designed to detect at least the general cause if not the root cause of the problem. The more boilerplate information (accessible by serial number or phone number) the system can deliver to the CSR's workstation, the better.

Task 3: Conduct Root Cause Analysis

Locating the root cause of a problem may not be the responsibility of customer service, but gathering data on the general cause to guide subsequent root cause analysis is an important secondary responsibility, which may be that of a specific unit, team, or individual. Whether service or another unit is responsible will depend on the problem. The apparent problem or symptom of the problem may not be the root cause. For that reason, the analysis may begin in customer service and then move to the department that is best positioned to discover the cause.

To effect this analysis, the IT system must support easy data entry, integrate data from all sources (including warranty claims and returns from various channels), and compile concise, readable reports for management. I'll discuss data classification schemes in Chapter 5 and ways of structuring such an IT system in Chapter 7.

With a fully integrated complaint system, issues are clustered and reported to the proper area by the preventive analysis group. Issues that appear to be cross-functional or that have murky causes can be researched by the quality and customer experience functions if they rise to the appropriate level of importance. Not everything gets analyzed. Problems that have less financial impact should be rectified individually with no further investigation unless there is a simple fix to eliminate them.

However, eliminating the root causes of problems precludes their recurrence and boosts company productivity. For example, one organization found that a significant percentage of the 35,000 calls it received *each month* were simple billing questions. By installing a voice response system to answer routine questions, the company decreased the number of calls received and gave customers virtually instant answers at any time of day.

Task 4: Triage to Solve/Resolve Systemic Problems

Once the causal analysis has been done, the preventive analysis team within customer service or the cross-functional customer experience management team reviews all the current issues and sets priorities for action. This triage results in three possible outcomes: prevent by education, prevent by process or product fix, or respond whenever the problem occurs and is reported. Prevention has an advantage in that it also helps those who do not complain. At Xerox, proactive education and preventive maintance dramatically reduced emergency repairs and raised satisfaction due to fewer breakdowns.

Task 5: Provide Feedback on Prevention

The data that reps gather contribute to a preventive database and the preventive analysis described in Task 3. This database enables the organization to identify and classify problems, understand their causes, prevent them when possible, prioritize them for solution, and then solve them. For example, when customer expectations for the life of consumer electronics and laptop batteries rose, longer-lasting batteries became part of DIRFT. Additionally, a surprising number of problems can be prevented through customer education, changes in marketing and sales messages, and changes in procedures.

Task 6: Confirm Improvement of Product and Service Quality

The entire feedback loop is designed to improve the customer experience. Once the causes of problems have been identified, the preventive action, product or process improvement, or enhanced resolution can be implemented. The final step is not only to confirm that the problems are fixed but also to notify customers and distributors that you have done so. The manufacturer of a leading detergent sent letters with coupons to the roughly 2,000 customers who had complained about its scent. The letter described how the scent had been modified and included a coupon and a request to give the product another try. Over 60 percent of the coupons were redeemed, and the company received dozens of letters to the effect of, "I am amazed that a big company like yours actually listened to a few consumers, acted to change your product, and remembered my letter."

Regardless of the solution or resolution, future reports on problem levels and on data from surveys and returns can tell management whether it worked or proved acceptable. Follow-up surveys with customers who complained will also quantify the effects on satisfaction and loyalty. With a consistent system for solving customers' problems, a company can continually improve its products or services and thus the customer experience. However, creating such a system will probably require changes in management viewpoints, organizational structure, and operating procedures, and some of these changes may seem unconventional.

UNCONVENTIONAL MANAGEMENT WISDOM

To implement a systematic approach to enhancing the end-to-end experience, the organization must create the proper conditions. In my experience, creating those conditions requires management to rethink several conventional ideas regarding quality, complaints, salespeople's roles, and customers' honesty. In rethinking these ideas, management must take a somewhat unconventional approach and:

- Redefine quality.
- Aggressively solicit complaints.
- Get sales out of problem solving.
- Assume that customers are honest.

Redefine Quality

Some managers define quality as delivering the product according to its specifications. Yet a product that meets its specifications might not meet customer expectations, and those expectations—and the customer's resulting experience—are the most important measure of quality. Other managers assume that the problem was caused by the functional area in which it surfaces, such as installation or customer service, and that's typically not the case. Still other managers define the problem as being the customer who is registering the complaint, the solution being to stop the complaining and reduce complaints. All of the above only exacerbate the problem and continue the downward spiral.

The more useful (and logical) approach is to define the quality of a product in terms of its ability to meet the reasonable expectations of customers who have been educated about its use by employees who have been trained to do so. Also, it's best to view customer questions and inquiries as symptoms of problems waiting to happen. Many managers dismiss customers' questions, as well as the befuddlement that causes them, as insignificant. For instance, when customers contact the company for explanations of service charges that they see as unexpected and unwarranted, this is a problem even if the company classifies it as a question. Why? Because customers see being charged fees that they believe to be unwarranted as a problem. If it is valid, anticipate the question with a clear explanatory message on the statement.

Aggressively Solicit Complaints

We have shown that service can fix only problems that are complained about and that noncomplainers are much less loyal, leading to lost revenue. Therefore, you want customers to complain, and you need to encourage complaints at every touch point. Part of this is convincing employees that you really believe that they are not the primary cause of complaints—as we pointed out in Chapter 2.

Get Sales Out of Problem Solving

While every company has customer service, virtually all salespeople, especially in business-to-business (B2B) environments, emphasize their dedication to service during their sales presentations. They urge customers to call them directly if they have any questions or problems. But salespeople are often not immediately available and often lack access to all the tools and information that service can tap. They must therefore tell customers, "I'll check that out and call you back." At that point, you've lost first-contact resolution. Worse, salespeople often forget such promises, causing more dissatisfaction and inefficiency. Salespeople need to encourage customers to go to service after the sale is complete.

We take this issue up in Chapter 12. There are strong reasons to cast customer service as *the* problem solver, one of which is to free up salespeople for more remunerative activities. That's a rationale that most salespeople readily understand.

Assume that Customers Are Honest

Many companies are run by risk-averse executives who want to protect the company's money. They fear that customers will "game the system" to extract unwarranted refunds and other benefits from CSRs. However, most fraud and shrinkage is caused by professional thieves rather than by casually dishonest customers. You can usually identify the crook if they come back at you a second time—a supervisor at Swift Meat Company once told me their rule was "One turkey per customer," meaning if you reported on bad turkey, you got a refund no questions asked; a second request got much more scrutiny. While there is a need for systems to identify the thieves, these systems need to avoid hassling known good if slightly flaky or error-prone customers. This means moving from the controller mentality to the idea that the customer is honest until proven otherwise, which is the approach that American Express, Neiman Marcus, Canadian Tire, and hundreds of other companies take.

In this chapter, we've looked at how properly structured service and feedback systems can enable an organization to respond well to unmet customer expectations. Building these systems costs money, and those expenditures must be justified on a cost/benefit basis. Chapter 4 will show you how the revenue implications of building these systems typically average 10 times their cost.

KEY TAKEAWAYS

1. Assuming that customers are honest unless proven otherwise can dramatically enhance efficiency as well as customer satisfaction.
2. Stop repeatedly addressing recurring problems and reallocate some resources that are now used to handle escalated complaints to fixing the systemic causes of those problems. However, not all problems can be cost effectively prevented—a triage process must make that distinction between prevention and handling.
3. If you don't log it you can't analyze and prevent it.
4. When customers encounter problems, apologize without admitting blame, regardless of who or what created the situation and ask what would make them happy.
5. Enhance first-contact resolution by providing front-line CSRs with Flexible Solution Spaces™ that allow them to adapt the response to customer circumstances.
6. A quick refund may solve a problem or placate a customer, but in some situations a clear, believable explanation is the better solution—don't throw money at every problem, it may leave the customer feeling that you are buying them off.
7. Tell your customers and employees what you've learned from your feedback loop and inform them when problems have been fixed. Feed back the impact of their feedback!

CHAPTER 4

Fixes and Finances

Making the Financial Case for Customer Service Investments

A NUMBER OF YEARS AGO, we were working with a leading automaker. The service area had identified an engine hesitation problem that was causing a significant number of escalated complaints, but senior management seemed to have bigger fish to fry. Doing a quick analysis similar to what follows in this chapter, we estimated that the profit impact over the next year would be about $50 million. This got management's attention, but they only appointed a work group to "look into it." We then presented our calculations in such a way that the head of customer satisfaction was able to say, "For each month we delay action, it will cost us another $4.6 million." Management took immediate action. If you can demonstrate the cost of inaction, you can precipitate action.

Organizations measure the performance of customer service in various ways, few of which are very useful. The reason is they have seldom accounted for the effects of good and bad service on customer satisfaction, loyalty, and word of mouth, let alone on financial results. Indeed, as noted in Chapter 2, most companies that track and analyze service metrics use the wrong measures. Some even use the results in ways that can undermine the customer experience, systematically creating dissatisfaction.

Strategic customer service demands a new financial view of service and of investments in improvements in the end-to-end customer experience. The strategic view is to see customer service as a revenue preserver and generator and to aim to maximize its impact on revenue.

The payoffs for companies with the strategic view are measurable and significant. For example, the traditional cost-center approach argues for increasing the productivity of service reps by increasing the number of calls each rep handles per shift. However, this approach can actually raise costs, because customers who fail to obtain resolution of their problem on their first contact often "shop the system" by calling several times or escalate contacts to higher-level employees. TARP's studies show that resolving a customer's problem completely on the first call leads to an average 20 percent increase in satisfaction and *at least a 50 percent decrease in cost*, compared with second-call resolution. Those subsequent calls suck up additional time, and often that of a more expensive employee.

In this chapter, we address the translation of the effects of good and bad service into dollar terms and, thus, the resulting financial impact on the organization. We combine the implications of the customer behaviors we examined in Chapter 1 (satisfaction, loyalty, and word of mouth) and the customer expectations and company goals that we identified in Chapter 2 (process, outcome, and financial goals) with the concepts related to problem prevention and problem solving in Chapter 3. The key (and rarely asked) question addressed here is: Which problems should we solve, and which investments in improved strategic customer service should we fund?

As noted earlier, most organizations use extremely unscientific methods of prioritizing problems to be fixed. They either fix the most frequently occurring problems or take the squeaky wheel approach of fixing those problems that customers bring to senior management's attention. They also fund fixes out of either the general budget for customer service or the budget of the function responsible for the problem rather than creating a separate budget and a system of incentives for fixing problems. Most organizations don't even think of these outlays as investments, despite the fact that making or not making them directly affects future revenue and profit in measurable ways.

Therein lies the main mission of this chapter: to show you how to view outlays to improve the customer experience as investments in enhanced revenue and word of mouth that have a tangible financial payoff. Service can be viewed as a revenue savior and generator, rather than as a nice-to-have function that can be funded during good times and gutted during bad times. Quantifying the monthly financial impact of the current situation creates the economic imperative for making strategic service investments *now* rather than when it is convenient. For every month these investments are delayed, *X* million in revenue is being left on the table.

THE CASE FOR GREAT CUSTOMER SERVICE

All organizational goals should ultimately translate to revenue goals and, in a business, profitability goals. Even nonprofits aim to grow their membership or their scope of operations while meeting their budgets. So the key questions vis-à-vis customer service become: What is the financial impact of the current customer experience and your service function on the organization? and How much more payoff would accrue from an improved customer experience and customer service process?

Answering such questions actually goes beyond tactical problem solving to examining all customer touches across the customer experience. When any part of the customer experience is not perfect, it then expands to include the customer's interaction with the service process. In either case, word of mouth spreads and either reinforces your marketing efforts and generates additional customers or undercuts your marketing efforts and leads to fewer customers.

Figure 4-1 depicts a bucket with a hole in it, with the water in the bucket representing your customers. Your organization adds customers at the top via marketing and sales. Those customers who have a good experience remain loyal and attract more customers through positive word of mouth. Those customers who encounter problems and are not satisfied leak out through the hole. Problem prevention and tactical customer service reduce the size of that hole. As Bob Smith, the CFO of Electronic Systems Inc, a division of Xerox, says, "Investments in enhanced service,

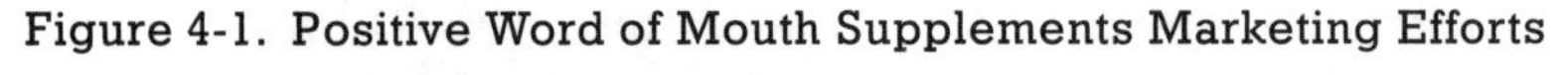

Figure 4-1. Positive Word of Mouth Supplements Marketing Efforts

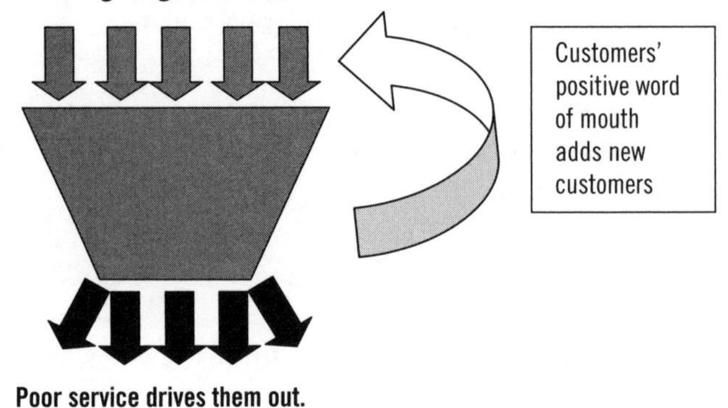

like customer service training, have a huge ROI because they reduce the cost of sales; our existing customers do our selling for us." If a company experiences very little leakage, as is the case for Chick-fil-A, USAA, Honda, and Lexus, then light marketing will reduce costs while positive word of mouth creates a continual flow into the bucket—or aggressive marketing will significantly increase market share by taking customers from others.

To quantify the current financial flows resulting from your customer experience and customer service, you calculate the percentage of customers who have a perfect experience, the percentage who don't and who don't complain to your company, and the percentage who don't and who request assistance from a customer service function or other department (or a channel like the retailer). Of those who obtain assistance, you determine the percentages left satisfied, mollified, or dissatisfied (or perhaps *more* dissatisfied). With that information, you have the basis for taking one or more of three key actions:

- Preventing problems through customer education, more accurate marketing and sales messages, or improved products and processes
- Motivating more customers to complain so that they can be satisfied by service
- Improving the performance of the service system to satisfy a higher percentage of those complaining

The challenge is to identify and prioritize opportunities for improvement in order to achieve the greatest impact on revenue and costs. In most organizations, the revenue implications of improved service are 10 to 20 times the cost implications. Every interaction, from prepurchase to billing and repurchase, is both part of the customer experience and an element of brand-aligned service that can be leveraged. Leaders like Bank of America, Disney, Starbucks, 3M, and Toyota view tactical service as part of the broader customer experience that constitutes their primary competitive edge. Meanwhile, many other companies capture and analyze copious data on satisfaction and loyalty, but then fail to compute the impact of those factors on revenue, word of mouth, and risk and regulatory expense (in addition to service cost). Those connections are what enable serious consideration of customer service investments by the CFO, also known as the resident skeptic.

HOW CFOs THINK

CFOs seek investments that will enhance the bottom line, and they support those investments that will improve it most by increasing revenue, reducing costs, or both. The investments that enhance the bottom line most are generally those that will yield the highest returns, consistent (one hopes) with the organization's business, mission, and goals. Investments in improved customer service typically earn returns well above those of competing investments. Returns of several hundred percent are not uncommon if all revenue impacts are included. Why, then, do CFOs and other executives often ignore these opportunities?

Historically, the financial impacts of improvements in customer service have been hard to quantify. The line from cause to effect has not been drawn as clearly as that from, say, new machinery to increased output, or even that from marketing expenditures to sales increases. Because the revenue implications of improvements in customer service are not necessarily immediate or readily attributable to those improvements, CFOs often view them as speculative or even suspect.

That's why TARP developed the Market Damage Model™ and the Market-at-Risk™ calculation. These calculations enable you to identify the revenue impact of specific experiences (that is, problems, questions, and points of pain as well as delighters) by customer or type of customer.

Most CFOs will be far more impressed with conservatively modeled financial data than with customer satisfaction data. The resident skeptic has long questioned the link between satisfaction and financial performance. That link is loyalty, which, as noted in Chapter 1, is measured by surveyed intentions to repurchase and recommend intentions validated periodically by measurements of actual repurchase behavior. Therefore, the Market Damage Model translates investments in customer experience improvements into pure financial terms. Likewise, the Market-at-Risk analysis addresses the financial impact of preventing specific types of problems. Jan Postma, CFO of the Museum of Modern Art, recently commented, "Satisfaction surveys and complaints are less concrete, tenuous indicators of future revenue. When you can translate specific problems' impact on loyalty into member revenue at risk, it makes a more compelling case for investment and action."

QUESTIONS TO GUIDE MODELING THE CUSTOMER EXPERIENCE

A good analysis is driven by clear questions whose answers can be directly applied to the current situation. Therefore, let's be specific about the needed questions.

When problems occur or unanswered questions arise, the customer has a negative experience, or at least is left perplexed. We call the problems that do significant damage to loyalty "points of pain," and we call those that don't "squeaky wheels" that don't deserve grease because they do little damage to revenue.

Every organization must periodically ask itself four questions:

1. What questions or problems have customers encountered in their recent experience with our ourganization?
2. To what extent are we not hearing about such issues?
3. What are our customers' key points of pain and squeaky wheels?
4. What are these points of pain costing our organization in lost revenue and extra cost?

The customers' pain affects loyalty and word of mouth in a way that can be translated into direct financial impact at both the overall organizational and problem-specific levels. At the organizational level, the Market Damage Model calculates the revenue you lose by failing to prevent problems and to fully address them when they do occur (the water flowing out the bottom of the bucket). It even considers the effects of new customers lost as a result of bad word of mouth. At the problem-specific level, which deals with the payoff from preventing specific points of pain, the Market-at-Risk calculation is the most precise way to estimate the financial impact of specific problems and to prioritize problems for investments in prevention.

These calculations can become involved and sophisticated, so for simplicity's sake I'll only summarize them. Conceptually, both the Market Damage Model and the Market-at-Risk calculation assume that once you win customers, they are yours to lose if they have a bad experience. The models estimate the percentage of customers lost as a result of the problem and the service experience and then convert customers lost into revenue lost and negative word-of-mouth impact. A key component of the calculation is the value of the customer. While some customers can be flighty, searching for the best deal given their need at the moment, others will stay for long periods unless they encounter a serious problem. The average longevity of a customer enables you to calculate the revenue or profit value or "lifetime value" (LV) of a customer, which should be the beginning basis for any serious customer retention effort. I say beginning because LV tends to be such a large number over such a long time that finance tends to discount it. More on that later. Another issue is whether it should be expressed as revenue, gross contribution, or net profit.

The second component, in addition to the revenue value of a customer, is word of mouth. Companies benefit when customers spread good word of mouth and refrain from spreading bad word of mouth. Companies like Cheesecake Factory, USAA, JetBlue, and Chick-fil-A get the majority of their new customers from word-of-mouth referrals, with some getting over 70 percent of their new customers this way, meaning that marketing has to bring in only 30 percent of new customers. These companies can spend relatively little on sales and promotions. When things go right, customer expectations are met or exceeded, problems and pain are absent, and satisfaction and loyalty ensue. So the easiest way to enhance revenue is to plug the hole in the bottom of the bucket by minimizing problems.

THE MARKET DAMAGE MODEL: WHAT IS THE DAMAGE?

The Market Damage Model™ calculates sales lost as a result of dissatisfied customers. This is a gross number, describing the overall experience rather than one related to a specific problem. This calculation makes an overall case for retaining customers by providing an overall picture of the impact of customer dissatisfaction. One of the earliest models developed by TARP, the Market Damage Model came out of our original White House–sponsored study of complaint handling in both businesses and government agencies in the 1970s. This model is also the progenitor of the Market-at-Risk™ model, which came out of work we did for Xerox and Motorola in the late 1980s.

In keeping with the rigor we are establishing, let's first define market damage. At the highest level, we define market damage as:

- The amount of sales or revenue lost or at risk from customers who encountered problems, *minus*
- Sales that were lost as a result of factors other than problems caused and handled by the customer service function

To isolate improvements to be realized by changes in customer service, we exclude customers' behavior resulting from things other than service, such as the product or service's pricing, features, or performance. (Later we will show how using the Market-at-Risk calculation to quantify these other aspects can set priorities for the process of planning the overall customer experience.) Here we're focusing strictly on problems and on how they are handled or not handled by the service process. So, in this formula, we subtract the number of sales lost as a result of natural non-service-related attrition—factors such as price and product features and basic design performance—in order to focus on matters that we can address through improvements to the quality and service function.

To fully gauge the impact of dissatisfaction and lost loyalty, we must factor in the effects of negative word of mouth. We'll look at those effects after presenting the basic market damage calculation.

Data and Output

A calculation to measure basic market damage requires both internal and survey data. To keep things manageable, I'll use simple assumptions and round numbers:

- Number of customers with problems (100,000)
- Percentage of customers with problems who complain (50 percent)
- Percentage of customers who complain and wind up satisfied (40 percent) or mollified (30 percent) or remain dissatisfied (30 percent)
- Nonrepurchase behavior of each class of customer with problems (satisfied, 10 percent; mollified, 30 percent; dissatisfied, 60 percent; noncomplainers, 40 percent). This is typical—that those who complained and were left dissatisfied are actually more disloyal than those who didn't complain.

Figure 4-2 shows a sample of how the revenue damage part of the overall market damage calculation works at XYZ Company based on these four assumptions.

In this case, the model shows that this company loses more than a third of the customers who encounter problems each year. It also shows which factor causes the greatest losses. In this example, as in most real-life cases, customers who don't complain cause the greatest damage, with more than half of the customers lost (20,000/35,500 = 56 percent) coming from noncomplaining customers who leave without a sound. This supports my contention that it's wise to solicit complaints aggressively and to provide customers with easy access to service representatives.

The damage in terms of lost loyalty and negative word of mouth comes from three sources: (1) sales lost due to the noncomplainers (2) sales lost due to complainers who remain dissatisfied (3) sales lost due to customers who are mollified (somewhat satisfied).

On this last point, think about how often you've been left mollified. The telephone or cable company representative says, "We're sorry, the repairman won't be coming today, but I'll be happy to reschedule him for

Figure 4-2. Quantifying the Revenue Impact of Service

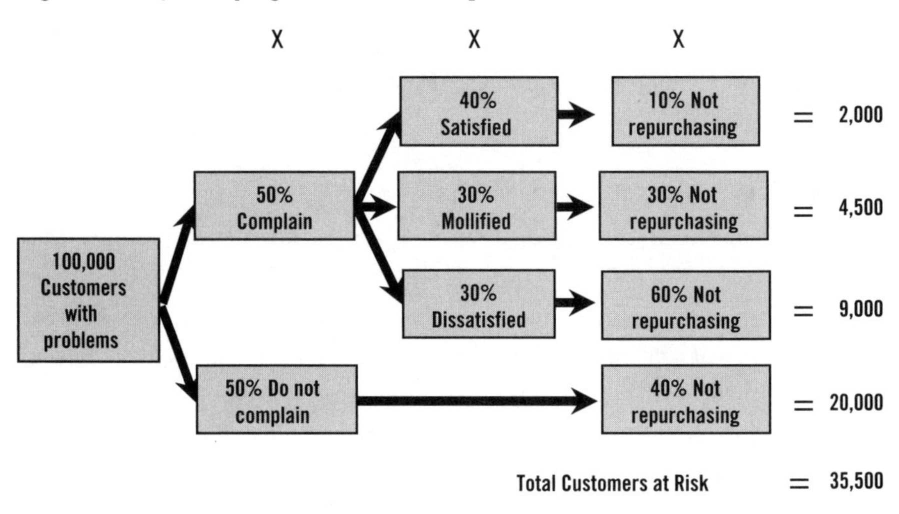

tomorrow" (so that you can stay home and wait for him again). Then there's the supermarket cashier who responds to a complaint about out-of-stock sale items with, "I'm sorry, we've reported it, but they're still having problems." They apologized, but you remained inconvenienced.

If a customer is worth $300 in revenue, then the revenue impact of the problems is $10.65 million. If handling each of the 50,000 reported problems costs $10, then the revenue damage of $10 million is 20 times the cost of handling the problems.

One other question arises about the 10 percent of customers who don't repurchase, even though they have been satisfied. We find that even if people have been satisfied or have had no problem, there are still about 10 percent who won't repurchase, either because they had a problem at all or because they now prefer an alternative product due to features or price.

The Market Damage Model shows which areas are likely to yield the greatest positive impact on sales if you improve them. In this case, at first glance it would seem sensible to satisfy complainers rather than mollify them or leave them dissatisfied. Also, preventing the problem from occurring would have a major positive effect. But the decision to fix or prevent a specific problem must consider the damage caused by that problem as well as the cost of fixing or preventing it. For that decision, we use the Market-at-Risk calculation, which we cover later in this chapter.

Financial Impact

As I mentioned above, expressing market damage in financial terms requires data on the lifetime value of a loyal customer. TARP has been shocked to find that many companies have not calculated the one-year, three-year, or lifetime value of a customer. *If you don't know how much your customer is worth, how can you decide how much to spend to retain him*—or, for that matter, to win him? Only with a value figure can you make fact-based decisions regarding sales and marketing methods, channel partners, pricing, and customer service. Executives often don't undertake these calculations because they believe the results would be too imprecise. Yet there is no need for to-the-penny precision; a broad, conservative estimate of the value of your average customer will support the Market Damage Model. In a pinch, just divide the number of customers into total annual sales and round down and you'll have a conservative estimate based on one year of sales.

While the lifetime value of a customer is a widely accepted measure, few finance people will invest based on it unless the value is estimated very conservatively. Therefore, we suggest using one year of revenue. If a product, such as a car, is purchased every three years, to be really conservative, estimate one-third of a sale. In such a case, you might, though, consider that many families own two cars and in effect buy one car every 18 months. In business-to-business (B2B) environments, you might consider one year of a contract or the price of the product along with that of incremental services that the client would buy.

The best approach is to ask the finance staff for the value it would use and then use that number or some slightly smaller round number—for example, if it is $1247, use $1,000—so that management can do the math in their heads. If an issue puts 5,000 customers at risk at $1,000 each, then that is a $5 million problem. The fact is that the positive revenue implications of service improvements are so significant that, regardless of how conservatively you calculate lifetime value, the analysis almost always favors improvements.

For instance, in Table 4-1 let's assume that the LV of a customer is $300. If that is the case we can see the impact of dimished loyalty on revenue as shown below.

The simplicity of these calculations belies their power, and numerical information holds incredible power. The fact that the calculations are

Table 4-1. Market Damage to XYZ Company in Financial Terms

Status After Having a Problem	*Number Not Buying Again*	*Lifetime Value of a Customer*	*Amount of Sales Lost in Dollars*
Satisfied	2,000	$300	$ 600,000
Mollified	4,500	300	1,350,000
Dissatisfied	9,000	300	2,700,000
Noncomplainer	20,000	300	6,000,000
Total Market Damage in Dollars			$10,650,000, or $887,500 per month

simple and logical appeals to financial mavens. Similarly, the sheer dollar amount of sales lost *every month* as a result of customers experiencing service problems motivates many executives to search out ways to staunch this outflow of funds.

What Is the Payoff if We Improve?

The Market Damage Model enables you to quantify the current revenue hemorrhage and to analyze the effect of improvements in the number of problems experienced, the accessibility of the service system (percentage of customers complaining), and service system effectiveness (percentage satisfied when they do complain). The model can also isolate the impact of problems related to quality (those resulting from product defects or performance) and to service (the accessibility and effectiveness of the service system in satisfying customers who encounter problems). But even with the baseline data from the Market Damage Model, you can estimate the impact of changing one or more of three controllable parameters:

1. Reduce the number and severity of problems.
2. Increase the percentage of customers who do complain when they encounter a problem.
3. Increase the instances or levels of satisfaction when customers complain.

This sensitivity analysis quantifies the response of the revenue stream to the three types of interventions available. I won't run the numbers, but instead point out that if you simply change the number of problems, the percentage of complainers, or the percentage of customers satisfied, the model will show the dollar changes in revenue. For instance, in Figure 4-2, if you reduce problems by 10 percent, you will reduce lost customers by 3,550, while if you just moved an additional 20 percent of complaining customers from dissatisfied to satisfied, you would save 5,000 customers. The question is then which strategy can be done for less money or more cost-effectively.

This analysis must be executed at a strategic level. The tactical customer service department cannot change the sales process to set correct expectations or change the packaging process to reduce damage complaints. Here again, strategic customer service looks at which action—prevention or handling after the fact—will be more cost-effective. To do this, you must understand the impact of specific problems on overall customer revenue and word of mouth.

It may also make sense to create the correct economic incentives to enhance the customer experience by charging the responsible department's budget for productivity or revenue lost as a result of problems (that is, causes) that the department has been aware of but has not corrected. After all, if a department incurred damage and expense because of a chemical spill, it would have to pay for it out of the departmental budget. So why not apply that logic to a misleading sales promotion that causes $500,000 in extra service costs and loses $2 million in revenue? Such a "chargeback" system provides a financial incentive for taking corrective action. Several major consumer goods companies now have service departments that routinely charge the cost of unnecessary calls about sales issues back to the product manager whose promotion or advertising caused them. However, it may make sense to charge the cost of solutions to an account created for that purpose rather than to the function's operating budget, to provide even greater incentive to eliminate root causes. For example, a tire manufacturer provides each store with a goodwill budget so that refunds are not withheld to protect short-term profits.

Objections to the Market Damage Model

Over the years we have used the Market Damage Model, we have heard several objections to its validity, usually along the following lines:

- **"Customers don't act in the ways they say they will on surveys."** In fact, British Airways, Delta Airlines, American Express, and several auto companies have all conducted longitudinal studies that show that customers actually do what they say they will do. In one case, we confirmed that about 60 percent of frequent flyers who said that they were going to change carriers reduced their miles flown dramatically in the next year.
- **"The more valuable customers are the ones who complain, and we satisfy them when they do."** TARP data from various markets—including high-net-worth investors and purchasers of aircraft—have shown that 20 to 60 percent of customers simply do not complain, even about problems that severely damage loyalty. Valuable customers' behavior is very similar to that of average customers.
- **"We will not realize the projected benefits that the model promises."** When organizations measure baseline loyalty and then make improvements, they see immediate increases in loyalty as measured by surveys. This usually tracks closely with future purchase behavior, especially if you go through at least one full buying cycle. The key is measuring the actual behavior of customers who have experienced the improved service or experience.
- **"Even if the service system increases loyalty by X, there's no guarantee that sales will go up by Y."** That may be true, because market factors other than service can affect customers and purchases. However, sales will still be proportionately higher than they would have been if loyalty had not increased by *X*.

Yes, skeptics abound, and that's good because it ensures rigor in analysis in a function that benefits greatly from it. In making the financial case for investments to improve service, it's best to review the model with the CFO's staff in advance. Involving finance in the original determination of the lifetime value of a customer, the calculation of negative and positive word-of-mouth impacts, and the data collection methodology can lead only to greater buy-in and acceptance. It can also decrease the rigor with which the case will need to be made. Remember to get the CFO talking about his personal last bad service experience and he will often get on board quickly.

THE WORD ON WORD OF MOUTH

Given the importance of word of mouth as a marketing tool—and the ill effects of negative word of mouth—it's remarkable that most companies have not attempted to quantify its impact on sales. Developments ranging from new theories of "viral marketing," to books such as Malcolm Gladwell's best seller *The Tipping Point*, to firms dedicated to "buzz marketing" and "social marketing" evidence a growing understanding of its power.

TARP's interviews with more than 400 marketing executives over a 10-year period led TARP to establish a conservative assumption that 1 potential customer lost for every 50 potential customers who hear a negative word-of-mouth message is reasonable. With the advent of viral marketing and "word of mouse," we have modified our parameters to *conservatively* assume that of every 20 consumers who hear either positive or negative word of mouth, 1 consumer acts. Our recent research for five companies suggests that of people hearing positive word of mouth, at least 1 in 10 takes action. In some cases related to popular consumer electronics products, 1 in 2 takes action, showing the ever-growing impact of the recommendations of others. Word-of-mouth calculations can and should be factored into the Market Damage Model. In fact, the actual number of negative word-of-mouth messages (and lost sales) can be included based on the actions of customers told as reported in customer surveys. For example, in one recent insurance survey, we found that two persons were told a positive message by a satisfied complainer, four were told a negative message by a mollified complainer, six were told a negative message by a dissatisfied complainer, and two were told a negative one by a noncomplainer. If you then add the conservative assumption on action taken, you can estimate the total impact on sales of word of mouth, as in Figure 4-4.

As Figure 4-4 shows, negative word of mouth is powerful. In the sample situation in the exhibit, despite the much higher 70 percent satisfied, the 30 percent dissatisfied customers generate net negative revenue every month because dissatisfied customers' negative word of mouth outdoes the satisfied customers' positive messages. Thus, it's essential to satisfy as many dissatisfied customers as possible, while maintaining the highest possible overall rate of satisfaction. If one were to take into account a third, larger segment of customers who were dissatisfied but non-complaining (which exists in almost every marketplace), the net negative word of mouth impact would be even greater.

Figure 4-4. Impact of Word of Mouth on Sales

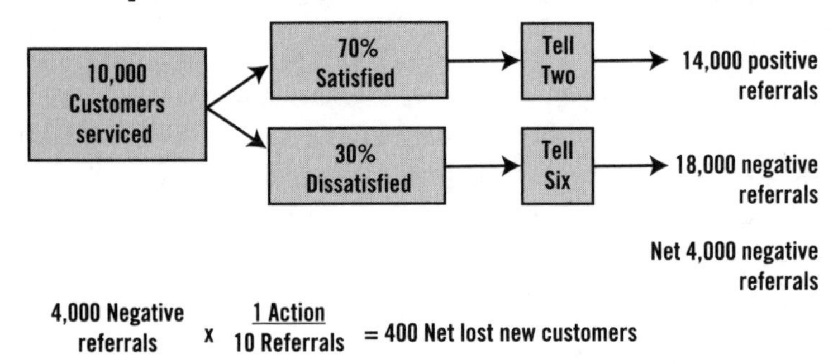

QUALITY AND SERVICE ALLOW YOU TO GET A PREMIUM PRICE

CFOs are always pressing product managers to increase margins. But there are only a limited number of ways to increase price and decrease costs. TARP has seen organizations, such as Neiman Marcus, John Deere, and Harley Davidson, show that you can charge a premium for superior quality and service.

In over a score of studies, TARP has asked survey respondents the following question: "How satisfied are you with the prices/fees charged by ABC Company?" TARP then analyzed dissatisfaction with price compared to customers' recent problem experiences. There is a strong—and certainly not surprising—relationship between problem experience and sensitivity to price, as shown in Figure 4-5.

In this example, among New York banking customers, only 10 percent of customers were dissatisfied with fees and charges if they had not had a recent service problem. Of those who had one recent service problem, more than twice as many (22 percent) were sensitive to current prices. If the problems were frequent, the percentage doubled again.

We found a similar experience with an airline. Of frequent flyers, only 12 percent of survey respondents without a recent problem were unhappy with the price. If one problem occurred, the number went to 24 percent, and further problems amplified price sensitivity.

When customers have bad service they say, "Given what I'm paying, this should not have happened!" If they get great service, they will say, "You're expensive but you're worth it!" Therefore, the message to finance

Figure 4-5. Percent of customers dissatisfied with fees rises with number of problems.

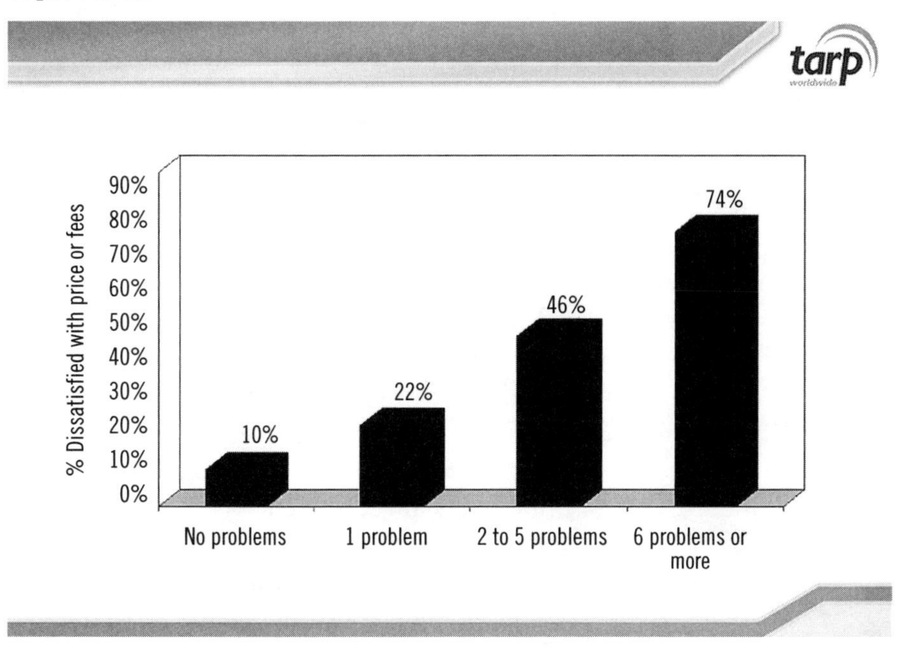

and marketing is, "If you want to charge robust margins, you better have few problems!"

THE MARKET-AT-RISK CALCULATION: IDENTIFYING CUSTOMERS' POINTS OF PAIN ACROSS THE WHOLE EXPERIENCE

I've found that most executives have no idea how much business they are losing in the normal course of operations until they think in terms of the Market Damage Model. When they consider the financial impact even in gross terms, they start seeing the strategic value of customer service in terms of problem prevention, service system accessibility, and better problem solving. The next question is usually, "Which specific problems should I attack?" That's where the Market-at-Risk calculation comes into play.

The Market-at-Risk calculation, as the name suggests, enables us to prioritize problems for correction on the basis of the portion of the customer base or market that may be lost or that is currently being lost on a monthly basis.

Typically, organizations are aware of the problems their customers face in doing business with them. However, surveys seldom provide enough detail to identify the specific problems that customers encounter, and they provide little guidance on the impact of a problem on revenue. In addition, "trained hopelessness" ensures that complaint data will indicate only the tip of the iceberg.

On the other hand, if you present customers with a printed list of issues and problems and ask them to indicate the ones they've encountered, you can bring to their mind forgotten issues related to the sale, account setup, installation, product features, use, maintenance, repair, and billing. Customers can then indicate which of these were the most serious and did the most damage to loyalty. Often, those problems *not* at the top of the customer's mind actually do more long term damage. For instance, at a copier company, the most frantic phone calls were prompted by breakdowns, but our analysis of damage by type of problem revealed that sales reps' broken promises concerning installation did four times as much damage, although customers seldom complained about them.

In practice, most organizations prioritize problems on the basis of frequency—how often customers complain—or on the basis of issues that are escalated to senior management levels. But, often neither frequency nor escalation indicates the most costly problems.

As shown in Figure 4-6, the Market-at-Risk calculation, performed on each problem, considers frequency and damage as measured by impact on loyalty, increased risk, and negative word of mouth. For each problem, the necessary data include the percentage of customers experiencing the

Figure 4-6. Market-at-Risk Calculation

Overall % Experiencing the Problem	×	% of Specific Problem Frequency	×	% of Customers Not Likely/Not Willing to Buy Again	=	% of Customers At Risk Due to Problem

problem, the percentage of interactions in which they experience the problem, and the percentage who say that they definitely or probably will not buy the product or service again. These data must usually be gathered by means of surveys, and can be verified or refined with internal records.

The goal of this approach is to enable the organization to allocate its limited resources to fixing those problems that have the most impact on loyalty, and thus on revenue. Again, as noted in Chapter 1, loyalty is best measured by continued purchasing intentions and behavior or measured by willingness to recommend. As Table 4-2 demonstrates, these calculations gauge the percentage of the customer base put at risk by a specific problem and permit comparison of the relative impact of a given array of problems.

The data in Table 4-2 show that the three problems that are most frequently reported at this company are back-ordered products (55 percent), missed delivery times (40 percent), and invoice accuracy (28 percent). However, although customers experience back orders about twice as frequently as they experience inaccurate invoices, the latter problem

Table 4-2. Market Damage Estimates for Top Six Problems at XYZ Company

Problem Experienced (40%)	*Problem Frequency (%)*[1]	*Percent Who Won't Buy Again*		*Percent of Customer Base Potentially Lost*	
		Will Not[2]	Likely to Not[3]	Minimum	Maximum
Product on back order	55	20	45	4.4	9.9
Missed delivery times	40	20	30	3.5	4.8
Accuracy of invoices	**28**	**40**	**90**	**4.5**	**10.1**
Product availability within desired time frame	18	5	10	0.4	0.7
Availability of sales rep to discuss product failure	11	50	80	2.2	3.4
Ease of obtaining credits/adjustments	11	20	35	0.9	1.5

1. Based on multiple problem selection.
2. Based on "will not repurchase" only.
3. Based on "will not repurchase" and "might not repurchase."

places a similar percentage of the customer base at risk. The percentage of customers potentially lost as a result of back-ordered products ranges from 4.4 percent to 9.9 percent, while the percentage potentially lost as a result of inaccurate invoices ranges from 4.5 percent to 10.1 percent. The second most frequent problem, missed delivery times, puts just 3.5 to 4.8 percent at risk.

In this case, the third most frequent problem, inaccurate invoices, places as much of the customer base at risk as the most frequent problem, back-ordered products. But when it comes to prioritizing problems, the cost of fixing them must be considered as well. We can assume that fixing the back-order problem by reengineering the production process or expanding inventories would cost dramatically more than producing accurate invoices. Therefore, the third most frequent problem—inaccurate invoices—would be the one to fix first.

Other costs and effects are also worth considering. For instance, missed delivery times could be addressed either by speeding up delivery, which may require significant capital investment, or by having sales reps give honest and accurate delivery times. Our research in B2B environments indicates that reliable time of arrival is actually more valued than speed of delivery. Plus, after priorities are set, there's the question of whether to prevent problems by making process changes or to solicit complaints more aggressively and resolve the problem more effectively when it occurs.

The Market-at-Risk calculation makes the financial case for customer service in the best possible manner—by isolating the relative performance of various areas of the customer experience and linking problems to customer loyalty. This analysis quantifies the portion of the customer base that is at risk and provides a customer-driven, financial indication of priorities. Again, as with the Market Damage Model, you can calculate the financial impact of these lost sales, as long as you have a conservative estimate of the value of the customer.

WHAT ABOUT CUSTOMERS WITH LIMITED OR NO CHOICE?

Some customers have little or no choice but to use a service. These include customers of many government agencies; utilities; government-granted monopolies, such as railroads; and internal departments of organizations, such as the IT or HR department. Such customers experience "forced loyalty" in that they more or less must continue their purchase behavior regardless of their level of dissatisfaction. Some authors call these customers "captives."

In such situations, customer expectations may be low relative to those in situations of choice, yet most customers expect reliable basic services. When that expectation is not met—for example, when the electric bill increases tenfold or the package is repeatedly delivered to the wrong address—customers will register complaints and demand additional service by escalating the problem to executives or to regulators, both of which cost the provider. In one instance, TARP found that responding to a complaint to the Public Service Commission cost the utility 600 times as much as responding to a regular complaint. Also, regulatory complaints can have serious legal and risk implications as well. Alternatively, customers may obtain supplemental services from independent vendors, which not only costs the customer more, but can erode the provider's economies of scale.

Customers may also exercise choice when they finally have the opportunity, as a result of changed circumstances. For instance, they may switch from oil to gas heat or vice versa when the burner dies, buy a car when they can afford to and forsake public transportation, or move to a city with better services for the given taxes when they decide to buy rather than rent. TARP observed a technical environment in which a key vendor gave relatively poor service. The vendor was warned that over half its customers said that they would migrate to a competitor as soon as one appeared. Two years later, exactly that happened, causing significant damage to the original market leader as the captives escaped with glee. (This might be a cautionary tale for Microsoft.)

When it comes to internal customers within an organization, such as those who rely on its IT department, the direct revenue impacts are nil. However, when we looked at issues that flow through to external revenue-producing customers *and* the cost of escalations to supervisors and staff time wasted doing workarounds, we could calculate a very credible cost of poor service for internal customers just as for external customers. Even when captives can't switch brands, they often find a costly "workaround." In one case, an operating unit in an oil company that was unhappy with IT withdrew part of its budget and hired its own programmers. The unit received more responsive service, but coordination and overall efficiency within the enterprise were damaged.

Such costs can be calculated or at least estimated with good accuracy, and the damage they create can be quantified. With that information, the utility, agency, or internal department with a captive market can prioritize problems and make improvements that relieve customers' sharpest pains and best control costs. True, in the absence of the profit motive, the economic imperative is often less compelling. Yet the experience of certain utilities in U.S. and European cities makes a strong case for a management focus on customer service in these situations.

IMPACTED WISDOM

The financial impacts described in this chapter should galvanize most managers to at least examine the complaint and purchase behavior of customers who encounter problems. Our key point is that the revenue and word-of-mouth impacts of the customer experience can be quantified. This requires a good amount of data, but the return on these efforts usually exceeds the cost by a huge multiple.

On the subject of data, customer service, market research, and operations all have reservoirs of underutilized, and often untapped, information from customer interactions and their impact. Strategic customer service requires that data from all those touch points be collected, integrated, and analyzed by issue when appropriate, and distributed to the proper parties, not only when problems occur, but as part of the ongoing VOC program. We take up that subject in Chapter 5.

KEY TAKEAWAYS

1. Even the best companies are leaving large amounts of revenue on the table (which can be estimated) as a result of customers not complaining about problems and quietly going to a competitor.
2. When calculating revenue at risk, be so conservative that even the CFO says you're being too conservative.
3. If you don't know what your customer is worth, how can you decide how much to spend to retain him?
4. Calculate what a 10 percent increase in satisfied complainers

would be worth and try to achieve that improvement by empowering the front line to resolve more problems.

5. Estimate the current levels of positive and negative word of mouth and the net payoff, then find ways first to decrease negative word of mouth and then to increase positive word of mouth. To further build the case, ask marketing how much they spend to win each new customer.
6. Enhance the credibility of calculations by periodically comparing purchase-intention findings from surveys with actual behavior from sales data for those same customers.

CHAPTER 5

Information, Please

Developing an Efficient, Actionable Voice of the Customer Process

I RECENTLY VISITED a major telecommunications firm and heard an executive say, "We know we have service problems, and we spend over $8 million annually on surveys, but we have little actionable data that points to where we can directly affect revenue." In other words, lots of surveys won't guarantee that you have an actionable Voice of the Customer (VOC) process. Surveys are important but are lagging indicators compared to customer contact data and internal metrics. These three sources, properly integrated—surveys, contact data, and internal metrics—make a world class VOC process.

Voice of the Customer means many things to many people. To engineers and quality professionals, it's a means of obtaining customer requirements for the ideal product. To marketers, it's a set of survey and research tools for specifying ways to enhance value and sales—seldom for preserving revenue. For chief customer officers, it is everything that describes the customer experience. To many managers, the term simply means "things customers said we should make or do for them." While everyone agrees on the importance of VOC, considerable confusion and disagreement surround both the term and the practice. But virtually everyone agrees on the importance of taking customers' viewpoints into account when making decisions that affect them.

Unfortunately, few organizations have effective VOC programs. In January 2006, a *Six Sigma* magazine study titled "VOC and Knowing the Customer" found that only 27 percent of 1,515 respondents said that their company always follows a defined process for analyzing customer feedback. That is a major reason for ineffective VOC programs right there, because you cannot act on unanalyzed data. When three-quarters of companies don't have a defined process for analyzing VOC data, the programs stand little chance of success given the mountains of customer data available. That also jibes with TARP's 2007 finding that only about half of companies have a coherent VOC process and that, of those, over half do not consistently get the issues that are identified effectively addressed by management. Again, that translates to three out of four companies lacking a truly effective VOC process.

This chapter will help you improve your VOC process, regardless of its current level of evolution. First, we'll examine appropriate objectives for VOC programs and the key building blocks: three sources of data and a unified analytical function. We'll also explore challenges in using each data set which must be included in VOC efforts. Then we'll define the eight attributes of an effective VOC process, show how to address two key issues in implementing VOC, and examine ways of judging the effectiveness of your current process.

THE OBJECTIVE OF VOC AND ITS KEY BUILDING BLOCKS

The best VOC process should describe the totality of customer desires and experiences throughout the customer life cycle, from marketing and prepurchase inquiry to purchase, use, repair, and billing. Thus, the VOC process should have the goal of *guiding management on how to enhance and redesign the end-to-end customer experience*. It addresses how to set expectations correctly, deliver on them, and anticipate and respond to customer needs in order to increase loyalty and word of mouth. To provide this complete view, an effective VOC must include surveys, customer contact data, and internal metrics. For instance, at a delivery company, the company often knows from its internal metrics before you do that the package will not arrive because it missed the flight. Then it gets your phone call, and then it does the survey. All three sets of data describe the same event from different perspectives.

An important clarification: VOC properly refers to systematic efforts to gather and analyze data on *existing* customers' wants and needs *and* to translate the results into action and increased profitability. A separate sector of market research focuses on winning new customers. Yet many managers and professionals view market research surveys as the mainstay of the VOC program or *as* the program. This is mistaken for three reasons.

First, the majority of market research is aimed at winning new customers. Therefore, combining market research and VOC confuses the study of existing customers with the study of the (usually much larger) noncustomer market. Customers provide a more knowledgeable, intimate, and immediately useful perspective on the customer experience.

Second, surveys taken days, weeks, or months after a purchase or an experience provide lagging indicators. They can measure loyalty and word of mouth, but events may have progressed. For instance, an electronics firm I worked with rejected customer surveys, saying, "By the time we get survey data, we're done making that model and often even the next model." The data were outdated.

Finally, surveys can be quite unreliable regarding prospective or hypothetical products and services. A cautionary example of the unreliability of customer "voices" on a hypothetical product occurred in the late 1970s. At that time, Citibank surveyed customers about automatic teller machines (ATMs), which the bank was then developing. Respondents overwhelmingly rejected the idea. They wouldn't trust the machines with their money, they wanted to interact with real people, and they feared getting mugged. But once they experienced round-the-clock access to their cash without lines, they became fans.

Surveys and most other VOC tools are most reliable when they are used for measuring *actual* customer experiences and the responses to those experiences. Surveys, focus groups, and recorded conversations can also provide insights into customers' emotional and psychological views of a product or service, and many VOC programs use them for that purpose. Nonetheless, most VOC programs are rooted in a small number of general surveys that capture relatively little data on the detailed customer experience. What's needed is a panoramic view of customers, and that view requires data from three different sources.

THREE SOURCES OF VOC INFORMATION AND WHAT THEY TELL YOU

When you look at an object with one eye closed, you have difficulty discerning how far away the object is because you only have one source of data and thus a limited perspective. The second eye provides a more complete picture of what you're seeing. Likewise, when you have only one type of customer data, your view can be dangerously skewed. Three sources of information—internal operations metrics, customer contacts, and customer surveys—will enable you to perceive the customer experience correctly.

As shown in Table 5-1, each source provides different data and relates to different time frames; therefore, all of these sources must be included in a robust VOC process.

Actually there is a fourth useful set of data, input from employees about the customer experience, which I'll discuss in Chapter 8.

Internal Metrics

Internal metrics drawn from operations tell you what's happening to the customer, often before the customer is aware of it, and thus serve as leading indicators. They portray the cause-and-effect relationship between a company's actions and its customers' reactions. These data can include returned mail, missed deliveries, and late charges assessed on customers

Table 5-1. Three Sources and Their Content and Time Frames

Source	*Content*	*Time Frame*
Internal metrics	• What you did or are about to do to the customer	Leading indicators
	• What you didn't do for the customer	Real time or lagging
Customer contacts	• Customer input	Real-time reporting
	• Employee input on customer problems	Real time or lagging
Surveys	• Customer surveys	Lagging
	• Employee surveys on customer experience	Lagging

after statements have been mailed late, all of which enable you to predict customers' negative responses. Other useful internal metrics include returned products, warranty claims, and invoice adjustments.

Operating managers tend to trust this kind of data more than survey data and complaint data, and, given that operations departments produce it, they find these data hard to refute. Yet internal metrics in exception and error reports, like those on late deliveries and inaccurate orders, are rarely viewed as being actions that affect customers negatively, even when they do—as, for instance, when items are out of stock. If you have data on short deliveries of chicken breasts to your store and you know the number of customers who buy them on an average day when they are on sale (for example, 300), you can estimate how many customers were disappointed when chicken breasts were out of stock for two days (600). Saying that 600 customers were disappointed sounds a lot worse than saying that chicken breasts were out of stock for two days. Furthermore, when you combine data from internal metrics with data on customer behavior, such as reduced response to the next sale, you can estimate the revenue lost as a result of a "minor" logistical error.

Customer Contact Data

Customer contact data are often produced in real time from customer interactions with the service system, mainly by phone, interactive voice response systems (IVRs), and e-mail. For example, the customer has just encountered an unpleasant surprise, such as unanticipated late charges, or is trying to assemble the toy the night before Christmas and is missing screw H. Like internal metrics, these data are more timely than surveys, but they can be harder to interpret because only a small percentage of consumers will call about certain problems, like late charges, whereas many (but not most) will call if screw H is missing. Customer contact data often have palpable emotional content; for instance, playing recordings of customer complaints when presenting complaint statistics to management has far more impact than statistics alone.

Customer contact data from all sources—including call centers, Internet interface, and technical support—represent the most robust data on the customer experience. Service reps know about problems as soon as the customer calls, and can disseminate that knowledge quickly.

Also, complaining customers typically identify points of pain experienced by a multiple of their number (recall that this multiplier can often reach 100 to 1 and in a few cases, 2,000 to 1), while providing valuable clues about the causes of problems, including their expectations and actions. All of this can help you prevent problems from recurring. For instance, a packaged foods company received complaints about mold in spaghetti sauce shortly after it eliminated preservatives for marketing and health reasons. Analysis of discussions with consumers revealed that complaints increased when consumers left the opened jar of sauce in the fridge for over two weeks. Simply adding "May be refrigerated for up to seven days after opening" to the label dramatically reduced complaints.

Contact data, properly extrapolated using the multiplier (percentage who call) and the impact on loyalty, will allow you to estimate the total revenue and word of mouth damage done by each type of problem including for those customers who didn't complain. This enables you to gauge the potential payoff from solving or preventing problems. Thus, by calculating the revenue earned or preserved and the cost of the improvements—as shown in Chapter 4—you can prioritize improvements in the customer experience on the basis of their potential returns.

For all these reasons, including customer service data in VOC programs truly amplifies the customer's voice.

Survey Data

Survey data, as noted, are valuable but have their limitations. However, surveys are the best source of satisfaction, loyalty, and word-of-mouth impact of a product or service or of an interaction with your organization. Also, if based on statistically sound samples, they can be more representative of customer needs and experiences than complaint and contact data. Just be aware that survey data can have drawbacks, including the potential for bias created by survey design, administration, and sampling techniques. Also, the cost can range from $20 to $200 or more per completed survey.

Indeed, each source of data on the customer experience has its pros and cons, the most significant of which are summarized in Table 5-2.

The strengths and weaknesses of each data source represent the best arguments for collecting and integrating data from all three sources in your VOC program. Note that these data come from different parts of the organization: internal data come from operations, contact data come

Table 5-2. Strengths and Weaknesses of Information Sources

Source	*Strengths*	*Weaknesses*
Internal metrics	Credible to management and useful in problem solving (to the degree that it describes factors that are important to the customer) because it is operations data	Provide a limited view of the customer experience based on only the aspects of operations that management measures (such as billing errors, late deliveries, etc.)
Customer contacts	Very timely and descriptive of the actual customer experience	May not be the exact data you want, and the data must be extrapolated to the customer base
Surveys	Data can be projected to the customer base and markets (with proper sampling), and ongoing comparable measurements are possible	Significantly more costly and often less timely than data from internal metrics and customer contacts

from the call and contact centers, and survey data come from marketing. Therefore, you need a function that combines and analyzes the data and translates it into a unified picture with believable financial implications. As noted in the *Six Sigma* magazine study quoted earlier in this chapter, the lack of such a function is a major reason that few organizations have a robust VOC process.

This VOC analytical activity typically is fragmented among operations improvement, call-center reporting, and marketing services. The internal operations data are usually collected routinely and thus are available at little or no incremental cost. The customer service data are a by-product of handling contacts and are being collected or can be collected at a small incremental cost. Survey data are the most expensive because they entail research and questionnaire design, sample development, fielding the study, and analysis. Ironically, the data that are most often called VOC—survey data—are the least timely and the most expensive, while the most useful data on the customer are already available in house *if* you know where to look.

For instance, a Midwest bank received sixteen complaints in a month from customers who had not received their monthly checking account statements. Management wondered whether there was a serious problem or whether a few envelopes had been lost by the Postal Service. Whenever I hear about missing mail, I ask the mail room supervisor if he receives returned mail. In this case the answer was, "Truckloads, every day." I asked, "Does that include checking account statements?" The supervisor pulled out a report and said, "Last month we had 3,463 statements returned for bad addresses." "What do you do when that happens?" He said, "We send a form letter to the address asking if there is a problem with the address." (Consider the efficacy of that action!) I asked if he sent the report to the quality, complaint, or VOC unit. He said, "No. No one has ever asked for it." The chairman's office was trying to decide if 16 complaints indicated a severe issue when the guy in the basement had an exact snapshot of the scope of the problem, but no one knew it.

To hear the Voice of the Customer, you have to question, and listen to, the people involved in the processes that affect the customer experience. Comprehensive analyses of customer experiences have also shown that the *single best predictor* of loyalty is whether or not the customer had a problem and how it was handled. Thus, data from customer service interactions describing problems must find their way into any VOC program worthy of the name. As noted, for any problem or question, only a percentage of customers will call. Thus, it's important to extrapolate contact data to the customer base and the marketplace so that it can be tied to survey and operational data (as I'll demonstrate later in this chapter).

In sum, the factors that create or erode customer satisfaction and loyalty are complex and therefore cannot be captured by any single method. Furthermore, every data source has its strengths and weaknesses. That's why every organization that aims to build and maintain customer satisfaction and loyalty needs an effective VOC process that draws upon multiple sources of information.

THE ATTRIBUTES OF AN EFFECTIVE VOC PROCESS

We have found eight attributes associated with really effective VOC processes:

1. Unified management of the program
2. A unified data collection strategy

3. Integrated data analysis
4. Proactive distribution of the analysis
5. Assessment of financial implications and priorities
6. Defining the targets for improvement
7. Tracking the impact of actions
8. Linking incentives to the VOC program

Unified Management of the Program

The data feeding into most VOC programs don't fit together. Given free will, each functional area will collect the data and use the formats that are easiest and most useful for it. When this happens, the data won't yield a coherent picture. I have literally found up to seven "owners" of the VOC program in some companies.

The remedy is to put one executive in charge of the VOC effort, or at least to chair a committee mandated to ensure compatibility. This tends to be the role of the chief customer experience officer, where such a job exists (see Chapter 12). Where it doesn't exist, I ask, "Who has the customers' best interests at heart?" The answer varies, but the head of quality or the chief marketing officer is often named. In such cases, the VOC program may report to one of them or, in several cases, to the chief operating officer. I've also seen heads of service take on the role, typically with good results, if they have the skill or clout to get the process rationalized.

A Unified Data Collection Strategy

I'm not stating that all VOC data must be collected at one point. That would be virtually impossible in any large organization. I am saying that the data must be collected in a manner that allows it to fit together and be reconciled. At least at a macro level, the *classification schemes* must be unified, or at least coordinated. At one auto company, the factory engineers, the sales and marketing functions, and the dealer service technicians all had different methods of describing customer problems. The engineers talked about subassembly failures and customer abuse, while the service technicians talked about symptoms like brake pulsation and engine hesitation. A cross-functional perspective demands a data collection approach with a compatible problem and experience classification scheme. That way, you can construct a *single*, clear, complete picture of the customer experience and the implied needs and gaps.

Keep in mind that every company has blind spots. For example, in most companies, no data exist on the effectiveness of handling prepurchase queries—truly important contacts given that the customer will be lost if they are not properly handled. At one bank, current business customers had to call an average of three times to gather enough information on cash management services to make a purchase decision! Meanwhile, the relationship managers were busy chasing new customers.

Integrated Data Analysis

Data from all of the sources and channels must be combined and reconciled to create an accurate picture of customers' unfulfilled expectations, the sources of the resulting disappointment, and the impact of this disappointment.

The challenge here is twofold: First, the data must be compatible in terms of categorization of expectations, problems, causes, and impact. Second, contact and operations data must be extrapolated to the marketplace in order to be comparable to survey data, which tend to describe the marketplace as a whole. I show how to address these challenges at the end of this chapter.

Proactive Distribution of the Analysis

One of the more depressing occurrences at any company is learning that a problem could have been avoided if only product design, or marketing, or production, or sales, or somebody had had a piece of information that somebody else in the organization already possessed. To do their jobs, people need the right information. Given people's workloads and the pace of organizational life, this means proactively distributing not just data but actionable analysis that "connects the dots" for the parties that require it. Interested parties should be able to pull data, but pushing the data and the connected dots out to those who'll need them is most important. This does not mean distributing all data to everyone. Data overload creates more problems than it solves. Those in charge of the VOC program must know who needs what information, take the risk of filtering and tailoring the information to their customers' goals and needs, and distribute a summary proactively.

Assessment of Financial Implications and Priorities

Again, as indicated in Chapter 4, customer expectations and behavior have an impact on revenue and profits. Assessing that impact and apprising management of it (*and of the impact of inaction allowing the status quo to continue*) transform inert data into actionable information. Since the best decisions are based on financial information, the implications that customer data hold for satisfaction, loyalty, and word of mouth must be translated into at least general financial impacts. Unless the economic imperative to act is highlighted on the first page, VOC is just a feel-good or feel-bad exercise that will not provoke action.

The major weakness in this area is that most analysis simply outlines the cost of customer problems, such as warranty service expense. This implies that if we could reduce complaints, costs would decrease and the bottom line would improve. In fact, the revenue damage is probably ten to twenty times greater than the potential cost savings, so the key is to estimate the revenue and word-of-mouth implications of each issue and opportunity.

Defining the Targets for Improvement

Once an issue has been identified and the cost of not acting has been calculated, there are two other standard impediments to getting things fixed. First, the manager assigned to the issue is told to fix it, but he must start from scratch—while continuing to do his day job. Second, the manager is rarely told what would be considered a successful outcome of addressing the problem, as total elimination often is not possible. Therefore, suggested actions and achievable targets for improvement must be part of the VOC process. Some VOC analysts fear violating the prerogatives of line managers, but I have found that managers are thankful for suggested starting points and targets.

On the subject of targets, one of the silliest exercises I've observed in many companies is "satisfaction planning" for the following year. In this exercise, a company that is at, say, a 76 percent level targets a level of 80 percent for next year. Why 80 percent? Because it's higher than 76. This is irrational target setting. Instead, use Market-at-Risk analysis to identify which improvements to make, assign responsibility for implementation, and suggest the expected lift in loyalty and satisfaction along with estimated cost and return on investment. Such analysis enables people to implement the kind of decision making explained in Chapter 4 and equips management with rational plans for moving the needle and hitting satisfaction and loyalty goals.

Tracking the Impact of Actions

Once the actions linked to improving both the customer experience and the organization's financial performance are assigned, there must be a process to ensure that things really get fixed. In most companies, if you file your action plan, you're done. No one goes back to check whether you actually moved the needle. Organizations require tracking processes to measure the percentage of issues raised by the VOC process that are actually addressed. That information should then be reported to finance and senior management, or the VOC process will have little or no impact. We'll examine methods of putting these processes in place in Chapters 10 and 12.

Linking Incentives to the VOC Program

If you accept that VOC has the goal of proactively responding to customer needs and increasing loyalty, then you accept that the VOC process must be linked to both strategic and day-to-day decision making. This linkage occurs when senior management accepts the strategic importance of VOC, links incentives to suggested actions, and funds those incentives. The VOC manager must also have a seat at the decision-making table and generate buy-in across functions. We generally find that for VOC to make a positive impact (meaning that management addresses most of the identified issues), at least 20 percent of incentive compensation must be linked to identified VOC initiatives.

THE TWO MAJOR CHALLENGES IN USING CUSTOMER CONTACT DATA IN VOC PROGRAMS

Assuming that it is agreed that you need a VOC process based on integrated data generated by your customer service system and internal operating metrics in addition to surveys, the two most difficult challenges you will face are: developing a unified, actionable data classification scheme, and extrapolating the contact data to the larger customer base so it can be integrated with the other types of data.

Developing a Unified, Actionable Data Classification Scheme

I met with the EVP of a major communications company who said, "I get seven reports on quality each month, three of which say life is great, three say it's OK, and one says we're having a disaster. Who is telling the truth?" How often have you been in a meeting where someone says that the company has a problem and presents supporting data, only to hear someone say, "You're mixing apples, oranges, and kumquats. The data are not comparable"? Information from customer interactions, surveys, and internal metrics must be coded in uniform ways that various functions can use. If data from different sources are coded in different ways by different functions, neither the functions nor management can combine, analyze, and act on the data, and you're doomed to having multiple contradictory reports.

To the degree possible, the data must uniformly describe the symptom, problem, expectation, cause, and impact for each experience. Furthermore, data on the product involved, the type of customer, and the geographic location will almost always be useful. When there has been extended customer contact or investigation, it may also be possible to code information on potential root causes of the problem, actions taken to remedy it, the resulting satisfaction or impact on loyalty, opportunities for improvement, and the outcome of the contact.

A universal classification scheme must enable people to describe the problem and its cause in a manner that they all can understand and use to remedy the issue. While the following classification scheme must be customized for a specific organization, it contains the basic types of categories that an actionable scheme will require:

- **Reason for contact/symptom.** This is the problem or symptom from the customer's point of view, but in terms that are useful to the company.
- **General cause.** Did the issue arise from a customer error or

expectation, or from a product defect, policy, or process? (Ideally, this comes from the CSR.)

- **Root cause.** This is the specific error, marketing message, or process defect that led to the problem. Often the cause will not be known because investigating the cause of all issues is wasteful. Focus only on big issues.
- **Escalation code.** If a complaint was received at headquarters, why wasn't it handled in the field? If a problem was escalated to a manager, could the CSR have handled it? The answers often point to communication or empowerment issues.
- **Specific product or service description.** This includes specific product details like the model, serial number, sales channel, and date of purchase.
- **Geographic location or unit.** This helps identify local management and geographic influences.
- **Action taken to resolve.** Reviewing the resolution action often provides a different perspective on how the customer perceived the problem.
- **Outcome.** This indicates the resulting satisfaction and loyalty impact according to the contact record and follow-up surveys.

Each data element should be numerically coded to allow data processing and analysis. For example, the general cause (second bullet point above) guides the CSR toward the appropriate response and the preventive analysis process toward the appropriate corrective action. The outcome (last bullet point) identifies which questions and problems cannot be systematically resolved. Not all data need be collected on every contact, however. Data on root causes of defects may have to be supplied by an investigative unit or an analyst in a functional area. Data on follow-up surveys may come from a separate research function or an outside firm. In high-volume organizations, capturing every item on every call may be too expensive, in which case a subset of contacts can be coded to provide a valid sample of the relevant population.

All codes must be actionable if they are to be useful. To be actionable, the classification must be comprehensive, specific, mutually exclusive, and arranged hierarchically, as explained here:

- **Comprehensive.** The full range of issues across the customer experience must be addressed, and the system must accommodate the addition and deletion of categories.
- **Specific.** Actionable data result from specificity and differentiation among symptoms, problems, and general and root causes. Avoid unhelpful generalities, such as saying that a food product "tastes bad" rather than being too salty or bitter.
- **Mutually exclusive.** Overlapping or poorly defined categories will generate misleading or useless data. For instance, "foreign object in product" is not precise enough; is the object gravel, seeds, or glass? A utility company used "poor service" and "missed appointment" as separate categories, when the latter is a form of the former.
- **Hierarchically arranged.** A hierarchical scheme permits flexibility as well as logical organization. For example, although two levels are often enough, even complex product lines, operations, and customer bases can be accommodated with a menu of up to three levels. In such situations, consider using five to seven Level 1 categories, five to seven Level 2 categories under each Level 1, and another five to seven Level 3 categories under each Level 2. That allows for 125 to more than 300 codes that are easily distinguishable.

In practice, CSRs should not be expected to memorize codes, but should instead select codes from short drop-down menus with not more than 10 subcategories. For instance, if the CSR selects the code for "statements," Level 2 might include up to seven subcategories, including "didn't receive statement," "received statement late," "lost statement," and "difficulty understanding statement."

Extrapolating Data to the Customer Base

The second major challenge is extrapolating the contact data to the entire customer base. The key here is knowing what percentage of customers who experience a problem go to any particular touch point. For instance, TARP found that about 20 percent of consumers encountering a rude airline gate agent will complain to a company touch point—but to different ones. Most will complain to someone at the airport, who rarely makes a record of the encounter. About 4 percent (or 4 out of 100 who had the problem) will complain to the toll-free reservation number, 1 percent to the frequent flyer number, and only 2 tenths of 1 percent via e-mail to headquarters. Such statistics enable you to estimate the number of total incidents affecting your customer base, as shown in Table 5-3. The exact way you combine the estimates can be weighted by the relative quality of the estimate or by a simple average, as shown in Table 5-3.

Once you have the unified classification scheme for all data sources and the ability to estimate the number of customers experiencing the problem, you can estimate the revenue impact with the Market Damage Model discussed in Chapter 4. For example, if an encounter with a rude employee damages loyalty by 22 percent and a customer is worth $2,000 per year, then we could say that 6,000 customers encountering rudeness (as shown in Table 5-3) will cost this airline $2.64 million per month (6,000 × 0.22 × $2,000). When the revenue impact is made explicit, you have information that will motivate management to act.

GETTING STARTED IN IMPROVING YOUR VOC PROGRAM

An effective, efficient VOC program calls for a number of building blocks and process steps. The first step is an examination of the materials at

Table 5-3. Extrapolating from Complaint Touch Points to the Customer Base

Touch Point	*Percent of Customers Using Touch Point*	*Multiplier (Inverse of Percent Using Touch Point)*	*Number of Contacts*	*Estimate of Incidents in Customer Base*
Toll-free reservations number	4	25	200	5,000
Frequent flyer number	1	100	70	7,000
Executive complaint	0.2	500	8	4,000
Recent survey of customers about rude gate agents				8,000
Best estimate of actual instances per month				6,000 instances (straight average of four estimates)

hand. Pick your best detailed survey, your most detailed complaint source, and one or two operational reports and connect them to one problem that has been affecting customers for months or years. This exercise will give you a more powerful case for taking action on the issue, and will show you how fragmented your data and classification schemes are and some opportunities for quick fixes.

Once you've done this pilot test, there are seven steps you can take to systematically improve your VOC program:

1. Coordinate the classification schemes of your main service or complaint-handling process with those of your main survey process that measures customer loyalty.
2. Enhance your surveys to measure problems, complaint rates, and word-of-mouth impact.
3. Identify the top five problems indicated by your complaint and survey processes.
4. Work with someone in finance to estimate the revenue damage from those five problems, then suggest fixing the top two based on revenue impact.
5. Find operational data (even anecdotal) that describe the same customer experiences from various company perspectives to reinforce the validity of your analysis.
6. Identify a viable approach to mitigating the problem and estimate its payoff.
7. Walk your most forward-thinking senior executive through the analysis to prompt buy-in, action, and, hopefully, your first success—leading to further support for VOC.

With these seven steps in place, you will have a foundation on which to build a truly effective and efficient VOC process that more than pays for itself.

KEY TAKEAWAYS

1. Your VOC must include survey, customer contact, and internal operational data to provide leading, real-time, and lagging information on the customer experience.

2. Your data must fit together, and the keys to achieving this are to create a comparable classification scheme across data sources, and to extrapolate customer contacts to the number of customers who encountered the issue.
3. Someone has to coordinate, or at least facilitate, the collection of data, the analysis, and the selection of priorities based on economic impact. Otherwise, the VOC will have little effect on the organization or its customers.
4. While the most cost-effective data collection is usually decentralized, the most effective data analysis is usually centralized, especially when it is executed by senior analysts with operations experience.
5. The VOC should be led by someone who has the customers' best interests at heart. This might be a quality or marketing executive, the COO, or the chief customer experience officer.

PART 3

Responding to Customers' Questions and Problems

CHAPTER 6

Defining Processes That Work for Customers

Using the Eight-Point TARP Framework for Delivering Service

I WAS RECENTLY TALKING to the head of service quality for a major computer company, and I asked him about his analysis of preventable types of inquiries and complaints. He said, "We're so busy answering the phone cost-effectively that we're not analyzing the content of the calls." Given that 20 to 40 percent of calls are preventable, this company's lack of strategic focus doomed it to handling millions of unnecessary calls per year.

Earlier I mentioned that customer service systems have changed radically since the complaint departments of years ago. Some changes have been wrought by information technology. Others have grown out of the sheer size and scope of today's organizations. And some have been driven by innovative methods of managing and growing customer relationships. Those factors—information technology, organizational size and scope, and customer relationships—demand a systematic approach to delivering tactical and strategic service in ways that achieve all four key goals of customer service, which are satisfying customers for whom the organization did not do it right the first time; proactively educating and communicating; cross-selling; and capturing the data needed to feed the Voice of the Customer, prevent problems, and support efforts to enhance doing it right the first time.

In a majority of companies, customer service is still defined only as tactical service, or complaint handling. This reinforces the stepchild status of service, which often leads senior executives to position customer service as a backstop, cleanup, or maintenance function rather than as a proactive strategic resource. Some executives think of customer service only as "the call center" and thus extend "the complaint department" metaphor to current times. Such thinking limits service's contribution to the organization. Customer service can broaden its contribution to strategic objectives only when the process is properly conceived, designed, built, staffed, and managed. This chapter presents a framework for the conception and design of that process. (Chapter 7 addresses technology and the user interface, and Chapter 8 covers the human resources aspects of the process.)

FRAMING THE WORK

Given that customer service is a process, it can be defined logically and approached logistically. TARP has identified and charted eight functions—four tactical service functions and four strategic service functions—which are further broken down into distinct activities.

Tactical functions comprise the procedural, day-to-day tasks involved in receiving and responding to customers who interact with the service function: input, response, output, and control functions that deal directly with the customer at the time and point of contact.

Tactical functions ensure that CSRs:

1. Capture the information needed to classify and solve individual customers' problems and answer their questions, and, if necessary, route to best resolution point.

2. Provide assured, satisfactory responses to customers during the initial contact or soon thereafter.
3. Store the outcome information on transactions, problems, responses, and solutions and distribute it to people who will analyze problem frequency and costs and eliminate root causes.

Strategic functions—analysis, evaluation and incentives, staff management, and awareness—include activities that enable the organization to improve the experience for most customers. These activities analyze and leverage all available information on the customer, improve contact-handling policies and procedures; prevent unnecessary contacts; engage customers to complain and to educate and delight them; and recruit, manage, and motivate staff.

Strategic functions ensure that:

1. Customers' contacts and requests are handled in such a way as to maximize the value of the customer experience and revenue.
2. CSRs receive appropriate support from internal functions, such as IT and legal.
3. Customer service data are used to analyze and, when it makes economic sense, correct the root causes of problems.
4. Communications foster a strong two-way relationship with customers.

Table 6-1 organizes the 21 tactical and strategic activities into 8 functions and organizes them into a framework.

Like any framework, the one in Table 6-1 identifies and organizes the elements of a process, in this case the process of handling customer contacts at the tactical level and managing information, workflows, and human resources at the strategic level. The original functions in the complaint-handling framework were derived from an analysis of more than 500 corporations and from extensive research conducted under the auspices of the White House and the National Science Foundation.[1] It has proved to be extremely durable and, with minor modifications, has been fully capable of incorporating developments such as Web- and e-mail-based customer complaint mechanisms and customer relationship management (CRM) strategies into the customer service process.

Table 6-1. A Framework for Organizing Customer Service Activities by Function

Tactical Functions

Intake	*Response*	*Output*	*Control*
• Screening • Logging contact data • Classifying contacts	• Response investigation • Response formulation • Response delivery	• Coordination • Storage, retrieval, and distribution	• Internal follow-up • Referral follow-up

Strategic Service Functions

Analysis	*Evaluation and Incentives*	*Staff Management*	*Awareness*
• Statistical generation • Opportunity analysis • Input to the organization	• Evaluation • Incentives • Accountability	• Recruitment • Training • Supervision and scheduling	• Contact solicitation • Proactive communication

In this chapter, we'll examine the activities in this framework and how they fit together, as well as best practices. While a list of 21 activities may seem long, it is a complete checklist for a world-class strategic customer service process. The following two sections briefly describe each activity.

TACTICAL FUNCTIONS

The four tactical functions follow standard process mapping: intake, response, output, and control of the transactions to ensure that nothing falls through the cracks.

Intake

- **Screening** separates contacts by type and, as needed, forwards them to the appropriate channel.
- **Logging contact data** records a description of the complaint or inquiry on electronic or paper forms.
- **Classifying contacts** codes each contact according to a predetermined scheme.

Response

- **Response investigation** looks at individual customer requests and identifies all the facts needed to decide how to respond to the customer's problem or question.
- **Response formulation** uses the investigative findings and response guidelines to develop an appropriate response to the customer's complaint. Response guidelines are flexible and empower employees to provide the optimal response that will leave the customer feeling that she has been treated fairly, given her circumstances.
- **Response production** transmits the response content to the customer via voice, email, letter, text, or other mode of communication.

Output

- **Coordination** ensures that all relevant groups in the organization are made aware of the customers' issues and that appropriate action is taken.
- **Storage, retrieval, and distribution** stores complaint files in a central location and ensures their availability for subsequent uses. These uses may include anticipating when the customer will welcome an offer of assistance or analyzing data to identify defective products.

Control

- **Internal follow-up** monitors the progress on, and disposition of, complaints handled in-house through defined monitoring techniques.
- **Referral follow-up** monitors complaints handled by other areas or offices in headquarters and the field, or in other organizations, such as third-party repair centers.

STRATEGIC SERVICE FUNCTIONS

The strategic functions use the data from contacts to enhance the rest of the customer experience and help service employees to succeed.

Analysis

- **Statistical generation** aggregates data on complaints received and handled. We used to call this "statistical reporting," but we found that reports were being distributed as analysis *without* any analysis or interpretation. This function feeds analysis.
- **Opportunity analysis** identifies systemic problems that damage loyalty, along with opportunities for product, service, and marketing improvement. This includes analysis of customer accounts to identify ways to deliver more value to specific customers.
- **Input to the organization** puts analytical findings and policy recommendations into final form and presents them to senior management and other constituents.

Evaluation and Incentives

- **Evaluation** periodically assesses the performance of complaint handlers and complaint-handling and VOC processes for effectiveness. The majority of the time is spent focusing on the effectiveness and outcomes of the response process, response rules, and VOC reporting, as most staff members are generally in compliance with protocols.
- **Incentives** provide CSRs with primarily positive rewards that encourage them to prevent problems and handle complaints effectively.
- **Accountability** assigns complaint-handling and problem-prevention responsibilities to specific offices and individuals—some in service, but others in areas such as marketing and quality—and evaluates their performance.

Staff Management

- **Recruitment** provides for the selection of the right mix of staff, which might include part-time and home-based CSRs as well as full-timers seeking advancement within the organization.

- **Training** addresses initial, transitional, regular reinforcement, and remedial training as needed. Staff members are trained with stories and role playing demonstrating flexible solutions, as described in Chapter 3. In addition, some staff members usually receive specialized training to allow them to become subject matter experts.
- **Supervision and scheduling** tailors the staffing pattern to the workload and the workers to make scheduling a win-win for the staff and the organization.

Awareness

- **Contact solicitation** informs customers that you want to hear complaints, and educates them about the availability and use of communication channels.
- **Proactive communication** preemptively educates customers on how to avoid problems and how to get the most value out of their purchases by placing the message in front of them just when it is needed.

Before examining how these functions fit together in the service system, let's look at the benefits of this framework.

WHY USE THE SERVICE DELIVERY FRAMEWORK?

The world has many frameworks—of what practical use is this one? I see four specific uses. First, it provides a checklist to ensure that you are doing everything needed to achieve the four key goals of customer service identified at the start of the chapter. Second, it supports process management and improvement. Third, it supports the application of technology to all aspects of service. And fourth, it allows the customer service staff and other departments to see how their job helps or hinders the customer experience and how your process can help improve service.

A quick comparison of your activities to the 21 activities outlined in Table 6-1 will probably highlight situations in which:

- You are not even performing aspects of certain functions, such as regular reinforcement training or classifying contacts, so that they can be tied to staff evaluations.
- You don't have metrics to measure the quality of the activity, for instance, whether customers were truly satisfied or only gave up and were still dissatisfied.
- You don't have the right people doing the right activities, for example, assigning line supervisors to opportunity analysis rather than having a full-time analyst, diverting them from coaching staff.

Viewed in this manner, the framework can serve as the basis of a self-audit. The framework also allows you to identify activities, map them into a process, and identify those that are not adding value. You can establish quality and productivity metrics for each activity, track delays, and locate bottlenecks. This approach is firmly rooted in quality improvement methods. When process improvement professionals arrive in any department, the first thing they do is map the department's processes. Very few service organizations have developed rigorous maps of their service systems.

Most of the major CRM software systems have at least a nodding acquaintance with this framework, which provides a road map for professionals who design, implement, and maintain IT systems that support customer service. In my experience, IT staff members like to see the framework presented as a flowchart (as shown in Figure 6-1) because that is their usual method of representing systems. Indeed, several IT groups have adopted this framework while helping their internal support organizations implement it for customer service. They recognize that IT support is an internal customer function with essentially the same goals as customer service.

Finally, the framework lets your internal staff and your external sales-channel partners see how they fit into the overall operation. Staff members see, for instance, that their logging and classification support the analysis that helps prevent the toughest calls. Your partners see that

Figure 6-1. Contact-Handling Flowchart

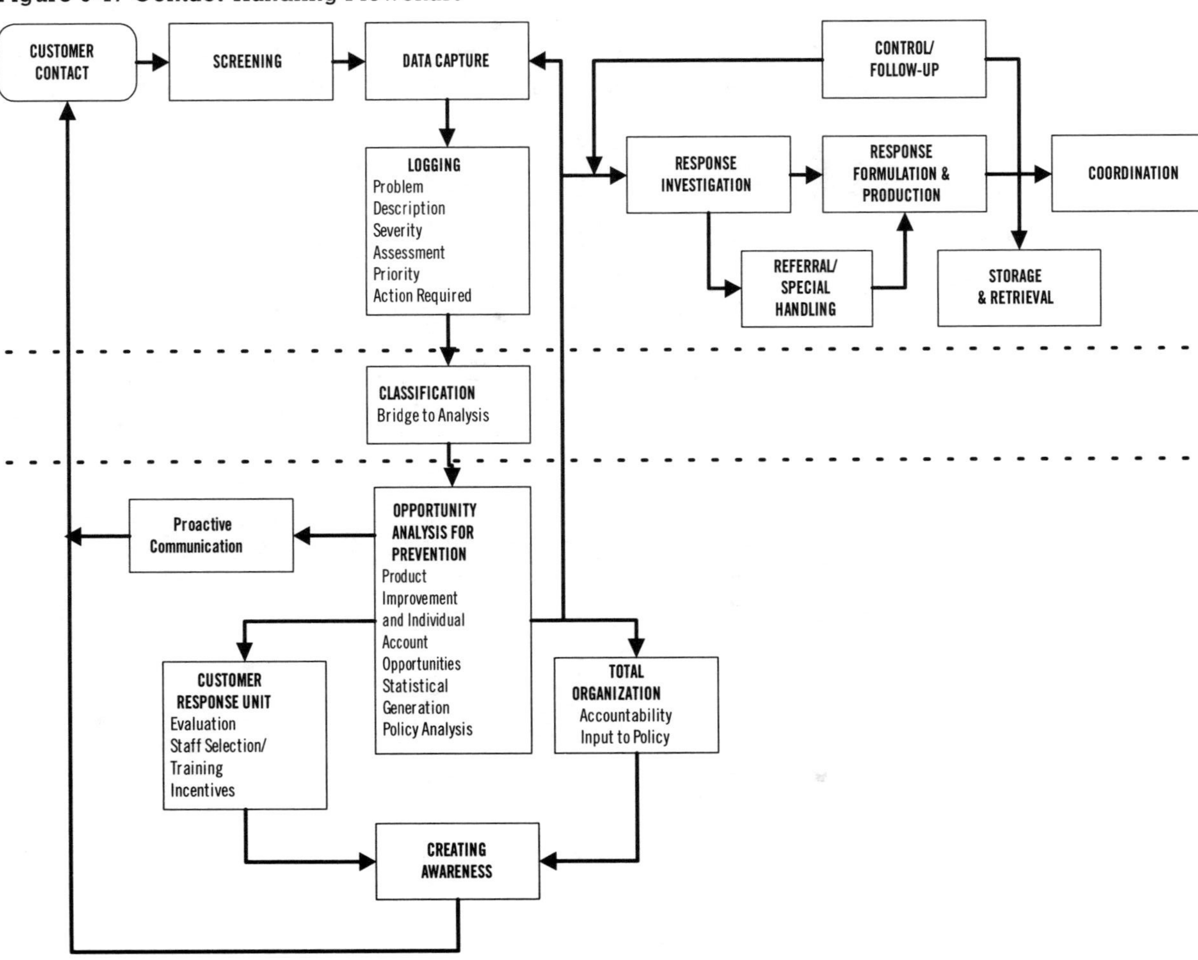

quickly notifying you of the effects of delays can improve service to their customers. In sum, the framework enables everyone who directly or indirectly affects your customers to know what role they—and others—play in creating the customer experience from the standpoint of customer service.

THE FLOWCHART OF THE FRAMEWORK

The flowchart in Figure 6-1 organizes the activities in the framework into a process with three layers:

1. The first (top) layer encompasses the functions involved in interacting with customers and in formulating and delivering the response.
2. The second (middle) layer—classifying the transaction, inquiry, or problem (using a scheme like the one in Chapter 5)—forms the information bridge to the third layer.
3. The third (bottom) layer includes the functions involved in improving the customer experience through problem prevention, proactive communication, and proper staffing and management.

In this flowchart, some activities in the framework are folded into others to simplify things. For instance, the Control/Follow-Up activity box in the top layer includes internal follow-up *and* referral follow-up. Also, a couple of activities are added for clarity, such as Customer Contact, which is the initial phone, e-mail, mail, or personal contact by the customer. Apart from these points, the flowchart is, as it should be, largely self-explanatory. Nonetheless, the following items are worth noting.

We show Creating Awareness (of the customer service function among customers) at the bottom of the chart because that step of soliciting contact from non-complainers should not be taken until you have first developed the ability to handle service interactions in ways that satisfy a high percentage of customers on the initial contact. Creating awareness of a service system that generates more dissatisfaction will only further erode loyalty.

When you are designing or upgrading a system, every function should be taken into account and provided for at some level. If you have a customer service system, you need every one of these functions in this system. Indeed, most of these activities are probably already being performed in your organization. The question is, how effectively and efficiently are they being performed, and by whom? Furthermore, bear these points in mind if you are outsourcing your service function or call center. Important functions such as Opportunity Analysis often get lost in the effort to reduce costs or obtain high service levels with a vendor or partner.

Someone must be responsible for each of these functions. Individuals such as CSRs can handle multiple functions, but each responsibility—logging contact data, classifying contacts, response investigation, and statistical generation—must be explicit. Each must be identified as an activity that is to be performed in accordance with certain standards. People must be trained to execute the tasks, and the data must be captured to measure their performance on the tasks using clear, fair, predetermined metrics.

When problems arise in the system, walking through this flowchart can help you identify deficiencies. For example, poor data capture or inaccurate logging will undermine classification and preventive analysis as well as the quality of the response given to customers. In general, as noted earlier, the fastest ways to improve service and to reap the rewards for doing so are almost always to improve the response to customers at the tactical level. When you do this, satisfaction and loyalty start to improve on the very next phone call.

The functions on this chart extend beyond customer service. For instance, Opportunity Analysis draws data and uses resources from outside customer service, such as warranty claims, repair records, data on late charges, and findings from market research surveys. All of these feed an analysis aimed at improving products, services, and operating practices, and thus the customer experience. (This analysis should also use the Market Damage Model and Market-at-Risk calculations to gauge the impact of problems on financial performance.) Similarly, Opportunity Analysis and input to the organization would feed findings and recommendations to every department, because each one plays a role in doing it right the first time.

For the system to work well, each of these functions must be performed to high standards, as recommended in the next section.

BEST PRACTICES FOR IMPROVING SPECIFIC FUNCTIONS AND ACTIVITIES

With the goals of handling customer problems, improving the customer experience, educating customers proactively, and cross-selling when appropriate, let's examine best practices for the most prominent functions individually. These are of necessity somewhat broad recommendations, but they apply across industries and to telephone, Web-based, mail, and personal modes of complaint handling. As you read this, consider how these activities are now structured and performed in your service system.

Activities Within the Tactical Functions

The tactical functions of input, response, output, and control include the following activities (as shown in Table 6-1).

Screening. The screening activity should get the customer to the proper location in one step (at most two). This starts with building customer awareness of the contact channels, hours of availability, and details like the phone tree and web site instructions.

Best Practices. In advertising your telephone trees, print the menu for the selections wherever you print the 800 number so the customer knows what to push before ever dialing the number. This increases satisfaction by 20 percent and reduces opt-outs to the CSR. For Web-based contact mechanisms, provide clear links for the top types of issues to help customers route themselves to the right areas. Also, keep a record of misdirected contacts so that they can be eliminated. Training is another key to proper screening and routing, which are essential to resolving customers' issues on the first contact.

Logging Contact Data. The logging activity creates a record of the complaint, accompanied by all relevant information. CSRs require tools and training that enable them to gather the necessary information efficiently and at the right time during the customer contact.

Best Practices. Require customers to log data into the web site in ways that are consistent with the guidelines for CSRs handling phone contacts. A template with a few items that must be completed before accessing the complaint-reporting section can accomplish this. In general, try to encourage customer use of the Web, and provide speedier service as an incentive.

Classifying Contacts. The classification activity assigns the complaint to a category so that the problem can be analyzed and response guidance given to the CSR. Recall that classification is the bridge between tactical and strategic customer service, that is, between handing a specific customer's complaint and eliminating the problem for all customers.

Best Practices. CSRs should be able to enter the general code into the computer and have the appropriate sub-codes automatically presented to allow rapid granular coding. This hierarchial coding produces greater accuracy and efficiency than scroll down coding.

Use an actionable classification scheme as discussed in Chapter 5, and ensure that the classification method supports rapid resolution of the problem. Also, review the classification scheme and problems periodically to assure that the categories are being used properly and that no more than 2 percent are coded "other."

Response Investigation. The response investigation activity gathers all the information needed to support a sound response to the customer as well as a resolution of the problem and the root cause. The investigation may be conducted by the CSR, a specialist, or an individual in the area where the problem originated, and is driven by the information logged by the CSR and the classification code.

Best Practices. Based on the customer's identity and the problem code, the computer should automatically gather and provide the CSR with relevant customer history and all information needed to make a decision. For example, if a consumer appeals a claim, one insurance company has the system deliver to the CSR all the information on why the claim was rejected (including, for instance, images of physicians' charts), along with guidance as to when an appeal can be accepted. That way, the CSR doesn't need to scan 10 databases. Give the investigator access to all relevant information, and enable the CSRs to investigate as many cases as possible, given the available resources, type of business, and complexity of the problems.

Response Formulation. The response formulation activity arrives at a decision and constructs the response to be delivered to the customer. This should include a clear rationale for the decision, conveyed with empathy and an assurance that the customer has been treated fairly.

Best Practices. Based on the problem code and the value of the customer, reps should have 2 to 5 responses (which include a clear believable rationale) which provide a Flexible Solution Space, as explained in Chapter 3. Such response spaces should enable resolution 95 to 98 percent of the time without going to a supervisor. Resolution should result in customers feeling that they have been treated fairly, regardless of the outcome.

Response Production. The response production activity delivers the decision to the customer in a timely manner, with the rationale and an apology, but without accepting blame.

Best Practices. Transmit the response to the customer via her preferred channel of communication—perhaps with a confirmation by e-mail if another channel was used. If the decision cannot be made immediately, set a specific expectation as to when a decision will be forthcoming, and update the customer regarding any delays.

Storage, Retrieval, and Distribution. The storage, retrieval, and distribution activity tracks the case and renders at least summary data that are electronically accessible for future reference and analysis.

Best Practices. Ensure that the problem classification code drives the automatic distribution of data to the right parties. For example, the information supplied should go to the unit responsible for analysis of the problem's cause, such as data on incorrect customer expectations go to sales, inferior product quality to manufacturing, or third-party actions to channel management. Information on problems must also facilitate counts of occurrence, types of resolution, and customer satisfaction with resolutions so that you can perform Market Damage Model and Market-at-Risk calculations. Distribution includes informing organizations about issues emanating from their areas, such as the marketing or sales departments creating customer misunderstandings as a result of confusing messages or exaggerated claims.

Internal Follow-Up and Referral Follow-Up. The internal follow-up and referral follow-up activities ensure that problems referred by CSRs to analysts or other parties are properly handled.

Best Practices. Track all referred cases and inform CSRs when problems have been resolved so that they will project confidence in the referral process to customers. Such confidence results in a reduction in calls from customers to confirm that the transaction was done or that the repairman will show up on time. The tracking process should report resolution to the CSRs proactively to eliminate the need for them to check on cases repeatedly.

Activities Within the Strategic Functions

The strategic functions include the following activities.

Analysis. The analysis activity puts the data collected by the tactical service functions to strategic uses.

Statistical generation produces aggregated data concerning problems, resolution, and customer satisfaction. Opportunity analysis identifies ways to eliminate problems, increase satisfaction and delight, and reduce workloads. Input into the organization provides analysis that compels management action to improve tactical and strategic service based on the financial cost of inaction.

Best Practices. Create a separate, strong, credible analytical function, staffed by professionals with at least five years of experience who can act as internal consultants. Their analysis should include recommended action to eliminate causes of problems, along with the monthly cost of inaction (in lost revenue resulting from decreased loyalty and bad word of mouth). VOC reports should be tailored to each executive audience rather than one report sent to a vast distribution list.

Evaluation and Incentives. The evaluation and incentives activity requires metrics that capture willingness to recommend for customers with and without problems by type of issue as well as by CSR. Rewards should include 20 percent of at-risk compensation as well as promotions. In addition, rewards should focus the attention of employees companywide on preventing problems and improving customers' experience rather than productivity.

Best Practices. Track satisfaction by issue and highlight issues that produce systematic dissatisfaction. Emphasize customer education, process and response-rule fixes rather than focusing on individual CSRs. Tie at least 25 percent of managerial and front-line incentive compensation to problem prevention, in addition to quality, productivity, satisfaction, and loyalty. Emphasize positive peer recognition, with storytelling in weekly team meetings, for things done right. Also, eliminate productivity metrics that motivate behaviors that erode satisfaction and loyalty. Incentives to create a great customer experience should go across the organization; for instance, in a packaged goods company, the service department charges the product management department for calls resulting from faulty marketing messages.

Training. The training activity provides staff members with basic communication and problem-handling skills (soft skills) as well as with flexible tools for specific issues and problems. Monthly reinforcement of key modules should be provided.

Best Practices. Always explain the rationale for policies and procedures that affect customers, especially those that customers may not like. Prepare CSRs for challenges that customers may pose to the standard explanation. Use role playing to build skills, and use storytelling to dramatize situations that employees will encounter and to demonstrate the best ways of handling these situations. In addition, hold "bragging sessions" that celebrate staff members who handle a difficult customer or problem particularly well to educate others on alternative approaches.

Building Awareness and Soliciting Complaints. The building awareness and soliciting complaints activity aims to encourage customers to complain. This recommendation seems wrongheaded to many executives, but, again, you can fix only the problems that you know about. Also, you must genuinely welcome and thank customers who bring problems to your attention.

Best Practices. Prominently display phone, web site, and (if available) e-mail information on your product packaging, welcome letters, monthly bills, newsletters, and e-mails. John Deere and Polaroid both embossed the toll-free number on the product (for Deere, on the dashboard of a tractor). This strongly signals that you want to hear from the customer. When it makes sense, provide a physical address, although relatively few customers now use the mail. You simply want to make it easy for anyone who has a question or complaint to get in touch.

Proactive Communication. The proactive communication activity sets proper expectations for product performance and warns customers of potential problems before they are encountered or created—or before they become worse.

Best Practices. In welcome kits and other communications, flag common product limitations or customer missteps and explain how to avoid them. Have CSRs proactively suggest problem-avoidance strategies to customers as well as methods of self-service. Additionally, educate CSRs to recognize potential cross-selling and up-selling opportunities and to understand that proper cross-selling creates delight because you are filling a customer need. When a customer displays interest, the CSR must either start selling or refer the customer to a salesperson.

Breaking down the process into these activities and applying these and other best practices to each one will automatically start to improve not only customer service but the overall customer experience.

IMPLEMENTING THE FRAMEWORK

To make the best use of this framework within your organization, start with the tactical functions and "clean your own house" before dealing with other areas. If you can demonstrate improved operations and results, you can then accumulate resources to build a robust, impactful analytical function, which will be your best ambassador to the rest of the organization.

Within the tactical service function, start by enhancing the complaint-handling process. That process is customer-focused and understood by all employees. It produces metrics that measure performance against clear standards, linked to the core operation. In companies that lack a well-designed, well-managed process, complaints are often not screened, logged, or classified in effective ways. Thus, a usual first step is to look at your definition of a complaint and expand it to include any question regarding the customer experience; for instance, "Why did I receive this service charge?" is not a question but a mildly stated complaint.

Then use the framework and best practices identified in the previous section to:

- Map the tactical service process with visual tools.
- Use employee and customer input to redesign the process.
- Tweak the technology to enhance tactical service.
- Create or strengthen the analytical functions.
- Enhance strategic service across the organization.
- Practice continuous improvement.

Map the Tactical Service Process with Visual Tools

Mapping a process with a flowchart, process map, or other visual tool fosters a clear, common understanding of the tasks that people in the service system must perform. When people see a flowchart, they see the functions and individual activities and how they relate to one another, and how their own job and function help to create customer satisfaction. I have seen many companies benefit greatly from the simple step of holding a session to create a flowchart. People find even simple flowcharts quite useful and often go on to develop more complex and graphic maps, and to develop a clear vision of their customer service process.

Use Employee and Customer Input to Redesign the Process

Your best consultants on how to improve tactical service are your customers and your employees. You need only ask each group two questions: "What are your top three frustrations in receiving service or delivering service?" and "How would you change it?" and then sit back and listen.

Tweak the Technology to Enhance Tactical Service

If you believe you need wholesale changes in technology to get improvements in your customer service, you're dead. It won't happen unless and until the CEO becomes a zealot, and you probably can't depend on that happening. Therefore, identify where minor tweaks will produce visible results and save significant technological changes for the strategic effort.

Create or Strengthen the Analytical Functions

Information is power to persuade. You need to strengthen the analytical activity so that it can make the business case for improving the strategic service activities. You get the other functional areas on board by appealing to their interests—they will be more successful and the organization will make more money if these activities are enhanced.

Enhance Strategic Service Across the Organization

The framework, supported by the analysis just discussed, can establish a common view of the service system when you interact with marketing, sales, operations, finance, or IT—and with senior management. If you currently have a purely tactical, just-respond-to-the-customer service system, you can identify the strategic elements you require and begin to develop them.

Practice Continuous Improvement

Continuous improvement means never being satisfied with your current levels of customer satisfaction, loyalty, and word of mouth. The best companies, which have over 90 percent satisfaction, recognize that each additional percentage point represents tens of millions in revenue. Therefore, senior managers monitor key performance measures and insist that the causes of dissatisfaction and problems be continually pursued. They reward improvement and view the system for delivering the customer experience as a loop, with the customer at the beginning and at the end, and the organization's processes in between. Only continual feedback from customers and employees and constant measurement of satisfaction and loyalty can assure continuous improvement.

GET YOUR SYSTEM FRAMED

This framework for handling tactical and strategic service has been used by regional, national, and global organizations to plan new customer service systems and improve existing ones. It has also proved useful in designing the technology platforms supporting contact handling and CRM and in setting up outsourced or offshored systems.

Each function within the process must be properly understood, staffed, resourced, measured, and managed if the entire tactical and strategic customer service system is to work effectively and efficiently. In the next two chapters, we examine ways of ensuring that the technological interface and human resources that support the process work to its advantage rather than its disadvantage in your organization.

KEY TAKEAWAYS

1. The key to effective response is effective investigation of the customers' issues followed by a flexible response that clearly explains the outcome and assures customers they've been treated fairly.
2. Only after customer service can resolve at least 75 percent of complaints on initial contact should you aggressively solicit complaints.
3. Classification is the bridge between tactical service and strategic service. If the classification system is defective, your analyses and strategic responses will be severely damaged.
4. Analysis should focus not only on contact-center operations and CSR performance, but should root out ineffective response rules and processes, which cause about 60 percent of dissatisfaction.
5. Evaluation and incentives should be at least 80 percent positive to confirm that everyone is satisfying the customer and to reward staff members who identify opportunities for improvement.

NOTES

1. "Serving the American Public: Best Practices in Resolving Customer Complaints," Federal Benchmarking Consortium, Study Report, March 1996; "Increasing Customer Satisfaction," U.S. Office of Consumer Affairs, 1984.

CHAPTER 7

Technology and the Customer Interface

Creating Systems That Customers Will Use—and Enjoy

I'VE HAD TWO RECENT INTERACTIONS with United Airlines that show they absolutely do not understand how to use technology to enhance the customer experience. First, everytime I call the Premier Executive Service Number (they know that I fly at least 50,000 miles a year with United and am a Million-Mile Flyer), they have messages on hold that are aimed at Aunt Tilly who flies once a year about how early to get to the airport, luggage limitation, etc. Secondly, they invite e-mail feedback, always asking for frequent flyer numbers and then have never, ever replied or even acknowledged one of my e-mails.

Perhaps this chapter should be called "Technology *Is* the Customer Interface," because in practice that is often the case. When a customer picks up the phone, sends an e-mail, or logs on to your web site, the quality of the experience—and customer satisfaction—will be dictated largely by the design of the technology interface and process between the customer and your organization. Often customers will interact *only* with technology—with a web site or an interactive voice response (IVR) system—but they are still interacting with your organization. They will judge your organization and their experience on the quality of that interaction, which will be determined largely by the ways in which you use technology.

Customers hold mixed views of technology. Most of them see it as a source of pain and a sign that the company doesn't care about them and would rather save money by not having humans delivering the service. At the same time, most people like printing airline boarding passes in advance, getting an e-mail confirmation that the birthday present has been shipped on time, and using ATMs rather than standing in line. Why the contradiction? It stems from how and when the technology is used.

Beyond the interface—the front end, so to speak—stands the technology that generates and directs the flow of information you need at the tactical and strategic levels. At the tactical level, that information enables you to deliver great service to individual customers; at the strategic level, it helps you detect, prevent, and solve problems for all customers. Technology also provides the metrics you need if you are to monitor the performance of the people and processes that make up your service system.

In this chapter, we'll first review why customers both love and hate technology, and what drives them nuts about it. Then we'll focus on appropriate roles for technology in tactical service and in strategic service. I'll also suggest ways of encouraging customers to use technology willingly—even happily—rather than reluctantly. Finally, we'll address nine technologies that you'll have to use and, without getting into the weeds, suggest how you can apply them successfully and avoid the most prevalent pitfalls.

WHY CUSTOMERS LOVE-HATE TECHNOLOGY

When customers love their experience, they will love your technology, and if they hate their experience, they'll hate the technology. It is the experience, not the technology, that drives their love or hate. That is, they don't love or hate the technology itself; rather, they love or hate what it is or is not doing for them as they seek to get their needs met.

When Customers Hate Technology

Customers are driven crazy by technology and judge it as undermining the service experience, primarily when they notice it and have to deal with it. It creates angst when it:

- Increases the amount of time that the interaction requires and wastes their time by requiring tasks that provide no value added (like requiring login when you only want to ask a simple question)
- Seems inflexible, as it does if it provides only one answer when there are several possible solutions
- Plays "Gotcha" by citing rules only veteran users might be aware of
- Benefits the company at the customers' expense or provides no benefits to them
- Appears to be insensitive to their plight, for instance, when it delivers marketing messages on the lost baggage hotline
- Provides incorrect or inscrutable answers to their questions like the "check engine" message that may mean nothing or impending disaster
- Prevents them from speaking with a human via endless IVR loops

You could usefully seek out these issues at your customer touch points by trying them yourself—you might be surprised at what you find.

When Customers Love Technology

Customers typically love technology for the same reasons that you do. Technology can provide faster, more accurate transactions, answers to questions, and solutions to problems. At a strategic level, technology can deliver the solution or inform customers of the opportunity before they even know they have a problem or a need. Think of the doorbell ringing and a guy standing there with a pizza and saying, "This is the pizza you were *about* to order"—what I call psychic pizza. Customers benefit from technology and find that it improves the customer experience when it:

- Enhances the convenience and speed of the process of obtaining an answer to their question or resolution of their problem on the initial contact
- Anticipates the response they need—and proactively provides the next response they'll need
- Avoids the need for service in the first place, via proactive communication. As former Amazon service vice president Bill Price says, "The best service is no service"—that is, there's no need even to interact with customer service
- Provides added value, for instance, by offering useful advice, more delivery options, tailored education or history, or telling you that your left rear tire needs air.

Both your customers and your company benefit from your effective use of technology. Customers want service interactions to be as efficient and effective as possible, just as you do. They don't want to think about the technology. They don't even want to notice it. To the degree that it is transparent, it does not evoke any reaction whatsoever aside from a brief, "That's slick!"

Here's another instance where putting yourself in your customer's shoes can help. Recall the last time you had to call customer service. Did technology serve as a facilitator or as a barrier to getting your question answered or your problem solved? Did it speed up or slow down the interaction? Did it clarify the situation or confuse you?

Furthermore, who you are and what your situation is at the moment can dictate radically different appropriate roles. If you are gregarious, you might place great value on a barista who asks you about your kids and your dog and schmoozes—except when you just want a cup of coffee and you're already late for your meeting with your boss. Then it's, "Give me my coffee and I'll leave the money and run." Similarly, if the IVR tells you that your flight is canceled, you want to be able to exit to a human immediately to rebook the flight, with your frequent flyer status taking you to the head of the line.

GETTING THE CUSTOMER-TECHNOLOGY INTERFACE RIGHT

To provide technology-enabled service that customers enjoy using, you must get the interface right. The first goals, then, are to include the characteristics that customers love and to exclude the ones that they hate. But how do you go about doing that? Chief among the challenges are to:

- Create a system that will save the customer time and you money.
- Educate and encourage customers to adopt the technology cheerfully.
- Start with a few functions to guarantee success.

Make the System Intuitive for Both Novices and Veterans

The Frequent Flyer and Aunt Tilly analog applies to all technology. You have new customers and veterans. The technology must accommodate both. Anticipate the situations in which customers will contact you, the questions and problems they will have, the information they will have and will require, and the ways in which they will use the system itself. For instance, companies that let customers identify themselves by their primary phone number, rather than by account number or confirmation number, have the right idea. So do those that realize that some customers will have problems while they are actually using the product, will typically want to back up a step (or two) rather than start over, and will not want to be dropped if they must leave the phone or the computer to obtain information.

Test the System with Live Users. Spare your main customer base by using focus groups, prototypes, and limited tests to ensure that the system works for mere mortals before you put it into wide release. Some companies do not use just their best customers to test systems, but also enlist customers who have done boneheaded things with previous products—the theory being that the less sophisticated customers will be the best test of how klutzproof the product really is. If novices have a bad experience, they'll never become veterans and will go to the call center every time.

Create a System That Will Save the Customer Time and You Money

Start by examining your processes and identifying any transaction that has a delay before its completion, as such a transaction is sure to generate contacts from the customer asking if it has been completed. You want to be like the American Express CSR who says, "It has been done, and you'll see it on your next statement or online within five minutes." Use the Market Damage Model and Market-at-Risk calculation to identify transactions that may benefit from automation.

Don't charge customers for making an online payment rather than mailing you a payment. Even if they are doing it to avoid a late charge, let them do it free via the credit card. Better still, make online payment an ongoing automatic function. Payment is more certain and much less expensive for you to process if it is done online.

Educate and Encourage Customers to Adopt the Technology Cheerfully

If customers don't adopt the technology or are forced to use it under duress (for instance, to avoid extra charges for talking to a human), the purpose of the system is defeated. When it comes to customer service technology, TARP's research usually shows that customers fall into three categories that are roughly equal in size: those who will readily use the technology, those who will use it for some transactions when it makes sense to them, and those who won't even try it. The latter group generally cites three reasons:

1. I can't easily do what I want to do.
2. If I have a problem with it, I'll need to call anyway.
3. It's not as personal.

Effective customer education is the key to defusing the first objection. You must demonstrate the range of things that customers can do—or, better yet, the three things they most want to do. For instance, AOL has users perform a couple of simple tasks and then has the avatar "Irene" show them how to do other things they want to do as they learn the ropes—a version of just-in-time education. You have to *show* customers that they can do what they want to do. Key Bank in Cleveland gave its CSRs time to educate the consumer on the IVR by conferencing them into the IVR and letting them push the buttons. HP encouraged CSRs to take consumers to the web site and show them the self-service function. Up to half of those educated customers then started using the self-service. Another important educational tool is a clear site map.

You can address the fear of having problems and having to call anyway by ensuring that users can see where they can go for help—and human contact—at the top of every page or at any time in a phone tree. The best web sites provide customers with all channels of support, rather than keeping them captive in the online channel.

If a policy or requirement may seem unusual or onerous to customers, explain why you have it, or at least provide a link on the Web page that says, "Why do we have this policy?" Just the fact you have such a link will make many customers feel better because you're acknowledging that it's irritating, just as most of us feel better when the pilot apologizes for the 12 planes in front of us awaiting takeoff. Furthermore, those who feel strongly about the issue will often click on the link and be convinced, or at least be more understanding. In many cases, TARP has found that explaining your policies can lead to a 20 to 30 percent increase in loyalty relative to the damage done without the explanation.

Some companies have made their interfaces more personal by adding a quasi-human touch. For instance, "Claire" at Sprint received high marks for being personal, and she was a cartoon. You could even ask her out on a date, and she would frown and tell you, "I don't go out with customers." Such underlying humor goes a long way toward humanizing interactions, which a significant minority of the population likes. Avoiding bureaucratic language and using a personal style and phrases such as, "We're doing this because . . ." and "You'll soon find that you can . . ." make users more comfortable. Other ways of personalizing experiences include enabling customers to maintain personal spaces, such as My Eddie Bauer and the Netflix queue, or having an avatar who looks like the customer try on clothes at the Lands' End site.

Customers will use technology if they benefit immediately. In a senior-citizen focus group on automated response systems and ATMs, the facilitator ignited a firestorm by saying, "I know you seniors don't like technology." One man said through clenched teeth, "We can push buttons with the best of them when it is in our self-interest."

You can't just lead the horse to water; you have to give it the first sip. Allstate has a two-minute tutorial on what's inside the firewall to entice consumers into its web site. You must help the customer up the learning curve. Union Pacific had its sales force show customers how to use the web site for tracking shipments, which doubled web site use. Sharp has My Sharp web sites tailored to the equipment and warranties that the customer purchased, with tutorials and troubleshooting hints prioritized by frequency of use. The sales rep would educate end users on how to troubleshoot using the web sites, resulting in higher satisfaction, lower support costs, and fewer complaints to the sales rep—the latter being the incentive for the rep to spend time doing the education.

Start with a Few Functions to Guarantee Success

To increase the possibility of success, focus on a few functions that most customers will want to use and get them right, then slowly add more. Both customers and CSRs can absorb only a few new functions at a time and need a series of successes to build their confidence. Think about the first time you used a cell phone or your iPhone. Also, think about the quick start page that comes with most technology. It focuses on two or three things—all your implementations should be like that.

Which Technology Should You Apply?

All of them—thoughtfully. TARP's research for a leading-edge car company catering to consumers aged 16 to 30 suggests that if you *don't* employ technology in relatively sophisticated ways, these consumers won't even consider doing business with you. But you can make a mess of any technology if you fail to consider your audience.

In the following section, we examine nine of the most prevalent technologies, their application in tactical and strategic customer service, and pitfalls to avoid.

NINE TECHNOLOGICAL APPLICATIONS TO CONSIDER

You've probably interacted with most, if not all, of these technologies. However, reviewing them here may prompt you to consider new applications that you can adopt and ways to improve current ones.

The nine technologies you should be applying or at least considering are:

1. Interactive voice response
2. E-mail and chat
3. Web sites
4. Web video
5. Automated Web-based self-service
6. Recording interactions
7. Mobile communications
8. CRM and data mining
9. Machine-to-machine communication

Interactive Voice Response (IVR)

Commonly known as phone trees, this technology is probably the most widely used by organizations and is the most maligned because it can be complex and confusing. This is so common that Tom Peters did an interview with me a while back entitled, "Push One, Push Two, Push Your Customer Over the Edge!"

Tactical Uses. IVR works best for delivering simple answers and information, such as status of shipments, account balances, and flight information. Potential problems start as soon as customers dial the number. What option do they want to select? Why make them listen to rapid-fire options that may confuse them? (Is that what I want, or is there a better option still to come? Was it option two or option three that I wanted?) Print the IVR options wherever the phone number is printed on literature or on the web site so that the customer can decide in advance which option to select. At one technology company, TARP found that putting the menu on the inside front cover of the user guide reduced misdirected calls by 20 percent and increased the completion rate by 15 percent. If you're in financial services or another privacy-conscious industry, don't ask all the security questions up front if, say, 40 percent of the queries don't require accessing the account data. That wastes your time as well as the customer's.

This technology can deliver more detailed information, such as the last five checks that have cleared, but don't force customers to listen to such information before allowing them to opt out to a human. Also, whenever the IVR gives an answer that will probably be unsatisfactory—"Your package has not yet been delivered"—you should at the same time offer a transfer to a CSR. Why make the customer call back and reenter his tracking number?

Strategic Uses. If you analyze the data that the IVR interactions produce to determine the most prevalent queries and avoidable problems, you can push the answers and solutions to the customer, thereby avoiding the call and creating delight. You can also use IVR with voice recognition to gather e-mail addresses and have customers update them. For instance, "You have checked on shipments six times over the last 30 days. If you give us your e-mail address, we can update you on the status of your delivery each morning that you have packages in transit." This eliminates the customer having to log in and answer security questions. Finally, you can call or text-message customers to avoid hassling them later. For instance, CIT Finance calls or even texts customers saying that a payment is due, and that to avoid late charges, the customer should hit 1 to make a credit card payment now. (CIT uses reverse billing, so the customer doesn't have to pay for the texting charge.)

To Avoid Problems. Limit menus to no more than five choices, including opting out to a human. Avoid changing the menu every month so that the customer never gets up the learning curve. (Do you really have to change it so often?) Avoid introductions of more than 18 seconds. Whenever possible, avoid dragging seasoned customers through information intended for novices, for instance, on a frequent flyer phone line.

E-Mail and Chat

These Web-based technologies can deliver more complex answers and information, such as directions for use, warranty details, and return policies. E-mail is typically seen as less expensive than the phone, but on a full accounting, it is often more expensive because it requires multiple back-and-forth interactions. When it is poorly implemented, it can cost five times as much as a similar phone call. Furthermore, e-mail is limited compared to the phone in that you can't hear the consumer's tone of voice and discern whether she is satisfied with your response or merely mollified. Therefore, we often see that for the same answer given to similar problems, e-mail achieves lower satisfaction, often 5 to 15 percent lower.

Tactical Uses. E-mail is best for handling issues that require longer explanations or investigation. You can post simple information on your web site and direct customers to pull it themselves. Always ask the customer to code the type of issue from a list of no more than 15 codes. Also, ask how soon he wants an answer and provide a set of closed-end response categories from two hours to two days. If the customer indicates that he needs the answer in two hours, you at least know his expectations and can either juggle priorities to meet that time frame or tell him how quickly you can respond. While you may not like his time frame, you at least know how urgent the customer views the issue as being, and, if necessary, you can adjust either your or his expectations.

Strategic Uses. Consider when e-mail or chat can substitute for the phone, and vice versa. I once listened in at Hershey's call center when a customer who was making fudge asked the CSR to hold for five minutes while it thickened. That's a great place for e-mail or chat. Conversely, if the issue is emotional or requires immediate action, direct the customer to a phone answered by a CSR. At an auto company, we recommended that if the customer coded a serious repair problem, the automated reply would say, "We're concerned about your problem, which is potentially serious. Please call us as soon as possible at . . ." and the number of a live rep.

Chat can also be used to intervene when the customer is "stuck" on the web site. For instance, one retailer has technology that identifies when a consumer has been inactive on the web site for more than a minute and sends a message—"Hi, I'm Sam. Do you need some help?" If the customer answers yes, the chat assignment is transmitted to a real CSR. The intervention can even be automatically keyed to occur only if the customer agrees to accept help from a live rep.

To Avoid Problems. Intervene when customers seem stuck on a page. Both Lands' End and a major delivery company have CSRs who intervene after 60 seconds. This reduces abandonment and frustration. Ideally, answers to questions should be one line long—AOL tries to never have the text "wrap" to the next line. Anticipate subsequent questions to avoid expensive back-and-forth exchanges. But avoid doing a data dump. Don't use reformulated e-mails with chaff mixed in with the answer the customer wants. Make your e-mails concise but clear and easy to read. No paragraph should be more than five lines long, nor should an answer exceed twenty lines in total. Remember, these communications will be read mainly on the screen.

Web Sites

Web sites provide tremendous convenience for customers and economies for companies in delivering marketing messages, locations and directions, and product and warranty information. As with IVR, learn why specific customers come to your site and offer to push the information to them via e-mail so that they can avoid logging on. This also ensures that they will keep their e-mail addresses current.

Tactical Uses. Millions of customers are comfortable using the Web to check delivery status, portfolio performance, airline seat availability, and so on. Additionally, customers can learn about new products and even emerging developments. For instance, at one pharmaceutical company's site, physicians can see snippets of recent research and tap into continuing education institutes. Anticipate questions on your home page and announce emerging issues under "news you can use."

Strategic Uses. Use your site to educate customers about products and services and to guide them to the right choices. Allow them to manage their relationship with you, for example, by stating their preferred communication channel. Consider links to other sites, search engine optimization, affiliate relationships, and other online marketing tools to increase market awareness and your accessibility. Depending on your industry, tools may include sponsored affiliate groups and communities of users, which have been quite successful for pharmaceutical companies addressing people with specific diseases.

To Avoid Problems. Don't load too much introductory content on your visitors, and allow veteran site users to skip it and go to their favorite transaction section in one click. Have the top five FAQs prominently on the home page, and update the list based on phone calls and e-mails on a weekly basis. Don't force customers to log in when they have a simple question. Make it easy for them to obtain forgotten user IDs and passwords (while ensuring their security). While your IT people will want to assign complex passwords to customers, let customers select their own. (My wife has been forced to have three pages of passwords for her various professional and consumer accounts, and it drives her nuts when she is not near her written list.) Provide a site map organized by customer concerns rather than by your internal structure. If necessary, provide a second site map for employees.

Web Video

Video delivered via the Internet can bring products to life, particularly those with a strong visual component. Filmed entertainment obviously benefits from Web-based marketing, but that differs from true customer service applications, which are still in the early stages. As production technologies and high-speed connections improve and proliferate, more service applications will develop.

Tactical Uses. When they are short (less than 30-second segments) and useful, video-based product demonstrations, assembly instructions, and customer education are worth considering. For complex tasks, use a half-dozen short videos rather than one long one.

Strategic Uses. Videos of the message-from-our-founder variety can provide a human touch, but use them judiciously. The entertainment industry and companies in youth-oriented categories (such as energy drinks, clothing, and extreme sporting equipment) use Web-based video to generate buzz. As YouTube-style videos become part of the cultural landscape, it may well become necessary to communicate with customers, or with certain customer segments, in this way.

To Avoid Problems. Get the basics of Web-based and e-mail customer service in place first, then explore the possibilities of this technology. Don't use video to show off while slowing the delivery of useful information. Don't have 45-second openings when someone first arrives at your site—even allowing customers to skip the opening creates a barrier and increases abandonment rates. If you use Web-based video, *keep it short* and be sure you have the right (which might not mean the glossiest) production values and message, or the result may be embarrassment.

Automated Web-Based Self-Service

I differentiate automated Web-based self-service from general web sites and Web videos in that the customer has arrived in search of a particular type of assistance or information. A successful Web-based self-service process provides easy search and lets customers find what they want, pay for purchases, and obtain a receipt without human intervention. The payoff for the customer is typically faster service. The reasons that the majority of self-service functions fail are inadequate search mechanisms, overly complex transaction execution, and inaccessible staff when more intensive service is needed. While some of the following descriptions may seem obvious, less than a third of the companies that try these functions are successful, and few have pursued the strategic initiatives.

Tactical Uses. Allow customers to execute transactions and to get the answers to simple questions and the status of transactions. In addition, a good self-service process can handle more complex troubleshooting driven by an index of problems and a search function tailored to plain English descriptions of issues and problems. If the answer provided is not going to be satisfactory, provide links to "Why we have this policy" as well as escalation to a live rep, possibly by chat. Also, after you answer a question, ask whether you actually answered it, and provide yes, no, and somewhat categories. If the answer is not yes, offer a connection to live service.

Strategic Uses. Allow customers to learn what is new in products and even the state of the art. Anticipate the top 10 questions on the home page and flag issues that customers are encountering—under breaking news. In addition, automated self-service systems, whether they focus on facilitating transactions or delivering answers and solutions, can produce a vast base of customer data to be analyzed for ways to improve the customer experience, in both self-service and other arenas.

To Avoid Problems. Avoid lists of more than seven items. If there are more categories than that, cluster them and allow users to see the subcategories via rollover technology. Test prototype systems with live users. Whenever possible, give customers the option of getting in touch by phone or having a rep on hand to help them. Having a prominent "call me" button or an easy e-mail contact link will assure customers that they can get help quickly. Finally, design rich data-capture capabilities into the system from the outset, even if you won't be using them all initially.

Recording Interactions

Most service operations can and do record interactions on the phone or via e-mail. For phone or online media, almost all recording is done digitally, often with the capability to see the keystrokes, which is much more expensive. Most organizations have listening programs (real-time and recorded) that managers use for quality assurance, performance evaluation, and training. Rarely, however, is the resulting information mined for the most important data—those that enable management to measure satisfaction and use the results to analyze likely loyalty and word of mouth.

Tactical Uses. Use recording and listening to improve the customer experience, not just to evaluate CSRs' adherence to procedure. Voice recognition technology now enables the identification of statements such as "very disappointed" or "my lawyer" in individual interactions. You can also use voice-to-text to categorize the call and enter key parameters into the customer record, such as the type of problem and the customer's level of satisfaction with the solution, which would otherwise be far too laborious to search out. Furthermore, if you link the call data to the rest of the CRM data, such as the value of the customer, you can use automated decision rules to determine whether to call the customer back and how to mollify or satisfy him.

Strategic Uses. Listen to calls to see which ones result in dissatisfaction even when the CSR supplies the "right" answer. This will flag response rules or processes that need to be fixed. If you have voice-to-text capabilities, you can analyze the types of calls being received. Also, you can "humanize" the Voice of the Customer data by presenting samples of recordings that reveal the emotions involved along with the relevant findings.

To Avoid Problems. Give feedback to reps within 24 hours if at all possible. Giving feedback weeks after the call took place dramatically diminishes the effectiveness of the training. Give four pieces of positive feedback for each negative one. Most recording is used to play gotcha and is highly demoralizing. It's much more effective if CSRs look forward to getting generally positive feedback and recognition.

Mobile Communications

Customers with cell phones and PDAs can use Internet and telephone-enabled communications such as text messaging and Twittering (a shorthand texting community that, if you're lucky and relevant, the consumer might allow you to join) to present inquiries and problems. Organizations can then respond via the same media. However, using these media for proactive communications (particularly for promotions) is often viewed as self-serving or as annoying spam.

Tactical Uses. These are like e-mails and videos—irrelevance gets you deleted and ignored. Send to PDAs only information that's important or that's guaranteed to engage the customer. These media are currently most important to youngsters and teens, but they are gaining usage among older adults. Notifying customers of genuine news and opportunities, such as the availability of an MRI appointment because of a cancellation or an open seat on a flight, will be appreciated. Send urgent information to e-mail with notification by text.

Strategic Uses. Again, gather and mine the data on customer preferences and behavior, such as which messages draw responses, and enlist customers in updating contact information.

To Avoid Problems. E-mail and text only important messages to cell phones and PDAs. Don't try to communicate too much or to initiate anything complex using these media.

CRM and Data Mining

An integrated, enterprise-wide base of customer data—on purchases, account activity, problems, warranty claims, repair experience, and satisfaction and loyalty—may be the single most powerful tool for improving the customer experience at both the tactical and strategic levels. At its best, this function integrates a customer's history with information on his value and his position in the customer life cycle. Many of these data, or the capability to collect them, exist in most large organizations; what's needed are the resources to mine and analyze the data and to apply the findings to customers.

Tactical Uses. CRM data enable CSRs to provide flexible responses that are tailored to the customer and her circumstances. They also help CSRs to anticipate needs and thus to discover potential sales situations and ways to communicate proactively to create delight. Once codes that identify the customer and the reason for contact are input, the system can guide the organization to a flexible response based on the circumstances. This can reduce training time immensely. Likewise, the CRM system can help you personalize the interface offered to the customer based on previous visits.

Strategic Uses. Go beyond the basics and identify services and actions that will increase your value to the customer. This may include cross-selling, educating about problems, and creating an emotional connection. A Washington, D.C., nonprofit invited me to a luncheon with its CEO where I was educated on the full range of their activities. The connection resulted in an increased donation. An insurance company identified physician practices that were submitting a high percentage of rejected claims that were subsequently appealed. It targeted the office managers of those practices for visits from the education team, which reviewed their submission processes and helped them eliminate reasons for rejection and lots of expense for the company.

To Avoid Problems. Don't work too hard to personalize or anticipate everything. Amazon got into a bit of trouble by offering people who bought one book on a controversial topic other titles that implied a particular political stance when customers held the opposite view. Also, don't flood your external customers with too many offers or your internal customers with data that don't suggest an immediate action. Design communication strategies that "learn" from problems and successes and slowly modify them to become more sophisticated and finely targeted.

Machine-to-Machine Communication

Sophisticated products, such as luxury automobiles and even many high-end multifunction office printers, can notify the manufacturer of accidents or mechanical breakdowns and "phone home for help" or for required service. Machine self-diagnostic and reporting capabilities that can nip problems in the bud are now available for products such as networked printers and copiers (and will soon be available for home appliances, such as refrigerators and washers). These diagnostics also ensure that service technicians have the right parts when they arrive. In the not too distant future, the fridge will also tell you when you're almost out of milk—and send an e-mail to the online grocery service to add it to your next delivery.

Tactical Uses. Machines that phone home allow almost any company to move into the psychic pizza arena, where you know the customer has a problem before she knows that she has a problem. Consider "on board" communication capabilities for high-end vehicles, electronics, and computers and peripherals. For example, General Motors' On Star calls a communication center if you're in an accident. Such security blankets resemble the GE Answer Center, a service that has been "productized" and an insurance policy that people will purchase.

Strategic Uses. Machine reporting can be extremely specific, giving warranty staff better, more timely information than can be extracted from a field service or dealer representative. You can get information on minor issues that customers would not bother to report or even notice. This technology also solves another problem that usually goes unrecognized—field service staff members often fail to note that the customer did something to cause a malfunction or breakage, in which case the warranty will not cover the service visit. The machine will report facts without emotion or "blaming" the customer.

To Avoid Problems. Try not to provide confusing or ambiguous messages to customers. For instance, does the "check engine" light on your dashboard mean that the air mix is slightly off and should be checked within 2,000 miles? Or does it mean that the engine is out of oil and your pistons are about to seize? Auto companies regularly receive furious complaints from customers who are given misleading messages and rush to the dealer, only to be told that it's no big deal.

A FEW WORDS ON "PUSH" COMMUNICATIONS

In this book and among clients, I've often recommended launching proactive or "push" communications. These can range from welcome packages to vital messages to genuine news to promotional messages, as well as survey results, "news you can use," and changes in a communication channel. Push communication can occur during a phone call, in response to an e-mail initiated by the customer, or via outbound calling, broadcast or individual e-mail, or mass or targeted regular mail.

Whatever the medium, the keys to effective push communications are to:

- Allow the customer to decide what he would like to have pushed to him. One great way to get permission for e-mail push is to break your permission request into four parts: Can I send you requests for feedback on what you have bought? Can I send you information on what you have already bought? Can I send you information on issues you have stated an interest in? And, finally, can I send you information on other opportunities? The first three will often draw forth yes responses.
- Keep informational communications separate from promotional communications—avoid selling when you're delivering information.
- Use only the customer's preferred communication channel.
- Provide a means of responding or giving feedback whenever appropriate (like "Thanks for the help," "Not really helpful," or "Waste of time"). Field occasional "so we can serve you better" surveys with no more than four short, targeted questions. To enrich your VOC program, offer to put customers on advisory, quality assurance, and new product panels. If you do, be prepared to give them continual feedback on how you are acting on what they have told you (not individually, but as a group).

The quickest way to destroy the value of push communications is by sending customers unwanted material. You must use sophisticated segmentation or you will turn off two-thirds of the recipients, who will then delete the next message that would have given them value.

Successful application of technology (with the exception of a few arenas like Wii games, where the technology is the product) depends on understanding that technology facilitates satisfaction with the customer experience. Make it proactive and easy to use, and your customers will actually enjoy using your technology.

As important as technology is, it is the members of the service staff that mainly determine the quality of the customer experience in all but the most basic interactions. They also provide the human connection, which usually has 20 times the impact of an electronic transaction. We therefore turn to the human resources component of the service system in Chapter 8.

Key Takeaways

1. Technology allows your organization to be proactive, whether it is intervening via chat or phoning home for help at the first sign of a problem.
2. Technology must eliminate the need for effort on the customer's part—filling in the history and handling most of the transaction without the customer asking.
3. You must lead the customer to the new technology and ensure his first try is successful; if you do, the investment in education will reap a tenfold payoff in reduced service expense and increased satisfaction.
4. Don't overcomplicate, overengineer, or overblow the technology—an IVR that does 3 things well is better than one that does 23 things adequately, and a 30-second video is always better than a 3-minute one.
5. Tailor the technology to be responsive to multiple segments—to first-time visitors and novices as well as to veterans—and make it intuitive for each segment.

CHAPTER 8

People Are Still Paramount

Four Factors for Creating Sustained Front-Line Success

IF YOU'VE BOUGHT a new computer and called for technical support, you've most probably encountered the standard challenges of two minutes of the CSR deciding if you deserve to get support (serial number, date of purchase, and extended warranty contract number, and/or credit card number) and then a rushed two minutes of "try this and this and call back if it doesn't work." This is not a way to foster positive word of mouth. Alternatively, another computer company has completely stopped screening for support entitlement, stopped enforcing time limits, and actually encourages CSRs to take the customer to the web site to show how to use self-service in the future. The shocker is that the latter approach is less expensive than the former cost-containment approach.

This will not be the standard chapter touting how a great leader can create a people-oriented culture in which everyone satisfies customers and there is minimal staff turnover. I don't deny that a gifted leader can foster such a culture. However, TARP's analysis of companies that deliver great service has found specific factors in every one of them: the right people with the right tools, training, and motivation. Having a charismatic leader who creates a customer-focused culture is great. But even without such a leader, you can still deliver great service by comparing what you currently have with what I describe and gradually implementing the recommended improvements.

This chapter presents a practical approach to creating a customer service staff that delivers both great tactical and great strategic service. It is based on one simple principle: *It is cheaper (and more profitable) to provide service successfully the first time than to do it and then have to redo it.* The key is positioning your front line to address at least 90 percent of inquiries and problems satisfactorily on the first contact, and to facilitate resolution of most of the other 10 percent without managerial intervention. That's the tactical service component. The strategic component calls for your front line to have effective channels for communicating opportunities for service process improvement and an environment in which they can innovate.

The investment needed to achieve this is affordable because the alternative, including decreased loyalty and increased negative word of mouth along with the need for more expensive staff, costs even more, if there is a full and honest accounting. In addition, the lack of first-contact success leaves employees feeling demoralized when they can't resolve problems, and saying, "I don't get paid enough to take all this hassle." And finally, customer escalations of complaints can be shown to directly drive legal, regulatory, and risk costs. Too often, however, organizations take a very different approach to staffing the customer service function—one that actually depends upon high turnover.

THE HIGH-TURNOVER MENTALITY AND ITS SUBTLE COST

Many management teams think "strategically" about customer service reps, but in a perverse manner. Instead of viewing CSRs as skilled employees who put the service strategy into action for customers, they see them as a fungible, expendable resource that you don't invest in and are content to see turn over every six to nine months. This view is derived naturally from viewing customer service as a cost center and a "necessary nuisance" rather than as a strategic function on a par with marketing and sales. Organizations with this view not only accept high turnover, but actually build it in as part of their service "strategy."

Although a high-turnover mentality is widely employed, it is deeply flawed because it fails to quantify three costs:

- The damage to loyalty and word of mouth caused by underpaid, inexperienced CSRs
- The direct costs of high turnover—money spent on employment advertising, interviewing, and new-hire processing and training (normally 20 percent of the fully loaded first year's salary)
- The loss of service as a justification for higher margins and as a market differentiator and brand builder. Second- or third-rate service people actively undermine the company's marketing and sales strategies, expanding the hole in the bucket that marketing needs to fill.

In other words, the "strategy" of accepting—or encouraging—high CSR turnover as a way of minimizing service costs is, for most organizations, wrongheaded, even for those that want to be the low-cost provider.

The Alternative to High Turnover

The alternative to this approach—and the key to both customer and employee satisfaction—is to make your employees consistently successfully in interacting with your customers. You do this by creating a service function that has the right:

- People (including positive attitudes and sound staffing level practices)
- Tools (including information, empowerment, and feedback channels)
- Training (including initial, remedial, developmental, and ongoing training)
- Motivation (including compensation, supervision, evaluation, and career ladders)

I am a strong fan of small successes rather than big disasters, so I will suggest a number of incremental things you can do to enhance the chances that most of your employees will be successful most of the time. The rest of this chapter examines these four success factors.

FACTOR 1: HIRING THE RIGHT PEOPLE

Hiring the right people means employing people with the right attitudes for the job and using the right mix of full- and part-time staff.

Positive Attitudes Make a Difference

As a representative of Giant Food in Washington, D.C., says, "We hire friendly people rather than try to teach them to be friendly." The best way to find such people is to see them in action. Several executives I've interviewed say that the best approach to finding the right people is to have your employees carry the business cards of managers or HR staff and give them out to people they come across who deliver great service. This is one of the most effective methods I've seen for identifying and recruiting great staff members. Each hire earns the employee who found the person a small monitary spiff.

The interview process can also be used to gauge prospective employees' attitudes. Ask about the kinds of interactions they enjoy and dislike. If they don't mention handling difficult customers, or if they say they dislike doing so, you probably don't want to hire them. The interview can also be used to identify risk takers by finding out if potential hires are comfortable in murky or emotional situations. If they aren't, they will not be as effective in defusing anger or applying flexible solution guidelines.

Proper Staffing Is Essential

Almost every service organization faces a variable service workload. Traditional full-time employees can certainly form the core of the service delivery staff, but given customers' expectations of round-the-clock service and the cost of commuting, traditional staffing models are seldom sufficient. Enter part-time and home-based agents.

Largely as a result of pent-up demand from the weekend, more customers call for service on Mondays, although 24/7 service can smooth this peak significantly (as we found at the GE Answer Center two decades ago). Without such measures, Monday's workload in many companies is 30 to 40 percent higher than Thursday's, while Friday's may or may not show an increase as consumers prepare for the weekend. The point is that trying to handle certain workload patterns with a staff working a level eight-hour day/forty-hour week can lead to overstaffing at certain times and a crunch on Mondays. An overwhelmed staff generates excessive errors and waiting times, as well as more angry customers who can further frustrate even the best of employees. Matching the staff to the workload will actually improve employees' attitudes.

There are at least three large and growing sources of part-time (and often home-based) staff members: retirees, college students, and stay-at-home parents. Part-time staff members often have other responsibilities, such as school or family, but they value their part-time income, and they tend to be stable. College students are often loyal for their four-year stint in the area. As for home-based reps, they tend to be more productive than even full-time staff. Companies such as HP, JetBlue, and 1-800-Flowers have found them to be 15 to 20 percent more productive than regular staff members—usually because they are thankful to be able to work in their pajamas from home and want it to be clear that they are very productive. More on home-based reps in Chapter 11.

Too many companies overlook one other potentially valuable investment in staffing: root cause analysts. A root cause analyst might be a troubleshooter and might work outside customer service—for example, in quality assurance—or a customer service specialist can perform this role. The role is to recognize emerging trends, investigate the causes of problems, and develop ways to prevent the problem or provide a solution. The root cause analyst must possess keen investigative and analytical skills, along with excellent communication skills (to convince CSRs to take the time to communicate emerging trends and to convince management that the issues are real), an orientation to detail, and a focus on follow-up.

FACTOR 2: PROVIDING THE RIGHT TOOLS

Every employee needs the right tools, and in customer service that means information, empowerment, and feedback channels.

Give Employees the Information They Need

Almost no one enjoys being nasty or hanging up on a customer. Think about the last time you snapped at an employee, or even at your spouse. Wasn't it because you felt frustrated, foolish, or powerless? I've asked employees to describe the last time they "blew away a customer" or hung up on someone, and their answers almost always pointed to a lack of information or authority. One airline employee said that she had yelled at a customer because he wanted to know how long the repair would take and no one in the airline could or would tell her. She said, "I was embarrassed because I *should have had* that information."

Generally, the more information that is given to the CSR or the desk clerk in advance, the better. In contrast to my airline example, we worked with Amtrak to create a process that would provide the conductor with information regarding the cause and expected duration of delays as soon as the delays occurred.

Employees generally need information on:

- The customer's history with and value—or potential value—to the organization, which should be readily available, given today's technology. Regarding history, customers should not have to recount previous problems and preferences. The value of the customer should include both revenue and word-of-mouth value, coded into groups such as A, B, and C customers. Having more than three categories is usually not cost-effective.
- The customer's specific situation and wants or needs, and the background in cases like the Amtrak example. What the customer wants or needs should come from the customer directly or indirectly, for example, from the information provided by the customer via interactive voice response (IVR) or an electronic form.
- The range of actions that the employee can take in response. This should come from the training and response guidance that empowers employees as well as from real-time sources. For example, for a delayed flight, the necessary information would include the availability of backup connections to the customer's final destination, as well as response rules regarding a potential upgrade.

Empower Them to Act

Once employees know the customer's value, history, and need, they should be able to take action to fulfill that need. If they lack the authority to do so, the CSR must either refer the customer to a higher-level employee, where the customer must retell his story, or go to the higher-level employee, tell her the story, and get permission to act while the customer waits. Neither situation makes the employee immediately successful, and both should be avoided whenever possible.

Why don't we empower employees to *always* satisfy the customer? There are only two possible reasons, neither of which makes much sense from a strategic perspective: First, we don't trust the customer, and, second, we don't trust the employee. The first stems from an auditor or controller mentality that fears that the customer will game the system to get an unwarranted refund or free service. The second stems from the fear that the employee will give away the store.

As previously reported, less than 2 percent of customers are dishonest. American Express's head of customer experience, Jim Blann, says, "We assume the customer is honest until proven otherwise. Why run the 98 percent through the gauntlet to catch the 2 percent?" Starbucks and L.L. Bean take the same approach. As long as you can track who gets what, you can quickly identify the few who are gaming the system. We have *never* found a situation in which more than 2 percent of customers were engaged in this activity.

By the same token, we've found that supervisors either refuse or overrule the front line's solutions in 2 percent to at most 10 percent of cases. Why double the cost to the company and frustration for the customer for the other 90 to 98 percent of situations where the CSR could have acted immediately?

The controller at a credit card company told me that he allowed employees to spend up to $25 to satisfy customers with an average value of $1,500 in gross revenue. Employees who wanted to spend more or forgive higher fees needed permission from the controller's office. I asked, "What if I, as an employee, want to just say 'No' or even 'Hell no'? Do I need permission then?" He said, "Oh, no; employees never need permission to say no." To clarify, I said, "So I can drive a $1,500 customer away on my own authority, but I need permission to spend $100 to keep him, right?" The controller looked pained and said, "You're right, that makes no sense at all!" He changed the policy so that employees could spend what was needed (but be prepared to explain amounts over $200) and had to get permission to say no.

In general, employees should be trained to handle the top 10 most prevalent situations (beyond basic inquiries and transactions that are always handled to completion) within Flexible Solution Spaces. These spaces consist of the two to five appropriate actions based on the most prevalent sets of circumstances. For example the gold customer will be allowed to rebook his nonrefundable flight with no service charge while the nonpremium customer two months behind on his payments will be charged the full amount. A few stakes in the ground can guide an intelligent employee on how to make decisions without supervisory guidance.

Use Feedback Channels

Employees need to feel that they have control over their environment. Their sense of control diminishes when they get ambushed by misleading marketing offers or promises made by other departments. I can guarantee that if you follow your front line's advice about conceiving, developing, and delivering your products, you'll have better products and higher margins. In fact, one travel and leisure firm arranged monthly meetings between front-line employees and senior executives to give them feedback on specific parts of the operation. The employees would bring examples from their peers to show how promotions or policies led to customer dissatisfaction. The executives appreciated the unvarnished feedback, with one of them saying, "I get more from that 30 minute sit-down with the CSRs than from all the memos I receive the rest of the month!"

FACTOR 3: OFFERING THE RIGHT TRAINING

While the right training is costly, the lack of it is even more costly. High-quality training helps customer service attract and retain excellent employees while developing their skills, enriching their knowledge, and improving their job performance and results. These practices translate into financial rewards. For instance, Motorola reports it has achieved a return of $12 on each dollar invested in training.

Four Types of Training

In general, you must invest in four types of training for customer service reps: initial, remedial, developmental, and ongoing training.

Initial Training: Orienting New Hires. Front-line staff should be equipped to address the 10 most prevalent complex issues that they will encounter. The best approach is to provide them with the two to five alternative solutions (actions and general verbiage explaining the rationale behind the action) for each of these issues and role-play each approach. Initial training of new employees must prepare them to solve customers' problems and defend company policies without sounding like automatons.

Best-in-class service systems provide both formal classroom training and experience in a sheltered environment. The best way to do the training is to provide the logic and then stories illustrating the resolution. Typical new-hire training (prior to on-the-job training) ideally would be apportioned evenly among five areas:

1. General orientation to the company—its brand promise, products, services, and policies—and to the strategic role of the position.
2. Specific training in product and service knowledge, and in cross-selling or identifying potential sales opportunities.
3. Issue-oriented training on the two to five most appropriate responses for each of the top 10 issues. This allows CSRs to apply their judgment, based on the customers' circumstances.
4. Use of telephone, online, and information systems.
5. Customer service soft skills, such as communicating, listening, problem solving, and dealing with angry customers.

This fifth type of training is often the most critical. TARP's experience shows that techniques for defusing anger can actually decrease the cost of addressing customer problems (as indicated in Figure 8-1). Rational customers, whose anger has been defused via empathy, will usually accept a lesser remedy than complainants who are angry. TARP's Defusion of Anger and IANA (Identification, Assessment, Negotiation, and

Figure 8-1. Anger Defeats Resolution

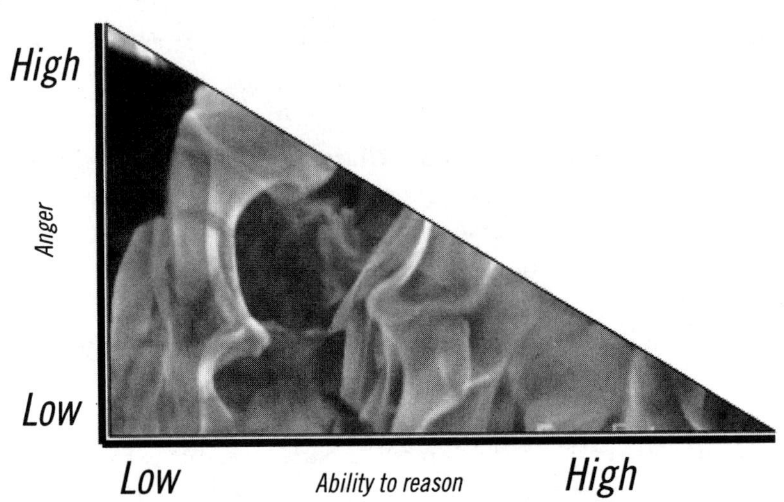

Action) Problem Solving training teaches front-line staff how to manage unhappy customers through techniques for defusing anger and a logical approach to problem solving. This process enables the CSR to ascertain all the facts pertinent to the resolution of a customer complaint, and allows the specialist to consider key aspects of the complaint before seeking a remedy. The process aims to create a win-win situation for both the customer and the company whenever feasible. However, when the customer cannot be satisfied, it provides guidelines for saying no in ways that maximize the potential for retaining brand loyalty.

Remedial Training: Getting It Right the Next Time. When a performance review indicates that a CSR needs improvement in a specific area, that rep must be retrained, tested, and then reevaluated periodically. Remedial training often addresses matters such as delivering positive responses, staying organized, or following up. Thus, the training often involves changing behavior and practicing skills, which can take time and depend on the employee's motivation.

Developmental Training: Preparing for More. Developmental training aims to prepare the service employee for special situations or new responsibilities, such as cross-selling or up-selling, or for a new position, such as customer service specialist or supervisor. It also can include training for moving outside of service, such as into product management or field management. This training should consider employees' career goals and desired responsibilities, the knowledge and skills they will require in order to pursue those goals and responsibilities, and, of course, the needs of the organization.

Ongoing Training: Keeping Current. Ongoing training is critical but can be dangerous. I recently asked a field service tech about training and he said, "They showed the customer service video, *again*." The minute he said *again*, I asked, "What did you do during it?" "My grocery list." Ongoing training reinforces a refresher on the material covered in initial training, as well as familiarizing service staff with new products and response rules as they are developed. The training must be fresh and new! Reviewing the basics should then be followed by stories from the staff on how they have applied the guidance. The new stories make the training fresh every time. For example, Toyota teaches one of its modules for dealing with a difficult customer for one hour each month on a rolling basis with the staff illustrating from recent calls. We have found that best-in-class contact centers provide 70 percent more ongoing training than other contact centers (a median of 68 hours annually versus less than 40 hours for every front-line representative).

In general, while supervisors should be responsible for coaching, formal training should be conducted by professional trainers. Many companies make the mistake of asking any available supervisor or seasoned rep to conduct training. This generates tremendous inconsistency in understanding and execution of policies and procedures, as well as inconsistent employee expectations. In fact, the chief goal should be to generate consistency—and accuracy—in all of those areas, which only professionally conducted formal training can do.

FACTOR 4: SUPPLYING THE RIGHT MOTIVATION

Motivational tools include competitive compensation along with great supervision, recognition, and evaluation by supervisors and the prospect for advancement. Gallup has published compelling research that indicates that most employees leave organizations because of their immediate supervisor. I agree that the supervisor can make or break both tactical and strategic service. Unfortunately, most supervisors either are not adept at evaluating and coaching employees or fail to allocate enough time to do it well. One reason for this is all the other things that supervisors are asked to do in the course of their work. In the section on supervision, immediately after the next section, I suggest a time allocation scheme that generally works well.

Competitive Compensation

In most situations, you get what you pay for, and this is particularly true of CSRs. Leading companies typically pay CSRs above-average compensation. For example, Ritz-Carlton pays at least 20 percent above the average to attract and retain superior employees. Bear in mind that, to motivated employees, "total compensation" includes the potential for promotion, which means that they consider the prospect of higher future compensation to be motivating as well as the "psychic income" of feeling successful.

Superior Supervision

Great supervisors:

- View their role as making the front line successful, promotable, and happy
- Have first-rate quality improvement and supervisory skills
- Use up-to-date call management, information, and monitoring systems
- Coach people in positive rather than negative ways, for instance, by citing four positive observations for each negative one. CSRs should look forward to their next evaluation rather than fear it
- Spend at least 50 percent of their time monitoring and coaching their staff

Many companies fail to hire enough supervisors given the size of the service staff. Best-in-class contact centers provide a supervisor/employee ratio of between 1:15 and 1:8 and specify that supervisors spend most of their time monitoring calls and coaching employees. The best ratio for your contact center will depend on the complexity of the calls, the experience of the reps, and the employees' ability to perform administrative tasks.

Table 8-1 gives a suggested time allocation for a supervisor.[1]

Proper supervision represents a key success factor in customer service, and more than repays the investment.

Table 8-1. Suggested Supervisory Time Allocation

Supervisory Task	*Percent of Time*
Monitoring calls, coaching, rep development	50–60%
Preventive analysis, developing enhanced responses	20–30%
Administration (scheduling special projects, etc.)	10–20%
Handling escalated calls	5%

Excellent Evaluations

Employees want and deserve fair, objective evaluations, and management wants to measure employee performance. Each party can get exactly what it wants. The key is setting both process and outcome goals as described in Chapter 2 and using a mix of measures to evaluate progress toward and achievement of those goals. Therefore, the criteria used in evaluations should be:

- Linked clearly to customer satisfaction, because reps become frustrated when they are told to invoke policies or follow procedures that lead to dissatisfaction and are then held accountable for the dissatisfaction
- Objective, so that reps know what to remedy and can see "the needle move" when they remedy it
- Calibrated and promulgated, so that all supervisors give consistent evaluations
- Structured, so that internal and external evaluations are linked and so that management can predict customer satisfaction and loyalty

The evaluation should focus on the effectiveness of the processes and the response rules as well as on people's execution of them. For instance, if 10 reps receive low marks when answering calls concerning warranty repairs on a specific product, it's likely that either the training or the responses geared to that issue, rather than the reps' performance, is the cause.

In general, you should evaluate people only on metrics (1) that drive the outcome you desire and (2) that employees can affect. As noted in Chapter 2, outcome measures gauge the results you aim to achieve. For instance, if the objective of your call center is to satisfy customers and increase their brand loyalty, then you must measure the satisfaction and loyalty of the customers who contact the call center. If your objective is increased sales, then the most useful outcome measure would be sales attributable to the call center.

In contrast, process measures are internal measures of how people perform an activity. Process measures should include productivity, skill, and quality, and 10 to 20 percent of incentives should be tied to input for problem prevention and process improvement to assure ongoing strategic service improvement.

Figure 8-2 displays an overview of this balanced approach to performance evaluation and a suggested weight to apply to each area. Notice that outcome measures should make up about half of the total evaluation.

Outcome measures at the department and CSR levels—customer satisfaction, customer loyalty, and cross-selling—can be readily quantified and measured. The satisfaction and loyalty measure should be based on a

Figure 8-2. Overview of a Balanced Evaluation

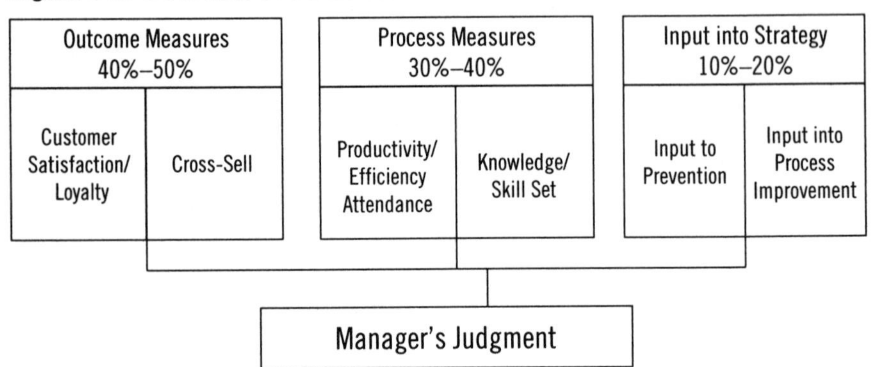

three-month rolling average index from an ongoing satisfaction tracking system (as noted in the next section). The most useful cross-selling measure is the percentage of cross-selling opportunities converted. This metric (like cross-selling itself) may not apply to every company, and the challenge is usually to develop good definitions of cross-selling opportunities.

The process measures at the department and CSR levels—productivity/efficiency and quality/effectiveness—are even more readily measurable. Productivity measures are based on the goals set for the process as described in Chapter 2, specifically those for accessibility, response, follow-through, education, and problem prevention. Some of these, such as goals and measures for system accessibility, are applicable only at the departmental and enterprise levels. Others, such as those for response and follow-through, can be measured and evaluated at all levels.

Capturing the Metrics. All of the measures discussed can be captured in one (or more) of the following four ways:

1. Automatic capture by the system
2. CSR entries in a case-tracking system
3. Observation or listening by a supervisor or quality monitor
4. Surveys of customers

Each means of measurement presents its own challenges, so the following sections provide some hints on how to go about implementing them.

Automatic Capture by the System. Systems can now capture the type and length of calls as well as recordings and even keystrokes for future review. The challenge is finding meaningful patterns in this mass of data, but vendors are now providing powerful analytical tools. They tend, however, to be too expensive for all but the largest service centers. You really need to know the type and length of call by rep in order to tie the call to observation evaluations and satisfaction surveys.

CSR Entries in a Case-Tracking System. Metrics such as "percent resolved on first contact" and any metric based on "percent of cases logged" rely on the rep to enter data into a case-tracking system. While some may argue that such a system is fraught with problems, TARP has found that it is rarely an issue. Reps' tampering with the system quickly becomes apparent when the data is correlated with customer satisfaction tracking or data quality monitoring. Reps must be trained to understand the system and its uses, and to recognize the importance of accurate data to the organization and the customers.

Observation or Listening by a Supervisor or Quality Monitor. While some coaching and monitoring is based on direct observation of employees on the job, listening programs have become standard in most large customer service functions. Of course, employees must understand the reasons for and the nature of the monitoring system, and the need for it to be random. The best test is that reps feel that the observation is fair and look forward to it as a time for celebrating their good job and getting tips on doing even better. The emphasis must be equally on which reps as well as which response processes need improvement.

Surveys of Customers. Surveys are the most effective method of measuring customer satisfaction with service interactions. The options for survey methods include direct mail, e-mail, and telephone follow-up of random samples or specific cases. The survey itself should be brief. It should measure the reason for the call, overall satisfaction with the contact and the result, customer's intention to recommend, and a few characteristics of the response process and the CSR.

Feedback to CSRs and specialists should be prompt and professional and should differentiate between the rep's actions and policy and process issues.

Avoiding Problems with Satisfaction-Based Incentives

To tie employee and management incentives to customer satisfaction, you need reliable data on satisfaction and must use them properly. Obtaining those data and using them properly means avoiding seven common pitfalls, which I'll detail here.

Corrupt Survey Distribution or Sample Identification. If people who are subject to the incentives can control the survey sample, they will exclude customers whom they see as not completely satisfied. One technology company found that ratings from the sample provided by the sales force were five to seven points higher than those obtained from independent sources. Therefore, survey sampling and distribution must be independently—or centrally—executed.

Ballot Box Stuffing, Intimidation, and Gaming the System. People who are being evaluated have been known to fill out surveys on themselves or to offer customers bribes or freebies for positive comments. Also, staff members can pressure customers by saying, "I'll get in trouble if I don't get a 5 rating." You can combat this with a survey question asking whether the customer was pressured about how to complete the survey. A yes answer results in a score of 0 for the survey.

Poor Survey Response Rate. Customers often overlook or discard surveys that are enclosed with a statement, bill, or product. This results in a negative response bias as well as low (single-digit) response rates. The best methods of distribution are stand-alone mail and e-mail, because customers can then complete the survey thoughtfully at their convenience. Telephone surveys are increasingly viewed as invasive and have a strong positive bias.

Inappropriate Use of Surveys to Evaluate CSRs. TARP has seen many organizations where a supervisor will use three surveys received on one rep in a month, one of which is negative, as the basis for a coaching session. Instead, a minimum of 20 surveys accumulated over a period of time should be used for formal coaching.

Appeals or Attempts to Exclude Negative Surveys. Those who are being evaluated often argue that a survey should be excluded because the customer was unreasonable. Disallowing specific surveys is dangerous because there's no reliable definition of unreasonable. TARP has found that unreasonable customers tend to be randomly distributed, so the scores of all reps will be more or less uniformly affected. Therefore, no customers should be excluded (except perhaps those in litigation), as long as the survey sample is random.

Comparison of Units Servicing Very Different Populations. Comparing different market segments or geographic locations on satisfaction measures is dangerous because expectations, definitions of satisfaction, and approaches to providing feedback vary significantly around the world. One solution is to ask about intention to repurchase and recommend rather than about satisfaction. TARP has found intention measures to be more stable and comparable across cultures. While there is some variation across U.S. regions, it's not enough to preclude comparisons, although comparison within the same region is best. That said, TARP has found—in four different countries—that urban customers tend to be more demanding than suburban and rural customers, giving lower satisfaction ratings for identical service.

Rewarding Only Absolute Levels of Performance and Not Improvement. Rewarding people for reaching an acceptable level of performance is useful, but it is potentially problematic with units that are well below the target level. The low rating can be the result of regional differences, historically poor management, or infrastructure factors such as older warehouses or computer systems. If a unit is at a 65 satisfaction rating and the target is 85, most managers will give up and focus only on revenue and profit goals. TARP has found that creating an incentive for improvement, regardless of the absolute level of satisfaction, will generate improvement and reward effort, even if the corporate target isn't met.

Recognition and Advancement

Recognition is as critical as compensation, and for many reps it is more important than another dollar per hour. One great approach is "victory sessions," which I first saw in a Midwest Blue Cross Blue Shield Plan. Every Thursday morning at a team meeting, each CSR had one minute to describe the toughest issue she had handled successfully in the previous week. Such "bragging" sessions assist in training and analysis while motivating reps to deal well with the next difficult customer—"This guy would be great to talk about next Thursday, if I can successfully handle him."

In terms of advancement, CSRs must see a future beyond the front-line position. One of the best managers I saw was at Toyota. He would ask reps where they wanted to be in five years and then facilitate the training and exposure that would allow them to get there. Given the importance of customers to every organization, it's amazing to me that few managers view customer service as the gateway position it can and should be for employees.

PEOPLE ARE THE SOLUTION

Ultimately, the performance of a customer service function depends mainly on how well your organization hires, equips, trains, and motivates the people who are answering questions and solving problems for your customers. It's no place to skimp, and because too many organizations believe that it is a place to skimp, developing such a staff is one of the surest ways to gain a competitive edge and win long-term loyalty.

With the customer service staff hired, trained, and motivated—and with the basic system for handling customer contacts in place—you are ready to pursue what I call aggressive customer service, brand-aligned customer service, and customer delight, which are the subjects of Part 4.

KEY TAKEAWAYS

1. Staffing practices that use full-time, part-time, and home-based service staff flexibly will be more effective and less costly.
2. Lack of a full-time root cause analyst dooms your service system to firefighting mode forever. One analyst for every 25 full-time service staff should be asking why you are getting these calls.
3. Empowerment should not be given in blanket fashion, but issue by issue by means of Flexible Solution Spaces.
4. Evaluation should be focused on celebrating staff doing it right 80 to 95 percent of the time, followed by fixing the processes that the front line is asked to execute; deemphasize catching reps doing things wrong.
5. Effective incentives should include recognition and clear opportunities for advancement beyond the service arena.
6. The biggest management flaw in most organizations is the front-line supervisor who fails to allocate enough time to developing the staff and who cannot give constructive feedback and celebrate good performance.

NOTES

1. Based on TARP's research, consulting, and training.

PART 4

Moving to the Next Level

CHAPTER 9

The Ultimate Customer Experience

Boosting Revenue by Creating Delight

AT LUNCH RECENTLY with an executive at Chick-fil-A, I mentioned a client who was in the business of delivering emergency road service, and the executive immediately described how his wife had locked their toddler in the car with the engine running. In desperation, she called and asked him to speed the 40 miles to her location with his key. Prior to starting out, he called AAA and was told, "You are our top priority. We'll have someone there to unlock the car in under 20 minutes." AAA delivered as promised, and he said, "I am a AAA customer for life." A minor juggling of call priorities by an empowered CSR had a tremendous effect on loyalty and word of mouth.

Once you can consistently fulfill the basic customer expectations that you have set, it's time to start exceeding those expectations *when it makes economic sense to do so.* Exceeding customer expectations creates the response known as customer delight. Dennis Gonier, TARP's CEO and former executive vice president of AOL, defines delight as, "a surprise that is clever or rule-breaking that provides extra value, either spontaneous or well thought out, but not in between." There are various ways to go about creating delight, and although many of them cost money, creating delight also preserves and generates revenue and profits. It makes economic sense to create delight when the revenue preserved or generated outweighs the cost of creating it by a reasonable margin.

In almost all organizations, customer delight occurs haphazardly—and all too rarely. When it does occur, it usually depends on the personality of the front-line associate. A rep may recognize that another product will solve a problem and take the time to educate the customer about it. Yet customer delight need not be created haphazardly. Instead, it can be created consciously, systematically, and reliably, and that's the subject of this chapter.

In this chapter, we'll first examine those aspects of the customer experience that lend themselves to delight and those that are "table stakes" and are always required. We'll also suggest the types of activities where very high performance probably will not create delight and thus will have little or no payoff. We'll then show how to measure the economic payoff from delight because not all delight has the same payoff or cost/benefit ratio. We'll also address five broad approaches to creating delight within the customer experience. And finally, we'll discuss cross-selling and up-selling, which, surprisingly, can also be a source of delight for customers and can generate extra revenue.

First, however, I want to emphasize that this is an advanced topic. This chapter assumes that the organization's service system consistently handles customer inquiries and complaints at high standards of performance at the tactical level. You cannot delight a customer who has just been disappointed. This is one of the most prevalent problems I've seen: Companies announce that they want to exceed customer expectations when they still fail to meet them 20 percent of the time. This chapter also assumes that your information systems are providing the data necessary to support strategic efforts to create customer delight. Delight must be dispensed intelligently, or you can look foolish at best and incompetent at worst. Ideally, the information would include the customer's value and history. On a foundation of competent service and solid information, you can build profitable, delightful customer experiences.

WHAT IS DELIGHT?

Many of us have been delighted when our low expectations have been exceeded. Perhaps a task that should take 10 or 15 minutes—say, renewing a driver's license or making an insurance claim—actually took that long, or less. Or perhaps a contractor finished a job on time. Or perhaps an auto mechanic said, "No charge; it was just a loose wire, and I knew where to look."

We've all also experienced the delight of having an organization exceed our reasonably high expectations or provide us with a truly pleasant surprise. We've seen our vehicle returned with the repairs completed—and the exterior washed—within two hours when it was promised that day. Or a company representative called to tell us that our monthly charges were being decreased. Or a health-care professional took the time to sit at our level and help us understand a complex problem, or perhaps an upsetting diagnosis, and made us feel better and more optimistic about the situation.

Note, however, that superb customer service can itself constitute a delighter in many product and service categories. Haven't you marveled at the efficiency, effectiveness, and personal touch of well-trained customer service reps who know their jobs, their organizations, and your wants and needs, and can use that knowledge to create an outstanding experience for you? This "no unpleasant surprises" form of delight happens every day, but not to all of us and not in every organization.

The Kano model is a theory of product development and customer satisfaction developed in the 1980s by Professor Noriaki Kano. The model classifies customer preferences into three sets of categories, which have been translated into English in various ways, such as delighters/exciters, satisfiers, and dissatisfiers, and can be portrayed as shown in Figure 9-1.

Basic factors include such items as speed of answering the phone. A slow answer, for example, creates dissatisfaction, but a faster answer does not create more satisfaction, let alone delight. Likewise, courtesy is not a delighter; it is "table stakes," a minimum requirement.

Performance factors are expected, standard dimensions of the product or service, such as speed of delivery, where faster is always better. To a degree, price is the same type of factor, as is value. The better the value, the greater the satisfaction; alternatively, high value can offset a defi-

Figure 9-1. Kano Model

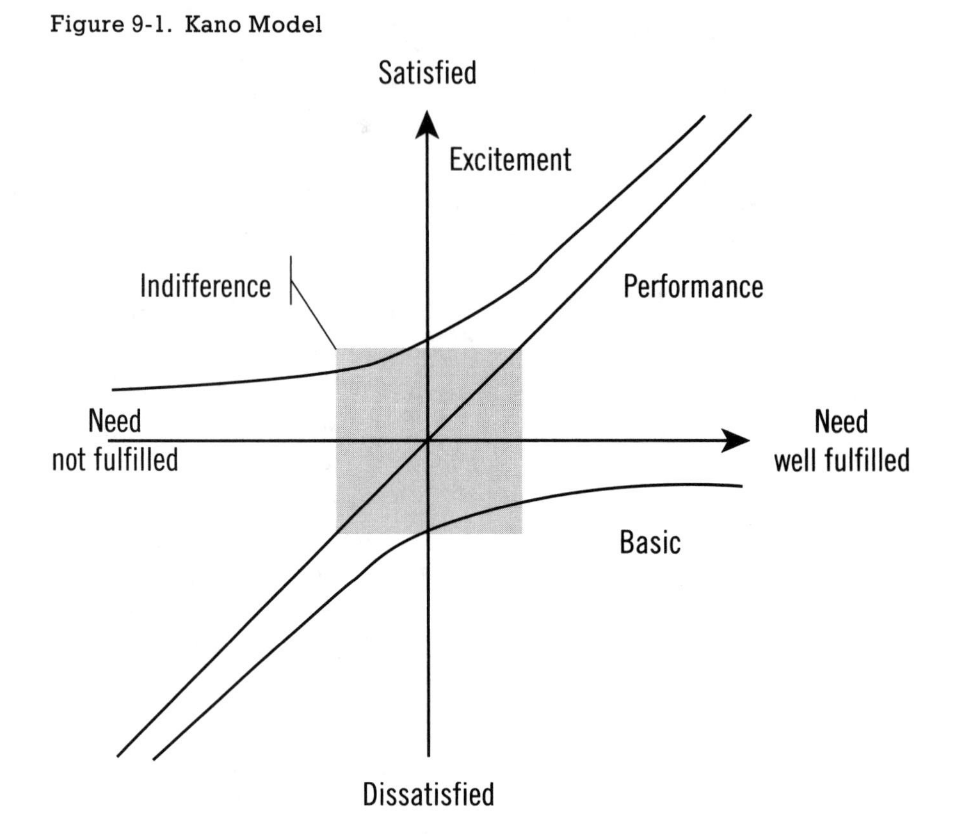

ciency in another dimension. For example, recently at an airport Starbucks, I ordered a regular coffee, and the associate said, "We're just making a new pot, so it will be two minutes, but because you have to wait, it will be free. Is that okay?" He turned the bad news of a wait into a perception that I was assured value (the price was certainly right) and increased the probability that my next purchase would be at a Starbucks. He increased the value to compensate for the longer wait time at a minuscule incremental cost to the company.

The same applies to ATM and Internet uptime and wait times at counters. Any downtime or waiting is a significant dissatisfier. Really fast service or extra value may cause delight, but here we are trying to move into the unexpected—the realm of delighters. If a delighter is not delivered, it doesn't cause dissatisfaction, but its delivery can cause surprise and delight. This points up the fact that a delighter that is delivered multiple times soon becomes part of standard expected performance. While this is bad news, it's also good news, because if your system can deliver this experience reliably, then you've raised the bar for the whole marketplace, as FedEx did with overnight delivery. Now anyone who doesn't offer it is not even in the running. But, again, it has to make economic sense.

THE ECONOMICS OF CREATING DELIGHT

It would be nice to delight customers to make them feel good, to brighten their drab or frustrating days, or to practice the Golden Rule, given that we all want to be treated in ways that delight us. However, there are important strategic, competitive, and financial reasons for creating delight, and the most important of these is increased loyalty, which means increased revenue.

A delight experience usually raises loyalty by 10 to 30 percent, depending on the type of action. Table 9-1 sums up the analyses of thousands of delight experiences. The first two categories are what I call heroics. Two applicable quotes from survey respondents were, "He drove it to my house in the middle of the day" and "She balanced four years of back checkbooks for me after my husband died." Both actions are labor-intensive and disruptive to operations. On the other hand, the 90-second

Table 9-1. The Impact of Delight on Loyalty

Delight Experience	*Average Lift to Repurchase*[1] *(Top Box)*
Service beyond expectation	12%
Assistance during life event	14%
No unpleasant surprises	22%
90-second staff interaction	25%
Personal relationship over time	26%
Tell me of new opportunity	30%
Consistently good service	32%
Proactively provide information	32%

1. Percent increase in loyalty (top-box score) between general customer base and customers reporting a "delight experience."

interaction in the middle of the chart was characterized by, "She heard Fluffy, my dog, in the background during our phone conversation, and we stopped to talk about him, and I really connected with your rep, and you're a great company." A 90-second interaction produced an emotional connection and a 25 percent lift in top-box loyalty (that is, the highest rating on a five-point survey response scale).

Clearly, not all delight actions have the same impact or the same cost. Therefore, you must measure impact by type of delight action at least once to see, in your marketplace, which two or three actions make the most sense. Returning to Dennis Gonier's definition, delight needs to be either systematic and surprising or clever and spontaneous. You can plan the former and let your employees experiment with the latter.

Beyond increased loyalty, other impacts of delight include the following:

- **Highly positive experiences generate highly positive word of mouth as well as increased loyalty.** Positive experiences generate positive emotions, and those emotions motivate customers to tell their friends and acquaintances how they can experience similar delight. Such customers often want to see your organization do more business and succeed (if only so that they can continue to do business with you).
- **Delight dissolves price resistance.** When customers are delighted, they recognize the value of doing business with you, which enables you to engage in aggressive value pricing rather than competitive underpricing or simple cost-plus pricing, hopefully evoking the comment, "You're expensive but you're worth it." Delight can also help you overcome nonprice factors that can hurt your business, such as an inconvenient location or new competitors.

While attractive, these benefits do come at a cost, so any organization that contemplates an actual, systematic program of delighting customers must consider the economics of the situation.

The Cost of Creating Delight

It often will cost an organization more to delight customers than simply to meet their baseline expectations. As Table 9-1 implies, heroics will cost a lot in many cases, as in the case of balancing four years of back checkbooks from a box of papers. The best source of delight is personal interaction, either face to face or over the phone. One auto finance company found that 20 times as many customers said that they were delighted by a personal interaction as by any other experience with the company, such as ads or the web site. Furthermore, each delighted customer told *four* other consumers about the experience. Most striking, when asked, "Of those you told, how many acted on your recommendation?" they reported that one out of four did so. That means that each delighted customer told four people, one of whom acted; thus, each customer produced one new prospect who at least seriously considered the product.

Superb service often costs money in terms of longer talk time or an additional phone call. Creating delight may also involve direct outlays for extras, upgrades, discounts, freebies, and other pleasant surprises for customers. At times, even the hidden costs of creating delight can add up. The unoccupied first-class seat given as a free upgrade probably comes with complimentary beverages and food, and napkins and larger blankets to launder. Similarly, the first-class room will come with more complimentary items and, given its larger size, take longer to clean. I only suggest that you balance the costs against the loyalty and word-of-mouth impact.

The Cost/Benefit Analysis

As with the cost of preventing or solving problems, it makes sense to track and analyze the cost of creating delight. A policy of creating delight will often make intuitive sense, as is true of unconditional merchandise returns at many retailers. But the only way to know for certain is to capture, compile, and analyze the relevant data on the value of your customers and on how loyalty, word of mouth, purchase behavior, and revenue are affected by creating delight.

While creating delight costs money, the direct financial payoff is usually significant and takes the following forms:

- Proactively educating customers about how to avoid problems not only makes them happy but also saves you the money that would have been spent solving their problems.
- Creating delight generates word of mouth that reduces the need

for marketing because your customers do a good portion of your marketing for you.

- Cross-selling and up-selling create direct revenue as well as delight, which we address later in this chapter.

In other words, the "return on delight" can be calculated, just as the return on problems prevented or solved can be calculated. To calculate the return on delight, you first draw data from the customer service system and the entire VOC program that enable you to identify instances of delight and the effects on measures of satisfaction, loyalty, and positive word of mouth for those customers. Then you extrapolate the effects on those measures to the relevant segment of the customer base. Finally, you net out the average costs of creating delight by the means employed in these instances.

You may well find that some methods of creating delight, such as providing realistic delivery times and then delivering before the promised time, say, 20 percent of the time, may not only be much less expensive than other methods like driving an item to the customer's house but also create more delight more consistently. (Such a move may reduce costs as well by reducing calls regarding shipment status.) Indeed, it's worth taking the time to identify delighters for your business and your customers and to choose those that work best for both parties.

FIVE WAYS OF CREATING DELIGHT

TARP's research suggests that there are five basic ways to create delight, with at least a dozen specific actions possible within each of the broad approaches. These five ways, which include sources of customer delight created by your product as well as through service, are:

1. Enhanced product value
2. Enhanced transaction value
3. Financial delighters
4. Proactive communication
5. Creating emotional connections

Enhanced Product Value

Customers are often delighted by an alternative enhanced offering that better meets their needs. This includes product innovations, like the iPhone, as well as providing additional products via cross-selling or up-selling—accessorizing, if you will. It also includes enhanced or tailored service. For instance, Avis asks whether, to you as a customer, speed is more important than cost; if it is, it offers valet service to the airport rather than its shuttle. Any tailoring to the customer's needs can create delight. At Chick-fil-A, the counterperson will carry the tray while Mom shepherds her two little ones to the table. A major association found that if they used the reason for joining to drive the content of the welcome package (for example, travel vs. health-care or political advocacy) sent to new members, a significant percentage of customers were moved from satisfied to delighted.

Breadth of selection also serves as a delighter in certain product categories where mass marketing and high-turnover shelf-space management have resulted in limited choice. Amazon.com probably offers the largest selection of books and CDs of any major retailer. Yet enthusiasts in any particular category appreciate *depth* of selection, whether their obsession is hot sauce, automotive items, or shoes, as at Zappos.com.

Enhanced Transaction Value

An easier, more convenient transaction (or no need for a transaction at all if you practice "psychic pizza"—delivering the pizza you were about to order) delights many customers. This includes tailoring the transaction to the customer, as Chick-fil-A does. It also includes anticipating customer needs. Michael A. Johnson, Senior Vice President of the Automobile Club of Southern California, recently described two examples of anticipation that produced enhanced transaction with great impact. In a recent wildfire in San Diego, AAA called the customer, based on his address, before the customer could call them and had a check in their hand within a week that the customer described as "a very fair settlement; you can't ask for more than that". In the second example, the road service driver provided mother and children who were in the accident with bottles of water and an umbrella to shelter them from the 103 degree sun. She reported that, "just knowing I have AAA to call puts me at ease when I drive".

Financial Delighters

Given that everyone likes to make or save money, the Flexible Solution Space used for training front-line staff (as noted in Chapters 3 and 8) should define financial parameters within which the CSR can not only resolve problems, but also create delight. These might include waiving setup or other initial fees for a higher level of service, the free Starbucks cup of coffee, or not charging for a minor repair at the gas station. You can readily calculate the cost of financial delighters, so it's in your interest to do so, and to measure their effects. Providing financial delighters without calculating their cost and gauging their monetary effects makes little sense from an economic perspective.

Proactive Communication

Customers appreciate updates on the status of a problem, an important delivery, or a complex procedure. They also like follow-up after the fact, as this indicates that you were genuinely interested in solving the problem or ensuring satisfaction by checking on how the appointment went, whether the problem was solved, and so on. Similarly, while it's useful to provide welcome packages and Web-based information about products and services, it's never wise to rely on them completely. Customers love proactive education on how to avoid late charges or repairs, and they appreciate that you cared enough to help them avoid them.

Creating Emotional Connections

There are many ways of creating a sense of connection with and among customers. One is to provide a community where they can get valuable informational and emotional support. This can be done by sponsoring the community, as Intuit does for its users, or by providing, say, a diabetes patient or someone who is trying to quit smoking with links to a relevant support group. Customers associate the support with the sponsoring or referring organization, and you get part of the credit. Genuine empathy will create connections. For instance, Iams has pet loss counselors who have also lost pets and who will spend whatever time is needed to help customers deal with their grief, resulting in very high long-term loyalty and positive WOM.

Other ways of creating connection simply show customers that they belong and are appreciated. Some Chick-fil-A franchisees post Polaroid pictures of frequent guests. Also, taking an action that shows personal concern can create a strong connection. For example, at one high-fashion catalog, CSRs will advise *against* buying certain combinations that will not be flattering. At an investment company, advisors have received huge compliments when they have discouraged an investment and suggested redirecting the funds to pay down an excessive credit card balance. One customer said, "Thanks for having the guts to force me to deal with this debt earlier than I would have otherwise." Admittedly, you are forgoing a sale and may risk alienating the customer who is not genuinely looking for advice. However, if CSRs truly suggest what is best for the customer and present it in a logical, soft, caring manner, most customers will recognize the value of the advice and have stronger loyalty in the long run.

You will literally never run out of ways to delight your customers. It's merely a matter of finding out what, exactly, delights them, and there are proven ways of doing that.

DISCOVER YOUR SPECIFIC DELIGHTERS

While you may have a good idea of what delights your customers, a systematic program depends on consciously setting expectations and then exceeding them. This may mean actively managing your customers' expectations downward, like the airline that instructs pilots to announce that the midair delay will be 45 minutes when he believes it will actually be 30 minutes. This eliminates the rolling disappointment of optimistic estimates and creates a pleasant surprise if the announced time is accurate or, better yet, an overestimate. But it also means knowing exactly what your customers, particularly your best customers, expect. Specific sources of information on customer expectations and, thus, on opportunities to create delight include the following.

Listening Programs

Listening to telephone interactions or reviewing e-mail exchanges can help you identify delighters if you monitor customers' reactions to various solutions provided by CSRs. This includes both solutions within the

Flexible Solution Space and those in which a CSR chooses to move outside that space (hopefully, within his general range of empowerment). Listen for solutions suggested by customers as well. Even those who are bargaining hard or asking for something that at first blush seems unreasonable may sometimes point to a new way of creating delight.

Asking Customer Service Reps

Service reps live in the realm of customer interactions and can give you a good sense of what will dazzle most customers. If you ask your reps, either through surveys or in weekly meetings, about what delights customers, you will almost always get some good ideas.

Customer Compliments

Letters and e-mails describing CSR actions often suggest alternative cost-effective approaches to standard problems. Besides celebrating those actions with the CSR's unit (remember peer recognition!), look for new potential systematic delighters.

Surveying Customers

While earlier I stressed asking about problems in surveys, you should also ask what has turned customers on. Most companies gather verbatim comments from those giving negative ratings, but few do so from those giving top-box ratings. If you get top-box ratings, ask what you did to earn it. This is a great source of ideas. It's easy to assume that all your customers want it cheaper, faster, easier, and better, but they'll provide specifics that will often be different from those dimensions.

Be sure to ask customers about their last delightful customer experience, regardless of where it occurred. Remember, customers' expectations are set not only by experiences with companies in your business, but also by those with organizations in every business. When TARP asked on behalf of a power utility what Amazon and FedEx did that was better, customers mentioned specific Amazon Web features and noted that FedEx knew where its trucks were. In fact, to help our clients think creatively about delight, we have developed the Delight Matrix™, which outlines a series of generic delight actions across five delight categories that would apply to any business. What works for McDonald's might just work for Motorola or 3M as well.

Watching the Competition

When a competitor introduces a new customer service policy or procedure, or when a customer says, "Well, over at XYZ, they always do ABC for customers," ask yourself why. Typically, such policies and procedures stem from popular demand and make economic sense. Of course, when one company in an industry implements a delighter, such as unconditional returns, it may soon become an industry standard. In that sense, the higher bar becomes the new baseline.

That raises an issue. If a delighter becomes something that customers expect, then it soon ceases to be a delighter. It may continue to give you a competitive advantage, as long as competitors don't provide it or you can provide it more reliably or less expensively, but by definition delight is the response that occurs when an organization exceeds customers' expectations. When customers come to expect a feature, it becomes simply a feature of an improved—but now expected—customer experience.

In fact, there are two schools of thought on delight. The first is to spread it broadly to foster positive word of mouth, while the second is to bestow it only on the deserving, that is, premium or high-potential customers. The challenge with the second approach is that you may not recognize those customers, or that the customer behind them in line might demand the same thing, at which point you have to refuse and risk causing active dissatisfaction. Generally, I'd suggest following the first approach, especially with inexpensive delighters, so that the staff can always err on the side of delighting too many people.

The infrastructure for implementing strategic customer service includes a system for generating the data needed to identify problems and prioritize them for solution on the basis of their financial impact and the value of a customer in key customer segments. With that strategic infrastructure in place, your organization is also positioned to delight customers in ways that are conscious, planned, and systematic, and as a result can be replicated.

CROSS-SELLING AND UP-SELLING

Am I serious when I say that cross-selling and up-selling create delight? Aren't we all pounded so often with sales messages that we've long since ceased to find anything delightful about them? As Table 9-1 shows, customers see hearing about a new opportunity as a source of delight. That is basically cross-selling.

Whether cross-selling is a delighter in a specific instance depends on what, when, and to whom you are selling. It even depends on who is doing the cross-selling. Working with four different copier and office products companies, we have learned that if the sales rep says that you need a bigger machine (for an additional $2,000 per month), she just wants a sale. But if the service tech says that you're stressing the current machine and you need a bigger one, he's telling the truth. This is because the customer believes that the technician has her best interests at heart and is less biased.

Never forget that when customers call with questions and problems, they are among the minority who care enough, for whatever reason, to contact you. When they do, they expect you to help them, and they often have wants or needs that can be met with an additional, supplemental, or newer product or service that you can provide. The vast majority of customers are rational and do not expect you to provide this for free. If they have a want or a need that you can fulfill, they'll gladly pay you to fulfill it. After all, that's the basis of the relationship between your organization and your customers.

Common examples of situations in which organizations can create delight through cross-selling and up-selling include those in which:

- An upgrade or a higher level of service will meet the customer's expectations, which may have been incorrectly set by marketing messages, sales pitches, or sources beyond your control.
- A bit of advanced education is followed by an offer of a low-priced subscription to updated technical manuals, Web-based or DVD tutorials, or live training that will enable customers to realize greater benefits from their product.
- A service contract, an extended warranty, or another form of "insurance" will protect customers from further unexpected expenses or otherwise lower their exposure to risk. This is espe-

cially attractive when the current repair cost can be credited toward the cost of the extended service contract.

- A new offering provides the same (or better) performance for a lower price or better performance for the same (or a lower) price, or even better performance at a higher price.
- A rare, seasonal, specialty, or soon-to-be-discontinued item is currently available or on sale for a limited time. Bath & Body Works retains discontinued items in its warehouse and will sell the products in case lots to customers who inquire about them. In some instances, the demand warrants re-releasing the product online for a short time (for example, during the Christmas season), which enables the company to carry the product without incurring retail shelf-space and inventory costs. Delight and revenue both at once!

Regardless of your industry, it makes sense to at least consider opportunities to cross-sell and up-sell certain customers who contact your service system with certain questions or problems. However, selling efforts conducted in a service context must be carefully planned and executed with sensitivity.

The Right Way to Cross-Sell

As the author of Ecclesiastes may have said, there's a time to sell and a time to refrain from selling. Knowing the difference is the first step in establishing a successful cross-selling function. (I'll use the term *cross-selling* to include up-selling in this discussion.) The second step is to implement cross-selling correctly.

To the extent that it's practical, it's generally most effective to have the CSR guide the customer through the sales process as far as possible. If that's not practical or possible, the next best approach would be to hand the customer off to a specialist within customer service, preferably someone with a title that includes the term *service*, such as "senior service associate." Customers who call customer service have not called the sales function. Consequently, they expect a problem-solving process rather than a sales process, so the sales process must be secondary and very low key.

A CSR doesn't draw forth as much sales resistance because the customer doesn't perceive her as a salesperson and doesn't see the interaction primarily as a sales situation. As a result, the CSR's objectivity and the problem-solving interaction should be preserved and a transfer to sales offered only to someone who has been completely or almost completely satisfied.

Clearly, customers who are irritated or angry will rarely be interested in a conversation about expanding their relationship with the company, and unless the CSR can turn the situation around completely, cross-selling should not even be considered.

Establishing a Cross-Selling System

Converting inquiries and complaints into selling opportunities requires preparation, resources, and diligent execution. Therefore, in establishing a cross-selling system, it's essential to start small, get your CSRs to understand its value, and start with only a few specific items as a test.

Consider designing a pilot project or a limited test to learn how to make the program more effective before launching it widely. Use the listening program to see what works best, and continually improve it as the effort continues. Make adjustments as developments occur in your industry and your company, and among your customers.

Not every customer will be delighted to be cross-sold, but as Table 9-1 indicates, *soft* cross-selling can create delight. More often, the customer will be satisfied either to learn of an available option, to purchase the solution to his problem, or simply to enjoy better performance or service. If you have established a solid foundation of tactical and strategic service, at least consider adding cross-selling to your array of customer service activities.

FOSTER CREATIVE DELIGHT

Create delight by hiring good people; giving them first-rate training, tools, and information; and providing them with solid motivation and incentives along with caring, competent management and a good working environment—and widely celebrating actions that create delight. This means that the reps are acting on behalf of the organization and interacting with its customers, who hold certain expectations of someone in a customer service role.

The quality of the human interaction in the customer experience represents a true source of delight—or its opposite. So give your customer service staff the strategic and tactical tools they need to create delight, and give them the freedom to create it as well.

KEY TAKEAWAYS

1. Delight can be created only when customers' basic expectations are being consistently fulfilled.
2. Identify delighters by asking what caused customers to give you a top-box rating. There is a wide range of experiences that can be delighters, including appropriate cross-selling, proactive education, and 90-second friendly interactions.
3. Not all delighters have equal payoffs, and some are downright cheap to deliver.
4. Delighters are much more cost-effective when they are tailored to the market segment, making them both relevant and suited to the specific customer.
5. Today's delighter, systematically delivered, can become tomorrow's expectation and standard.

CHAPTER 10

Brand-Aligned Customer Service

Building the Service Strategy Into Every Function

WEBSTER'S DICTIONARY defines a brand as a well-known and respected name of a commercial producer. Companies invest huge sums to build respect for their brands. They mount advertising campaigns, develop corporate identities, design logos, register trademarks, and protect their brands from piracy, knockoffs, theft, and encroachment. A simpler way to achieve and maintain a brand is to follow Webster's definition, that is, to produce an offering that creates positive word of mouth and thus becomes well known and builds respect. If you can create a unique, remarkable offering and deliver it effectively, you can create and maintain an effective brand. Neiman Marcus delivers unique merchandise with remarkable service and can consequently command a significant premium. Chocolate Moose, a local Washington, D.C., retailer that carries unique gifts and greeting cards, follows a similar strategy. Like Neiman Marcus, it has created a remarkable brand through consistent selection of offbeat products and great service. In other words, a single local store and a major company can succeed in a similar way.

Such organizations create a service process that sets expectations properly through a clear brand promise and delivers a customer experience that is aligned with that promise. While the brand is the basis, the brand-aligned service builds upon and amplifies the basic brand offering by creating a remarkable experience.

Brand-aligned customer service begins with the realization that customer service is intrinsic to the customer experience. Brand-aligned service refers to service that fulfills customers' expectations for the brand and does so by aligning all the business processes, operations, people, practices, and communications with the brand promise. There are three critical requirements for achieving brand-aligned service. First, you must set the correct expectations. Second, you must have in place all the processes required to deliver on those expectations. And third, you must be able to adapt those processes to different types and segments of customers.

In this chapter, we present the concept of brand-aligned customer service and its benefits to an organization. We first revisit how customer expectations and the customer experience affect the brand experience. We then explore the nine factors that allow companies to build brand-aligned service and how those methods can be replicated in your organization. Finally, we examine ways of tailoring brand-aligned service to different levels of customers (gold, silver, bronze, and lead customers) to make them *all* feel valued. In this area, we also provide some counterintuitive suggestions.

This chapter focuses on delivering a consistent, emotionally satisfying experience through tactical and strategic customer service. This approach applies to any organization, whether it is starting up, establishing a new brand, or acquiring or reviving a brand.

CUSTOMER SERVICE AS THE GUARDIAN OF BRAND EQUITY

Although organizations often fail to see it in these terms, branding represents an extended exercise in setting expectations and then fulfilling (or exceeding) them. In all the touches—from product positioning and package design, through advertising messages and sales practices, to delivery of the product or service, to the ways in which service handles inquiries and problems—the brand and the customer experience must be completely aligned. If they are not, the result will be disappointment, unpleasant surprises, dissatisfaction, and loss of loyalty. It is, of course, the function of customer service to address, at both the tactical and strategic levels, situations in which customer expectations are not met. In that sense, service guards and bolsters brand equity.

Brand equity can be defined as the total value of a brand, and it can be extremely difficult to calculate in precise monetary terms. True, the accounting concept of goodwill can place a value on an intangible like a brand, but that becomes truly meaningful only when the company or brand is sold. Also, goodwill may or may not capture the full monetary value of everything that a strong brand can do for an organization and it seldom values the existing customer base, which I believe is an opportunity for improvement of the Generally Accepted Accounting Principles. A strong brand typically enables a company to do one or more of the following:

- Market and sell its current and new branded offerings more easily relative to competitors.
- Charge a premium over the prices that competitors can charge.
- Retain customer loyalty despite new competitors or new offerings from existing competitors.
- Increase revenue and profit through product and service line extensions and licensing arrangements.

Protecting brand equity depends mainly on two things, one of them a broad, risk-management issue and the other a narrower, day-to-day issue. The broad issue is to avoid a disaster. Tylenol's handling of its 1980s product-tampering case, where it immediately pulled all the product from the shelves at great expense but retained its market share, still stands out as one of the best examples of avoiding catastrophe through first-rate communications and crisis management. In contrast, Audi's handling of its "unintended acceleration" issue in the late 1980s, where it blamed consumers and resisted action, was far more damaging, although the brand ultimately did recover, but only after hundreds of millions of dollars in lost sales. (Note that a 1989 National Highway Traffic Safety Administration study found no mechanical faults and assigned the problem to driver error.)

Fortunately, disasters are few and far between. Therefore, most losses of brand equity are caused not by a tidal wave of bad publicity resulting from a mishandled catastrophe, but rather through the drip-drop erosion of customer loyalty resulting from dissatisfaction with the customer experience. (A chain of gyms was almost put out of business due to negative word of mouth about misleading sales tactics.) The surest way to build and preserve brand equity is for each part of the organization to do all it can to create customer satisfaction and loyalty by creating a customer experience that meets or exceeds customers' expectations.

CUSTOMER EXPECTATIONS AND EXPERIENCES

The brand promise sums up the expectations that the organization sets regarding the customer experience. Again, customers will bring expectations from other sources over which you have less control. However, you have tremendous control over the expectations you set for, and the experience you deliver to, your customers.

As shown in Figure 10-1, the brand promise is what people expect before a transaction or interaction between the company and the customer. The transaction or interaction generates an experience for the customer. The result of that experience is either an increased, a

Figure 10-1. Interaction of Brand Promise with Customer Experience

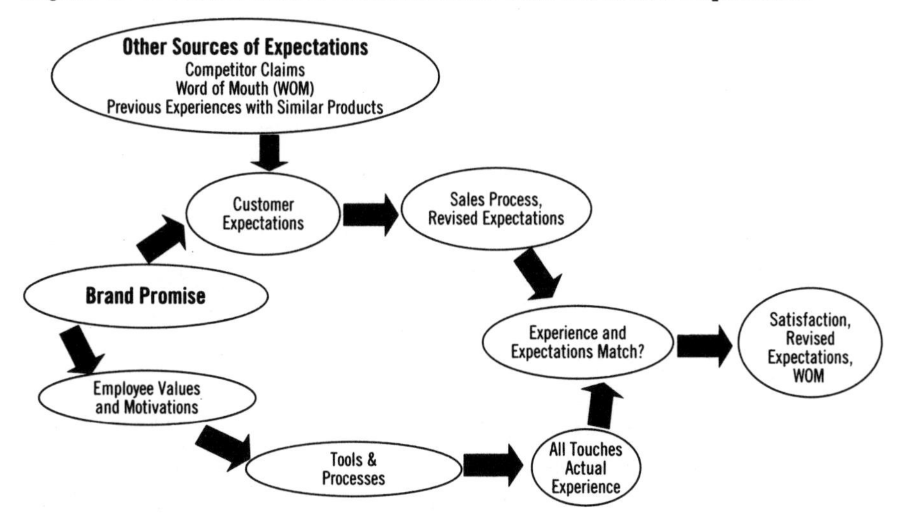

decreased, or the same level of satisfaction and loyalty on the part of that customer. I am defining *transaction* and *interaction* very broadly here to include calls to or from sales or service reps, purchases at retail stores, meals in restaurants, stays in hotels, and flights on planes. Indeed, a customer experience occurs for a cable TV company whenever a viewer picks up a remote, for a bank whenever a customer uses an ATM, and for a car company whenever a driver turns on the ignition. Whenever someone logs on to your web site, he's undergoing a customer experience.

Most executives see customer satisfaction as something of a steady state that can be captured in a snapshot or a single measurement. In reality, satisfaction is subject to change with every customer experience. That's why it's essential to focus on satisfaction at the level of the individual customer; waiting until aggregate satisfaction deteriorates before fixing problems at the tactical level is hazardous to your brand. That's also why it's important to measure the effects of management decisions on satisfaction. If, as indicated in Figure 10-1, the transaction or interaction generates an experience that fails to fulfill the brand promise and meet customer expectations, the result will be diminished loyalty and negative word of mouth. But if the customer is delighted, the emotional impact will drive increased loyalty and positive word of mouth. Every single customer touch or experience has the potential to enhance or diminish the power and value of your brand.

The value of a brand lies in its power to attract customers. Every brand connotes a certain level of quality, durability, and value for a product, relative to others of its type. Professor Emeritus Gerald Zaltman of Harvard Business School suggests that the majority of this value is the emotional fulfillment of a basic need, such as assistance along life's journey ("Don't leave home without it"), a resource for achieving one's goals ("You're in good hands with Allstate"), or the creation of a human connection (the Harley Owners Group).[1] The key point is that the brand suggests a particular experience from a product. For a service with no tangible, physical attributes, the brand is even more important in that it indicates a certain level of user-friendliness, expertise, and customization relative to others of its type.

All these attributes come at a cost, so a brand also connotes a certain price relative to that of similar products and services. Thus, a brand sums up the value proposition (benefits promised for payment made), which may range from low-cost and utilitarian to high-cost and luxurious. That proposition is realized (that is, made real)—or not—in each and every customer experience. Those experiences occur in every touch, transaction, and interaction between the company and the customer.

In fact, service in general, and customer service in particular, has become an integral component of many brands. A 2004 TARP study of the financial services industry, summarized in Table 10-1, revealed that superior personal service transactions have about 20 times the impact of advertising campaigns and corporate sponsorships on the customers' overall opinion of the company and its brand. At the same time, some people indicated that the online experience or the automated phone system had the greatest impact. Thus, while every touch has some impact on customers' opinion of your organization, service transactions often have the greatest impact. This held true in the automobile industry as well, where our research revealed that the experience at the dealership and over the phone with the auto finance company were the two major determinants of customer loyalty. Moreover, in virtually every service business—health care, hospitality, transportation, travel, financial, and personal and professional services—customer service *is* the product. Retail, technology, and many other companies dealing in tangible products also have a significant service component.

In a world in which technological innovations can rapidly be copied, with the effect of "commmodifying" most products, service is often *the*

Table 10-1. Impact of Customer Experiences in Financial Services

Specific Positive Experience	*% with Greatest Impact*	*Average Number Told About Positive Experience*
1. Great personal service transaction at retail store	29	4.3
2. Great interaction with telephone customer service representative	21	3.4
3. Did not feel pressured at the store	18	3.2
4. Store followed up to ensure that I was satisfied with the purchase	16	3.2
5. Access to account information online	4	2.9
6. Advertisement	1	3.4
7. Sponsorship	0	5.4

key differentiator for the brand. In actual commodity markets, service may be the only potential differentiator. For instance, a company selling mixed cement differentiated itself by enabling truckers to pull up to the giant mixer, load up, and expedite their purchases by making digital entries on keypads rather than going into the office to fill out paperwork. Few commodities are more basic than cement, but service made the "experience" of transporting the cement to the building site easier, faster, and cheaper.

Customers expect to be treated in certain ways, given the organization, the product they are buying, the amount they are spending, and their history as customers. They may or may not want the "warm fuzzies," as noted in Chapter 2, but they definitely want and expect genuine interest in their question, request, or problem and quick, friendly, competent delivery, whether it is the mocha without whipped cream but with a genuine smile or a solution when the organization fails to do it right the first time. Such appropriate touches are what former SAS Airlines chairman Jan Carlson called "moments of truth" 20 years ago. My point is that rather than just focusing on major moments of truth, you need to focus on every touch, because a small touch can turn into a damaging moment of truth if poorly executed (think about a date, wrong by one digit, for an airline return flight).

Ultimately, the power and value of a brand depend on two things: first, on how well an organization defines and communicates its purpose and promise to its customers, and second, on how well it fulfills and delivers on that promise. If the customer experience fails to fulfill the purpose and promise of the brand, then brand equity will erode.

THE NINE BUILDING BLOCKS OF BRAND-ALIGNED SERVICE

Starting in 2005, TARP has conducted qualitative research on how organizations align their strategic service with their brand promise to create a seamless customer experience. Our goal has been to identify the building blocks of brand-aligned service. Based on a wide range of executive interviews, consulting engagements, and published and proprietary work of companies with strong brands, this study suggests nine critical factors that assure that strategic service will build and preserve the value of brands effectively. These nine factors are:

1. Clear brand promise tied to the company heritage
2. Clear accountability for the brand
3. Focused values that reinforce and facilitate the brand promise
4. Measurement and feedback
5. Formal process for every touch
6. Ongoing communication to everyone
7. Planned emotional connection with the customer
8. Employees who deliver the brand
9. Customized brands for market segments

Another goal was to learn how companies align their strategic service offerings and customer service to reinforce brand loyalty. Again, we define brand-aligned service as service intentionally structured to fulfill the brand promise and to meet or exceed the customer's expectations across all touches. Delivering brand-aligned service requires the entire organization to align all of its business processes, operations, human resources, and internal and external communications to fulfill the brand promise and to drive business results. Absence of this alignment dilutes brand equity. Increasing this alignment fulfills the brand promise, protects brand equity, and increases brand loyalty, positive word of mouth, and revenue, all of which increase the value of the brand. Studies have shown that employee satisfaction and retention also increase, because employees enjoy working for an organization that has a strong brand and enjoy contributing to the brand's stature. For organizations with fully developed customer service functions, brand-aligned service will move service, and its value to the organization, to the next level.

Clear Brand Promise Tied to the Company Heritage

Companies with brand-aligned service have a clear brand promise that is illustrated by their history and is embodied by its role in building the brand. If you have a clear brand promise that can be articulated in a few words, and you can cite examples from your recent or ancient history, you have a firm basis for brand-aligned service. Bank of America used the tag line "Higher Standards" to illustrate higher levels of service than most banks. FedEx used "When it absolutely, positively has to be there overnight" to stress speed and reliability. Starbucks promised a great experience that barely mentioned coffee.

These companies use their heritage to inform their training, communication, and management practices. Disney has a particularly strong and proud heritage, as new Disneyland employees learn during orientation, where a "Traditions" class conveys the founding principles as they apply to the company's current vision and mission. The U.S. Postal Service also has a strong heritage and celebrates employees who embody its values of trust and dependability on its web site. Almost every day a mail carrier somewhere in the country saves a citizen's life, whether by finding an elderly person ill in her home, saving someone from a burning building, or literally catching a child who bounced too high on his bed and flew out of a second-story window (true story!).

Clear Accountability for the Brand

Organizations with brand-aligned service drive accountability for it in four ways: formalized structure, leadership, peer accountability, and employee empowerment.

Formalized Structure. Some companies establish a department or a cross-functional team to ensure that the organization delivers the brand's message in all communications and service design meetings. UPS's Brand Management Team defines the brand strategy, conducts brand training, and works internally to ensure consistency in the service experience.

Leadership. Senior executives in some organizations communicate that brand-aligned service is a priority, regularly referring to brand attributes and seeing that initiatives deliver on the brand promise. At a leading Internet company, the CEO often mentions brand attributes in planning sessions and communications, as does the CEO at UPS. Southwest Airlines' Herb Kelleher's stress on making flying fun earned *Fortune* magazine's title of "high priest of HaHa." These leaders understand that the brand is not just words, but a set of principles and promises that must be brought to life every day in practical situations. Therefore, they lead by example, as do the leaders at Disney, where all managers must spend at least one day a month working with the public.

Peer Accountability. Employees may also hold one another accountable for "living the brand." Starbucks's Green Apron program encourages staff members to recognize actions of coworkers that exemplify the company's core principles. More generally, a number of companies drive employee accountability through formal feedback programs. In these programs, employees agree to point out when someone practices or fails to practice brand principles and agree to use this feedback to improve. At Dell, most signature pages provide the employee's supervisor's e-mail with an invitation to provide feedback to the employee or their supervisor. In the best of these environments, the leaders ask for and accept this kind of feedback as well—even from subordinates.

Employee Empowerment. Companies that emphasize employee empowerment authorize and encourage employees to deliver the brand message actively and creatively. They provide Flexible Solution Spaces and encourage employees to ensure that customers are satisfied with the answers and solutions that they receive. And while they emphasize the importance of policies and procedures, they also confirm that customer satisfaction and loyalty is their primary goal.

Focused Values That Reinforce and Facilitate the Brand Promise

Brand-aligned organizations sum up their credo in mottos and *simple* core values that guide people in delivering on the brand promise. These clearly stated values prompt managers to make decisions and employees to create experiences that are consonant with the brand promise. For instance, Disney's core values are safety, show, courtesy, and efficiency, and everyone explicitly measures service planning and delivery against those values. Starbucks focuses on five principles: be welcoming, genuine, knowledgeable, considerate, and involved. At Levi's, the values are be real, confident, social, inclusive, and innovative. In well-led companies, leaders foster employees' belief in the brand by acting in agreement with brand values in their dealings with the employees, so that the employees, in turn, will convey that belief to customers.

Such values can help you in times of stress. Jane Yates, then a vice president at Johnson & Johnson, told me of the discussion among management about what to do when the Tylenol poisonings hit. She said the company's values, in the form of the J&J Credo posted in every conference room, clearly told the managers to put the consumer first, which they did; this dramatically simplified their decision making.

Measurement and Feedback

Brand-aligned organizations aggressively use measurement and feedback to ensure that their service delivery fulfills the customer expectations fostered by the brand. Metrics include process measures of the individual transactions or touches, such as ATM downtime, wait time in the queue, or empathizing with the customer about her problem. They also include outcome measurements of customer satisfaction, loyalty, and word of mouth from Voice of the Customer, and employee feedback.

One of the most difficult areas to measure is the impact of marketing and sales not setting correct customer expectations. It is easy to measure whether operations delivered the product according to specifications. It is harder to measure whether marketing set up the wrong specification in the customer's mind, which the customer then compared with what operations delivered. One useful approach is an *Index of Marketing Quality*™ that asks, "How much of the customer service workload was the result of marketing setting incorrect expectations up front?" As mentioned earlier, one of the leading packaged goods companies has set up a chargeback system in which the consumer affairs department charges the product management department the cost of calls where the root cause as determined by the CSR appeared to be incorrectly set expectations and confusion resulting from poorly designed marketing promotions.

Companies with brand-aligned service tie incentives to such measurements in useful ways. At Bank of America and Marriott, employees' goals are to improve the customer experience and the alignment of service with the brand. Toward that end, Bank of America uses daily phone surveys as well as mystery shopping (anonymous test visits by a market research firm), both tracked back to individual associates. Middle management incentives are tied to five service targets, such as rapid greeting, that have been found to be key drivers of satisfaction. These metrics are rolled up from the branch to the senior management level. At Ritz-Carlton (a division of Marriott), employees maintain an incident report (behind the scenes) so that any incident can be discussed in terms of both prevention via process improvement and the best immediate recovery strategy. Companies like these tie incentives to service metrics so that the customer experience fulfills the brand promise.

While these feedback systems can be expensive, without them you won't know exactly what went wrong, and therefore you won't know what to fix. How will you know, for example, whether one employee needs retraining or whether the whole process is broken?

Formal Process for Every Touch

Brand-aligned companies have formal processes for developing new services and integrating acquisitions to ensure consistency with the brand, and they implement these processes early in the development or acquisition cycle. They also use them to ensure consistency across the organization without creating robotic responses. For example, Starbucks aims to create the same welcoming atmosphere in all its stores by means of design, furnishings, product offerings, and employee-customer interactions. Bank of America uses playbooks that describe ideal processes for product introductions, mergers, and transitions of new branches to the brand, across the company and in all channels. Allstate defines key moments in the customer experience and their emotional and operational aspects; for instance, when a claims adjuster assesses a damaged car, she is trained first to empathize with the customer and then to explain the procedure.

Formal processes may be seen as undermining empowerment. They aren't, however, because their goal is to enable employees to achieve an objective within a general structure, but to do so using their own style of communication and one of the range of actions drawn from the flexible solution space.

Ongoing Communication to Everyone

Brand-aligned organizations communicate from senior levels to all other levels in ways that demonstrate and reinforce brand principles. This occurs in three ways.

Training, Briefings, and Meetings. Companies ensure brand-aligned service through initial and ongoing training and meetings. Most of the companies that TARP reviewed hold weekly or even daily briefings. While these often address local matters, they also include consistent reinforcement of the brand. Marriott uses Daily Basics sessions to focus on a single service principle at a time. A leading Internet company circulates stories about the difference that its service makes in people's lives. Southwest Airlines has a Culture Committee at every location that plans Spirit Parties and other events that reinforce the brand image of fun. Much of this activity consists of storytelling that conveys the brand history and success stories similar to the "victory sessions" mentioned in Chapter 8.

Periodic Newsletters and Web Site Stories. Organizations with brand-aligned service publish weekly or monthly print and electronic newsletters giving stories that tie employee actions to the brand's characteristics. The aforementioned Internet company, which has an image of fun and community, seeks stories that illustrate how people have fun and connect to others through its service. While e-mail and intranet sites have made newsletters much less expensive (and save trees too!), a printed newsletter still has an important place near the coffee machine, bathroom mirror, and elevator.

Universal Access to Consistent Information. Consistent service depends on consistent information. Disneyland gives cast members (its term for staff members) a fold-up guide with answers to the 100 most frequently asked questions and access to a web site that tracks character appearances. Levi's has a robust online training and reference tool, updated nightly, to help customer relations agents respond to customer inquiries.

Planned Emotional Connection with the Customer

Companies that stress brand-aligned service recognize the emotional dimension of their brands and the importance of emotional connections in forging customer relationships. This starts with a personal touch in employee-customer interactions. For instance, Starbucks encourages employees to get to know their customers and to remember customers' favorite drinks. Chick-fil-A operators often display a collage of photos of frequent customers at their stores. Harley-Davidson dealers often use customer photos taken at the time of purchase to help service writers recognize them and remember the customer's name when he comes in for service a year later.

Many companies, including Harley-Davidson and Triumph motorcycles, create communities of users through owners' associations, sponsored events, newsletters, and Web-based vehicles. In the pharmaceutical industry, Web-based efforts include retention sites that connect patients to the brand, to one another, and to other sources of support. The retention site for an ongoing treatment for rheumatoid arthritis has 75 percent of the medication's users as members.

Employees Who Deliver the Brand

Employees who believe in the company's brand or who somehow embody the brand can truly help a company deliver on the brand promise. For instance, Levi's customer relations department targets confident, outgoing, "real" people who already fit the core brand values. Whole Foods Market recruits new employees from the customers who frequent the stores in order to ensure that they share the customers' passion for natural foods. They especially focus on those who hang out in the coffee bars, because this shows that these customers really like the environment.

Customized Brands for Market Segments

International organizations must plan on a global basis, but remain flexible enough to meet market segment and regional needs. Bank of America varies its service specifications based on customer expectations in different markets, such as urban or suburban, and different locations, such as New York or the Midwest. HSBC has incorporated this into its brand promise—the world's local (hometown) bank.

Another aspect of customizing brands for different valued market segments is the matter of stratified or tiered customer service, which is a subject in itself.

TIERED CUSTOMER RELATIONSHIPS AND HOW TO HANDLE THEM

Tiered, or stratified, customer relationships, in which frequent flyers or hotel guests, gold or silver customers, or higher-value commercial customers receive higher levels of service than standard customers, have proliferated over the past 20 years. When these programs are well thought out and properly implemented, they provide a rational means of relating customer revenue and profitability to the cost of delivering the services that these customers demand. When they are not well designed and implemented, they generate excess costs, confuse customers, and create resentment among customers at all levels. A key issue is: How are the bronze and lead customers treated? This is important for two reasons. First, you should not have money losing customers; you should have profitable lower end customers. Second, your bronze customer of today may be your competior's gold customer who is just trying you—they could be *your* gold customer of tomorrow. American Express always looks at customers' potential value.

Tiered customer service is actually a brand strategy. The concept probably goes back to the first ancient markets when customers decided that the amount of business they did with a merchant warranted recognition, concessions, or extra service, and the merchant decided to accommodate these valuable customers. In modern times, the concept found formal expression in the 1940s at General Motors, which featured an entry-level brand (Chevrolet) and increasingly higher-quality—and higher-status—brands (Pontiac, Oldsmobile, and Buick), topped off by a prestigious, aspirational brand (Cadillac). Decades later, the American Express Gold Card (followed by the Platinum Card and, more recently, the invitation-only Centurion Card, or Black Card) applied the concept to financial services.

The challenge for an organization with multiple tiers of customers is that it must create and communicate a clear brand promise, set clear expectations, and then profitably deliver on that promise and meet those expectations for each level without creating confusion and dissatisfaction. To design and implement tiered customer service, you must know the monetary value of your customers. In B2B relationships, "silver" customers are often more profitable than "gold," given the discounts that each level of customer receives and the level of service that each expects. This is because the gold or top customers often leverage their volume to squeeze the maximum amount of margin out of the transactions. On the other hand, silver customers tend to spend a lot but not enough to demand the best margins, yet they are often treated like the bronze or "lead" customers. For example, at one domestic airline, silver customers who flew at least 25 times a year at business rates still had to check in with leisure-travel customers. TARP estimated that this one policy was costing the airline over $200 million in revenue annually. This principal of the biggest profit opportunity existing in your second tier is almost always true in B2B environments.

Tiered customer service must be implemented with care. Customers can accept that they spend less money or even that they are "less loyal" than other customers. But the system must also be "democratic," or at least rational. For instance, at the airport, everyone accepts the fact that frequent flyers and Million Mile Club members get special treatment because they spend more money with the airline (and more time suffering through air travel). However, both a bank and a communications company have recently suffered public relations disasters when they decided to "fire" customers who were less profitable.

While some experts have suggested getting rid of your least profitable (what I call *lead*) or money-losing customers, we suggest that you set prices for them at which you will make money if they stay around, and give them options. In this regard, explicit service pricing and minimum prices are effective *if* you explain the rationale for the pricing and show customers that they are being treated fairly. For example, working with one computer company, we explained to the very low-end customers that, given what they were paying, the company couldn't afford to provide them with live human technical support and that the self-service was pretty good once they understood how to use it. However, for an additional $10 a month, they could become bronze customers and receive live technical support. That gave the customer an option as well as an explanation. Those who remained lead customers were relatively happy because they understood the situation, and because when they decided to remain lead customers, it was their decision—not one that the company imposed on them. If, on the other hand, they chose to buy up to bronze, this became an additional source of revenue.

BRAND-ALIGNING STRATEGIC CUSTOMER SERVICE

Four important steps will increase the brand alignment of the overall customer experience, each of which will be discussed here.

Step 1: Identify the Brand Characteristics Your Company Wants to Reinforce

Representatives from marketing, sales, operations, and senior management must collectively assess each brand's promise and value proposition. This includes explicitly evaluating the brand's heritage and identifying the values that underpin the brand.

- What brand promise and value proposition have been communicated to customers and employees?
- Is the message consistent across communications and touches?
- What are the customers' expectations for the brand and the associated experience?
- What has been done to set those expectations?
- While these are key moments of truth (in Jan Carlson's words), remember that any touch that contradicts the brand promise becomes a negative moment of truth. Thus, in any customer touch, the initial line of the Hippocratic Oath—first do no harm—applies.

Step 2: Assess Your Current Level of Brand Alignment

The team must then assess the extent to which the customer experience across all touches fulfills the brand promise and delivers the brand value at the level of the customer experience. Measures of customer satisfaction at each touch point—as well as data from other Voice of the Customer sources and employees—should be included. Use the nine building blocks of brand-aligned service presented in this chapter to guide your analysis. It's essential that actual customer expectations, particularly from complaint data, be measured and considered. If this step reveals weakness in the company's delivery on the brand promise and expected value, the organization faces a decision: Should the brand positioning be changed to communicate a different promise and value proposition, or should the customer experience be changed to fulfill the promise and deliver the expected value? (It's also possible to change both.) For instance, a Mercedes-Benz dealership displayed the sign, "We give loaners for X, Y, and Z but *not* for A, B, and C."

Step 3: Identify Opportunities for Improvement

When any discrepancies between the brand promise and the customer experience have been identified, it's time to decide what you can do to achieve brand alignment. Use the Market Damage Model and the Market-at-Risk calculation to prioritize problems in financial terms. The goal here, however, is to view potential improvements in customer education, problem prevention, and the customer experience in the context of the brand. This means that you'll have to look across the end-to-end experience, not just within customer service.

Step 4: Measure the Impact

After you implement any changes, measure the impact on customer satisfaction, loyalty, and word of mouth, as well as the impact on internal functions' perceptions of brand alignment. Ultimately, brand alignment will be reflected in increased revenue as a result of repeat purchases and improved word of mouth, and in the increased power and value of the brand itself.

STAND BY YOUR BRAND

As a key component of the customer experience, strategic customer service must be aligned with the brand. Furthermore, all functions, departments, processes, and activities must be aligned with the brand and support customer service in its efforts to increase satisfaction, loyalty, and positive word of mouth. We take up ways of establishing this support in Chapter 12, but first, in Chapter 11, we examine several ongoing trends that are affecting customer service in most organizations.

KEY TAKEAWAYS

1. There needs to be a clear brand promise that tells customers and employees what the organization delivers and, more importantly, what to expect and what is expected of them (both employees and customers).
2. These expectations are most easily set by stories that illustrate

both the organization's values and the empowerment of employees to resolve problems.

3. There needs to be accountability for the brand at all management levels as well as at the front line, and management must walk the talk and reward employees for doing likewise.
4. Formal, measurable processes can and should be developed for all "moments of truth" and significant customer touches, including an index of marketing measuring the percentage of service expense incurred due to improperly set expectations.
5. When there are tiers of customers, the silver customers often present a greater opportunity for both satisfaction and profit improvement than the gold customers.

NOTES

1. See Zaltman's latest book, *Marketing Metaphoria* (Boston: Harvard Business School Press, 2008).

PART 5

Into the Future

CHAPTER 11

Ride Waves Without Wipeouts

Dealing with Trends in Labor, Technology, and Politics

RECENTLY A FRIEND OF MINE arrived late at Newark Airport and was given a Toyota Prius. The next morning, he pushed the start button and got a beeping noise but no engine turnover. Since there was no user's manual in the glove compartment and he was about to be late for an important meeting, he made a call to emergency road service, which resulted in his learning that after pushing the button, he had to wait a few seconds for the motor to start. Introducing new technology without enough up-front customer education can increase stress for the customer and costs for the company in the form of more complaints and problems for customer service to address.

New technologies and other trends that affect a company and its customers will also affect its strategic service function. As the company's eyes and ears, strategic service can provide both early warnings and impact assessments of trends, and thus is in a position to anticipate the problems and opportunities that these trends present and then instigate actions that will increase customer satisfaction and loyalty.

In this chapter, we examine several key trends that present challenges that strategic customer service must address. For convenience and logic, I've organized these trends as follows:

- Labor trends
  - Labor shortages in customer service
  - Outsourcing customer service
- Technology trends
  - Increasing product complexity
  - New communication technologies
- Political trends
  - Regulatory and safety concerns
  - Environmental issues

Although this chapter does not cover every trend affecting customer service, it does illustrate how these trends and others are affecting the service function. While there is no way to avoid these trends, management must determine how they affect customers' expectations and the customer experience, and then respond accordingly.

LABOR TRENDS: CHALLENGES IN ATTRACTING HUMAN RESOURCES

A majority of the customer experience is still delivered by people, especially via the call center. Call centers have become a cultural cliché in the United States—and not in a good way. The position of telephone CSR lacks the cachet of Starbucks barista or even FedEx or UPS delivery person (let alone a professional position such as attorney, accountant, or architect). Indeed, the job has negative connotations.

Companies themselves have done much to foster these negative connotations, some of which arise from the jobs having been outsourced (as discussed later), and some of which arise from widespread instances of bad service. When the "Your call is important to us" can serve as a punch line, and the comic strip *Dilbert* regularly addresses customer service, you know you have an image problem. This image problem and the resulting human resources problem, like so many problems in customer service, stem mainly from management's view and treatment of customer service. If management sees service as a cleanup crew and a cost center, then it will aim to get problems cleaned up at the lowest possible cost, leading directly to these negative stereotypes.

The strategic approach to customer service represents the solution to this image problem in that contact centers are viewed as contributors to the customer experience and to the top and bottom lines. In other words, this image problem is best overcome by genuinely celebrating the center's contribution and providing a work environment, a pay scale, and a brand banner that attracts people with superior skills and enables them to see a better future for themselves. Toyota, Neiman Marcus Direct, Zappos, and many other companies enable their people to feel good about the company, the brand, and their jobs, and thus to deliver a consistently great experience.

Addressing the Labor Shortage in Customer Service

The labor shortage in customer service is real, given the number of reps required in a developed economy and the demonstrated limits of our current educational system. CSRs must be able to explain complex problems and processes in a clear (both simple and linguistically understandable)—and sensitive—manner, often in writing. They must be flexible, empathetic, oriented toward problem solving, and able to work with a wide range of people and situations. Faced with a relatively limited talent pool, companies must compete vigorously for competent service reps, and hold onto those that they hire and develop.

In Chapter 8, I pointed out the importance of good compensation (including incentive compensation) and benefits, solid initial and ongoing training, and first-rate management and motivation, emphasizing career paths and opportunities for advancement outside the call center. Savvy companies such as Toyota have started to treat CSR as both an entry-level position and a stepping-stone to positions in field management, marketing, sales, and other areas. Merck repositioned its call center as a function to which it promoted successful salespeople! Granted, that center required extremely skilled and knowledgeable staff, given the number of physicians and pharmacists among the callers. However, the effort was so successful that the company spun off the unit as a separate entity that's now an outsource call center for other pharmaceutical and medical device companies. This shows the level of excellence that can be achieved when you put an appropriate amount of effort and resources into the call center. Similarly, Mark Scott, former CEO of Mid-Columbia Health System in Oregon, said that he marketed to his *existing employees* every day. His was one of the few hospitals with a *waiting list* of nurses who wanted to work there.

Despite even successful efforts to hire, train, and retain good people, CSR will not be a 10-year position for most people. Yet given the right conditions and the prospect of promotion to other positions in a company with a great reputation and respected brands, many people will enjoy the job for three or four years. One model is to hire college students in their freshman year and you'll keep most of them for four years. Many CSRs enjoy earning a second or part-time income or highly valued perquisites, including travel benefits at airlines, merchandise purchased at generous employee discounts at retailers, or health insurance benefits.

Aside from employee selection, training, and management best practices, many companies have tried to address the labor shortage and associated human resource costs by outsourcing part or all of the service function. The results have been decidedly mixed.

Outsourcing for Better or Worse

Many woes associated with customer service stem from the image and reality of outsourced call centers. By outsourced, I mean both foreign-based vendors of outsourced services used by U.S. and Canadian companies and U.S. and Canadian vendors of those services, and this discussion applies to both. (Here I use the term *company* to refer to the company that is outsourcing its service function, and *vendor* to refer to the organization providing the outsourced service.)

Any outsourced customer service operation, and particularly the call center, presents challenges. Essentially, these challenges stem from the fact that you are placing quality, communication, and control at risk in an area that depends on effective human behavior and interactions. Daily personal and telephone interactions between CSRs and other company functions, such as billing or shipping, become impossible, impractical, or simply rare. Certain types of information also become more difficult to obtain, particularly unfiltered information. In addition, given that a major goal of outsourcing is usually cost control, an implied decision about quality—namely, that it may to some extent be sacrificed for cost savings—may accompany the decision to outsource.

The overall record of outsourced call centers is indeed mixed. While not all call-center service vendors employ a low-price, low-cost, low-standard business model, many of them do. This model provides a limited set of constrained response specifications and limited investment in measurement and management. These limitations result in a gap between what the vendor's employees could do for customers and what they're permitted to do. For instance, the flexible solution space for difficult or complex issues as described in Chapter 8 is often limited or nonexistent. In many situations that fall in a gray area, the answer becomes no because it isn't a clear yes. Often the company doesn't trust the vendor and its employees to make nuanced decisions, so the company provides and permits a limited repertoire of highly structured responses; if this then that. The vendor is told, "Here are the questions and problems that you should pass on to us. Here are those that you should handle yourself, and in this manner." This leaves a huge number of situations in which the vendor cannot respond effectively, but rather can give only a yes or no answer. Given the conflicting incentives of reducing the percentage passed on to the company while holding costs in check, the easy out always becomes saying "no," causing great damage to loyalty and word of mouth.

In practice, many companies view outsourcing as a "fire and forget" situation; they offload customer service to the vendor, and then minimize their future involvement. One symptom of this problem is inadequate measurement through call monitoring and surveying. I saw a company with 3 million credit card holders outsource its service function and then listen to 5 calls per week. The company monitored 20 calls out of some 200,000 per month—or 1 in every 10,000. This is nobody's idea of a quality assurance effort. But monitoring without surveying is also inadequate, because while monitoring, as usually conducted, ascertains whether the CSR is adhering to the approved policies, procedures, and scripts, it does not measure the effects on satisfaction of her doing so. This erroneously assumes that the company can measure quality *without* asking customers about their satisfaction with the levels of quality actually delivered (let alone about loyalty and word of mouth). Therefore, satisfaction must also be measured by type of issue after the case is closed. Postcall interactive voice response (IVR) surveys will tell you whether the CSR was nice, but not whether the promised follow-through actually happened.

You can outsource your service function successfully, but you must provide the right decision rules, monitor activity and outcomes to allow the vendor to maximize customer loyalty, and manage the relationship carefully. (The U.S. Postal Service placed its own full-time manager on site at a vendor.) You get what you pay for in terms of competent CSRs and their training. Be prepared to spend 3 to 6 percent of your service budget on the in-house management and monitoring of your outsourced activity so that you can remain aware of the loyalty and word-of-mouth impact of your service system.

The following are the general upsides and downsides of outsourcing customer service.

The Upsides of Outsourcing. The key benefits and positive effects of outsourcing include the ability to:

- Lower capital investment, because the vendor supplies the physical plant and equipment and the latest technology, and spreads the cost across all its clients.
- Shift costs to a less expensive location.
- Respond more quickly to fluctuations in contact volume, because the vendor can have partially trained staff already available to shift to the workload.
- Provide 24/7 service without staffing three shifts (in fact, many companies outsource the two off-shifts and keep the day shift in-house).
- Make a professionally managed call center available to a relatively small company at a cost it can afford.

The Downsides of Outsourcing. The potential difficulties and negative impacts of outsourcing include:

- Reducing the linkages between the call center and marketing, sales, and operations, which reduces market intelligence; month-end reports cannot replace the daily interaction between CSRs and the rest of the organization.

- Lack of direct local control, which slows responses to changes in the marketplace.
- Vendors having little incentive to prevent unproductive, misdirected, or wasted calls because they are paid to handle—not to decrease—the volume of calls.
- Significant high-level in-house staff is still needed to train the vendor's staff, monitor ongoing quality, analyze call content, and handle escalated cases.
- Higher turnover due to lack of a career ladder, leading to higher training costs.
- Less ability to cross-sell as effectively as in-house reps, given the required tools, training, and incentives.
- The fact that savings may be limited when the costs of all management time, quality safeguards, and market intelligence are totaled.

Six Steps to Successful Outsourcing. To maximize the benefits of outsourcing without risking disaster, you can take the following six steps:

1. Get finance and marketing to agree that while the primary goal of outsourcing is to achieve flexibility and save some expense, quality and revenue preservation are still paramount, or more damage than good will be done.
2. Require the vendor or a third party to measure customer satisfaction continually through mail or e-mail surveys to random samples of callers *after their cases are closed.* Clarity of response, the CSR's ability to address customer needs, whether the customer felt he was treated fairly, follow-through, loyalty, and word of mouth should all be measured.
3. Obtain *direct* weekly feedback from the vendor's CSRs to your management, rather than through the vendor's management. Face-to-face or videoconferences are best, supplemented with immediate submissions of unfiltered e-mail from the front line on what isn't working and what customers love.
4. Require the vendor to capture detailed data, including causes, on

repeat calls, unproductive calls, and calls that are not resolved on first contact.

5. Provide the vendor with response guidance that gives CSRs all the necessary authority, tools, and information (including the value of the customer) to resolve your target number of calls on first contact and enough product knowledge to cross-sell effectively.
6. Ensure that your staff members spend several hours per week monitoring calls and that you visit the center to do side-by-side monitoring with CSRs that *you select randomly* for several days per quarter.

Outsourcing has a place, even in strategic customer service, although compared with in-house service, it has severe limitations. Do it right or don't do it!

TECHNOLOGY TRENDS: THE CHALLENGE OF USING TECHNOLOGY INTELLIGENTLY

I, like most readers, have four remotes in my family room, and I have given up calling my cable company for assistance. As this situation illustrates, the key trends in technology center on addressing product complexity and using communication channels effectively. In general, when it comes to product complexity, it's useful to ask whether a feature or an application will make a product or a task simpler and easier or more complicated and more difficult. If it's the latter, it's best to avoid adding the feature or application, or at least to help customers avoid the problems it creates. When it comes to communications channels, it's best to learn how and what customers want to hear from you and then to communicate accordingly.

Addressing Product Complexity

Dealing with product complexity means finding ways to:

- Add actual value and make new products easy to use.
- Gear education efforts to the majority of customers.
- Reach out to the "technoweary."

Add Actual Value and Make New Products Easy to Use. Despite the difficulties customers encounter with complex products, companies continue to introduce them. Why? Because certain market segments truly like and want to use them. However, those segments may be smaller than companies imagine. Consider the nature of market research questions: If you ask consumers if they would like a phone that can take photos or a TV remote that can zoom in by various degrees, many of them will say something like, "Yeah, that sounds cool," but this often echoes Citibank's ATM survey problem (albeit in reverse). When they're considering prospective products and features, respondents often don't know what they're agreeing *or* disagreeing with, nor can they envision all the assets and liabilities of these products and features in actual use. On the other hand, many new products and features clearly add value, such as a printer that tells me that my ink will run out in two weeks and offers me a new cartridge at a discounted price—and then connects me to the web site where I can place my order. In fact, that's both added value and greater ease of use.

Ease of use demands good design, which can be elusive. Most television remotes serve as excellent negative examples. Consider that, in addition to the power button, there are three other buttons for the functions that viewers use most often: channel, volume, and mute. Yet those three buttons are often the same size as those for the other fifteen functions that viewers rarely or never use. This is akin to making a car's gearshift lever the same size as the button for resetting the clock. Make the basic features easy to use and then do just-in-time education on the more complex applications.

Gear Education Efforts to the Majority of Customers. Many companies seem to gear their education efforts primarily to innovators and early adopters. That's a huge mistake. As Figure 11-1 shows, the product adoption curve, based on the idea of "diffusion" first proposed by Dr. Everett Rogers, divides users of a new product into categories based on how soon they start using that product after it's introduced.[1] The first 2.5 percent of new users are considered innovators, and the following 13.5 percent are early adopters. The next 34 percent and the 34 percent after them are the early majority and late majority, respectively. The final 16 percent are the laggards. (Of course, people can be in different categories for different products. Early adopters of new snack foods may be late majority adopters of new automotive products.)

Figure 11-1. Product Adoption Curve

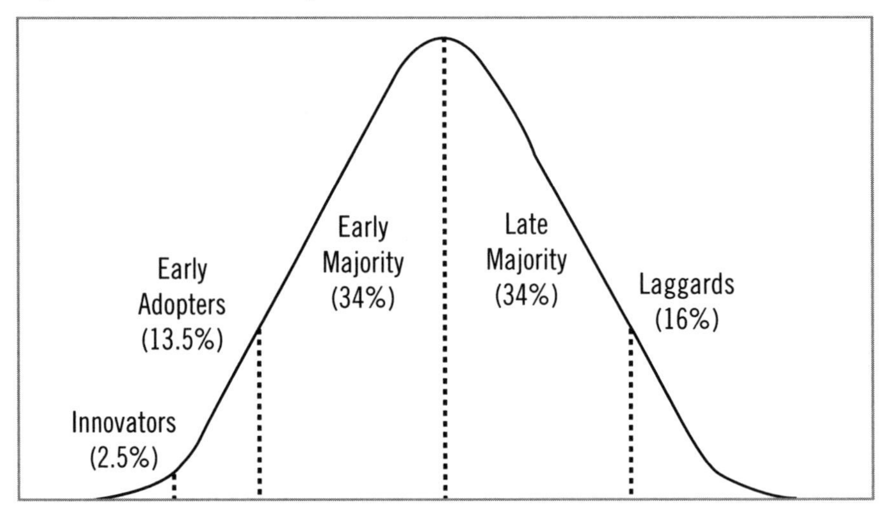

In fact, innovators and early adopters often don't need much education because they either take to the new technology readily, learn about it from their friends, or enjoy figuring out how to use the product. This does not describe the early and late majority, nor the laggards, which total three quarters of the market. Those groups need clear instructions on how to use the product, and this is typically a customer service issue. If you have a mass-market item, gear your education efforts to the early majority and provide education via multiple channels, including hard copy, online, and embedded tutorials.

Reach Out to the Technoweary. In 2007, the *Washington Post* headline for its review of a BMW automobile noted that the car was frustrating for "technoweary" consumers. Another car company actually had to set up two additional call centers, one for Bluetooth and one for the global positioning system (GPS) in its vehicles. At that point, the head of customer satisfaction asked the engineers not to introduce any new technology until customers could intuitively understand how to use it. Meanwhile, the Jitterbug cell phone promises customers that it only makes phone calls. It offers no photographic, texting, or other capabilities to complicate its operation. Simplicity is its major attribute! It's inexpensive, and it has nice, large buttons. This single-purpose device represents a reasoned response to technology proliferation. For those dealing with complex consumer electronics, there are now fee-based web sites that enable users to key in a diverse range of home entertainment and computer product models for instructions on how to achieve connectivity.

All of these are instances of and responses to product complexity. Complex products create problems and many support calls, as well as frustrating customer experiences.

Forward-thinking companies now use their CSRs as test customers for prototypes of new features and products. The CSRs understand the customers' mindset, expectations, and capabilities, as well as the ways in which they use products and features.

Before developing your next product, ask customer service to identify calls that could be prevented by more user-friendly technology, simpler directions, and improved, proactive customer education for your existing products.

Using New Communication Technologies

In Chapter 7 we discussed the need to communicate with customers through their preferred media and only about things they want to (or need to) hear about. All appropriate touch points should be used to both deliver the experience and manage tactical service. Lexus, among other organizations, asks customers how they want the company to communicate with them. These companies also lead customers to the water and give them those first sips, even if it means providing an online tutorial or having a CSR guide them through a Web-based self-service transaction to assure a first-time success. This is another area where it can pay to gear your strategy to the early majority rather than to assume that the innovators and early adopters are representative of the entire market.

To ride new communication trends, customer service must stay ahead of technological developments related to the customer base in question. This will enable you to develop capabilities that can be introduced to customers if and when it makes sense to do so. Such capabilities may include e-mail, texting, Twittering, automatic warnings issued by chips embedded in a product, and communications through other media that have not yet been developed. The worst mistake is to wait until a communication trend is big before addressing it. For instance, the cost and risk of fixing an e-mail system are much lower when you're handling 1,000 e-mails a week than when you're handling 100,000.

Currently three aspects of this trend demand attention:

- Mobile communications
- Visual communications
- "Life management" communications

All three have significant customer experience implications and applications.

Mobile Communications. Mobile communications have arisen because consumer societies have become incredibly mobile. Everyone now has cell phones with text capability. Companies that use mobile communications to inform, warn, and otherwise serve their customers can dramatically improve the customer experience. I've noted the importance of sending only desired communications to customers, but this is absolutely essential in mobile media. People on the go lack the time and patience to deal with unwanted or trivial messages. You can, however, create a valuable customer experience (and often delight) when you deliver vital information via mobile media. People truly want to know when an opening for a CAT scan or a seat on a desired flight becomes available. Deliver such messages, and you've forged another link to your customer.

Visual Communications. The Web is an inherently visual medium, and companies that grasp this have the most interesting, user-friendly web sites. They're also poised to exploit opportunities presented by small-screen graphic capabilities. Indeed, they are already doing so. Avaya, a major communications equipment company, can provide an on-screen schedule of home games for your favorite professional teams, a seating chart for the stadium, and the ability to purchase tickets for a specific game given a ticket price range or seat location, all on your cell phone. When designing applications of this type, aim to allow users to select from graphic images as much as possible. While the screens can be small, they are steadily becoming both larger and easier to read, particularly on PDAs.

"Life Management" Communications. Several companies want to make their product the communications hub of your life. QUALCOMM and Apple want your mobile phone to form this hub, while Microsoft and, again, Apple want your personal computer to serve that purpose. Some people at Whirlpool want your refrigerator to occupy that spot. Your refrigerator? Their idea echoes that of the "smart house," first imagined more than two decades ago. In this scenario, your refrigerator has a screen that displays your calendar and your schedule and tells you where to go and what products you're low on, *and* it will place the order with the grocer. (Never run out of yogurt again!) Regardless of which device becomes the hub of your communications—the personal computer and PDA hold the lead—seamless, reliable, useful communications are the key. The devices must also "talk to" one another and, of course, to the customer.

Closer to the present, chips can already report auto accidents, networked medical devices and printers can "phone home" for technical service, and home appliances have gone well beyond low-battery warnings. At the same time, such capabilities must provide actual value and work properly, or they will annoy and alienate customers—and generate thousands of needless service contacts. (Again, the blunt instrument of the "Check Engine" dashboard light presents itself as a major source of aggravation.)

The driving forces on this front are the need for capabilities that help customers manage their lives and help them communicate. Those forces should generate service capabilities that make customers aware of needs such as maintenance, repair, replacement, and restocking, and do so proactively, quickly, and conveniently.

POLITICAL TRENDS: CHALLENGES IN REGULATORY AND SAFETY CONCERNS AND ENVIRONMENTAL ISSUES

Two other emerging trends affecting customer service can be described in general terms as political: regulatory and safety concerns, and environmental issues. This section addresses the customer service and revenue implications of these trends, which have been amply demonstrated in the tobacco, pharmaceutical, food and beverage, automobile, air travel, consumer electronics, and other industries.

Consider that in the past several years alone:

- Trans fats have been banned in restaurants in a number of cities, including New York, and in California.
- Bottled water has come under attack as unnecessary and wasteful.
- SUVs have become symbols of gas-guzzling excess—and difficult to sell.
- Leading companies are being forced to accept responsibility for dangerous foreign supply chains such as rural Chinese production facilities.

A single event, such as the concern over *E. coli* in salad greens and beef in 2008, can put lives as well as brand equity at stake. Thus, these trends are among the most serious that companies face.

Coping with Regulatory and Safety Issues

Here's the key to addressing this trend right up front: Listen to your employees and connect the dots. In almost all regulatory or safety cases (and in the events of 9/11), an employee somewhere not only knew of the situation, but also had often documented it. Moreover, the original indication typically comes from customers who inform customer service—yet another argument for a smooth, fast, reliable feedback loop.

Indeed, that loop can be your surest path to reduced risk. Years ago, TARP worked with both the FDA and the USDA to set up adverse drug reaction and food safety reporting systems. However, we found that very few people who become ill because of something they ingested call a government agency to report it. A far greater number call the company or the restaurant that sold or served them the item. Yet the company usually goes into denial, avoids any implied liability, or settles the matter quietly. None of these represents an affirmative strategy for avoiding further, larger problems of this nature. In several regulated industries, where many types of customer problems must be passed along to the regulator, reports from customers are often not classified as "complaints" or "defects" or even "problems," but rather as "concerns," because the latter does not sound as serious and implies that the consumer might be at fault.

This embodies a basic problem and contradiction. Companies—in every industry—don't want to call a complaint a problem or a defect for fear that this will create larger problems, yet not knowing the full extent of a problem can allow it to increase in occurrence, severity, ramifications, or all three. Such an approach generates the very situation that it's supposed to preclude, and it stems largely from the conservatism of legal departments. I've had conversations with attorneys at auto, pharmaceutical, and insurance companies, and have found that many (but not all) of them would almost rather not know of a problem because of fear of legal discovery. While this may not absolve them of liability, in general liability must be associated with an identified pattern. This, unfortunately but logically, argues for *not* identifying patterns. Also, risk managers are usually told to keep risk costs low. This, again unfortunately but logically, argues for not sending problems to the company's attorneys or to regulators.

Granted, this can be a difficult area, fraught with issues of legal liability and allocation of responsibility. I recognize that senior executives must make decisions in environments of risk amid competing demands from customers, regulators, employees, investors, the media (which thrives on bad news), and the community. So the decision comes down to having good information—a must for any decision—and to drawing the line when the risks are high. If you err on the side of the consumer's interests, you'll always come out ahead in the court of public opinion as well as law and regulation.

Customer service must, of course, avoid crying wolf. It must instead systematically compile and analyze data and investigate the causes and patterns of occurrence of complaints and problems. Then management must be informed of potential risks, emerging risks, and actual occurrences and, as Johnson & Johnson did in the Tylenol case, implement what is best for the customer. The trust and positive public relations generated by such actions more than offset the short-term costs.

Addressing Environmental Concerns

The environmental concerns that affect any company are specific to that company's industry, scope of operations, and customer base. Some concerns, such as packaging and transportation, cut across many industries, while others, such as disposal of the product when it reaches the end of its life, are highly industry-specific. While various parties hold various views of environmental concerns, the following situations have already occurred, and we can expect more like them in the future:

- Mounting popular pressure—and demand—for truly green products, particularly in product categories focused on by activists, such as animal rights
- Increasing support for and payoff from green practices, such as recycling, energy conservation, and reduced packaging
- Rising production and distribution costs for formerly low-cost factors, such as water, energy, transportation, and waste disposal
- Increasing exposure to negative publicity or costs resulting from labor conditions, pollution, and other factors in upstream or downstream operations or channels

From a customer service perspective, it's essential, as always, to monitor customer inquiries, complaints, and problems, and to compile and analyze the relevant data. Customers—perhaps only a few at first—will usually provide the earliest warnings of developments in this area. For instance, certain customer segments and activist groups expressed early opposition to SUVs, large-scale farming, pesticides, and public cigarette smoking.

Early awareness can position you to take advantage of trends in various ways. Specific opportunities include providing green or toxin-free versions of products at premium prices, incorporating the trend into product development and operating plans, and promoting the company's response to enhance brand equity. "Being green" represents part of the customer experience for many consumers, and one that has a potentially strong emotional component.

Many companies have taken steps in response to environmental trends. In product development, many now consider "green criteria," such as carbon footprint, energy savings, and type and amount of waste in packaging and in disposal of the product itself. Hewlett-Packard runs an aggressive recycling program for inkjet printers and toner cartridges. Public and private waste management organizations are restricting the materials they will accept in the areas of electronics, computer components, and solvents. In marketing, companies now gear their messages as well as their products to customers' concerns. However, be careful that being green doesn't cause other problems; for instance, dim desk lamps in hotel rooms have become points of pain for customers. In becoming green, the overall quality of the customer experience must be preserved. Ask about customers' concerns in surveys, learn what they view as the highest priorities for your industry, and act on those concerns and priorities.

RESPOND, DON'T REACT

With all trends, the keys to success are monitoring the landscape through customer service, developing awareness of what customers want and don't want, and, most of all, understanding the current and potential opportunities that trends present. An excellent data gathering and analysis process with linkage to your VOC program will allow you to ride ahead of trends rather than get run over by them.

KEY TAKEAWAYS

1. Outsourced service must be managed as if it were an in-house unit, with the same quality standards and even more detailed measurement of customer impact.
2. Make adoption of new products and features painless for the late adopters and laggards via education to reduce service costs and customer dissatisfaction. Keep basic functionality simple and in the forefront.
3. Pilot-test and improve leading-edge communications before they become big and you'll avoid the larger costs of catching up in the future.
4. Rather than ignoring potential regulatory or liability problems, detect them early and act on them preemptively.
5. Go green, but take care to preserve the quality and convenience of the overall customer experience—or make being green a positive component of the experience.

NOTES

1. First published in *Diffusion of Innovations*, New York: Free Press, 1962.

CHAPTER 12

A Thousand Things Done Right

Translating the Strategy of Delivering Superb Service Into Organizational Behavior

A FEW YEARS AGO, during a chat with an office equipment executive, I said that one sign that a company may not be taking customer service seriously is the amount of money it spends on coffee mugs and posters of "The Customer Is King" variety. He gave me a pained look, walked me to the cafeteria, and showed me an expensive poster with a mirrored cardboard surface and the slogan, "*You* Make the Difference for the Customer!" He then pointed to stacks of ceramic cups with a similar slogan.

The purveyors of those cups and posters may have the best intentions, as may the managers who approve their purchase. But in my experience, those cups and posters are the extent of these companies' actual support for customer service. In fact, the ubiquity of those cups and posters and the prevailing low levels of customer satisfaction suggest that too many executives believe that slogans and encouragement alone can generate great customer experiences.

More cynically, many management teams simply minimize customer service expenses, accept high turnover, and hope for the best. For instance, a major automaker staffs its call center with part-time employees only, gives them no benefits, and accepts 70 percent annual turnover. The front-line managers, who cannot motivate those workers, rely on case managers to address problems—and half of *them* are temps. The result? Low rates of resolution on initial contact and high levels of frustration for customers.

In this chapter, I assume that you have already made or are willing to make the strategic decision to deliver superb service in your organization. Once you've made that decision, your attention then shifts to how to actually make it happen. As you've seen, this involves more than just crafting a few new procedures and spending a few weeks training customer service reps. It means making changes—some minor, some major—in the organization and its processes, as well as in policies and procedures. This chapter will focus on those changes and show how to implement them in practical terms.

Specifically, in this chapter we will discuss the emergence of the chief customer officer (CCO) as a way of achieving that alignment. As an example of how such an overview can lead to change, I'll examine the case study of the traditional role of sales and account management in customer service and how this can often be dysfunctional. I'll then turn to the matter of incentives and ways of linking them to useful metrics. It is this linkage, more than management directives (let alone slogans on cups and posters), that will move people to do the thousand things that create great customer experiences. Finally, I'll close with a discussion of creating a great experience when your customer is the customer of a retailer, distributor, or other channel partner.

APPOINTING A CHIEF CUSTOMER OFFICER

TARP has long recommended that a single senior executive be responsible for the end-to-end customer experience, which extends from an inquiry about a purchase, through the purchase and use of the product or service, to billing and repair, to the end of the relationship. I'll explain the responsibilities in this chapter, but they cover each function within the organization as it affects the customer, directly or indirectly. As of this writing, about one-third of major U.S. companies now have an executive with a title that implies such responsibility. Formal titles include chief customer officer (CCO) or customer experience officer. Informally, the senior marketing officer or the head of quality may have the responsibility for management of the customer experience. In some organizations, the CCO title is a second hat worn by another C level executive.

Actually, the successful CCO *facilitates* management of the customer experience. I use the term *facilitates* here because all the members of the executive team must buy in and be responsible for the roles of their functions in the customer experience. In order for the position to be effective, companies contemplating the appointment of a CCO must understand the rationale and prerequisites for the position, its proper functions, and how to make the position work.

The Rationale and Prerequisites for Hiring a CCO

The rationale for the CCO position is to create alignment among all departments and functions so that they pull in the same direction and work toward a single purpose. The need for alignment arises when parts tend to pull in opposing directions or to work at cross-purposes. Just as the wheels of a vehicle must be aligned or the tires will wear badly, steering will be difficult, and the wheels may come off, the functions in a company must be aligned or they will waste resources, undercut one another's efforts, and fail to reach their common goal.

In recent years, the most effective efforts to align business functions have focused on product quality. One could argue that the customer experience is simply a broader version of product quality. While product specs are cut and dried, the customer experience includes a broad range of service dimensions that depend upon human factors ranging from customer expectations and judgments to employee attitudes and behaviors. As a result, while product quality is formal, data-driven, and well defined, customer experience metrics are nowhere near as precise.

Delivery processes, including service and human factors, are much more complex and harder to improve predictably. This is mainly the result of the difficulty of modifying human behavior, which drives service processes, to produce a consistent result, as compared with changing materials and machines, which drive manufacturing processes. Table 12-1 lists contrasting elements in manufacturing and service processes, underscoring the difficulties of improving service.

The sharply contrasting characteristics of manufacturing and service in this table—and the intangible and behavioral aspects of service—are the chief reasons that, to my great surprise, many organizations have not mapped their key customer-touching processes. (As you may know, and as many articles and books explain, process mapping is a method of visually illustrating the flows of materials, activities, and touches that occur when a business produces and delivers a product or service. It helps managers to define, analyze, and improve production and service processes, as well as to align these processes.)

Table 12-1. Differences Between Manufacturing and Service Processes.

Manufacturing	*Services*
Linear workflow	Nonlinear workflow
Repetitive steps	Nonrepetitive steps
Standardized inputs	Variable inputs
Limited worker discretion	High worker discretion
Separate production and consumption	Simultaneous production and consumption
Aims to avoid variability, conform to requirements, and minimize defects	Aims to embrace variability, do what the situation requires, and minimize defections

I am not saying that the complexity and fuzziness of the processes and deliverables make alignment impossible in service environments, nor that customer service cannot be rigorously analyzed and its processes mapped. However, alignment is usually more difficult to achieve and maintain in service environments, and the metrics and activities differ from those in production processes. Thus, it is the human factor—the behavioral, emotional, and situational aspects—that makes customer service so challenging and the role of the CCO so important.

The prerequisite for creation of the position of CCO is that management accept three facts:

1. **A satisfactory customer experience is critical to long-term loyalty, positive word of mouth, and revenue growth.** The revenue

implications of an improved customer experience are usually 10 to 20 times the cost implications, but the CEO *and* the CFO must buy into this. They must accept the impact of the customer experience on loyalty and word of mouth, and therefore on revenue and profits, and they must believe that it can be quantified.

2. **Every major function contributes to the quality of the customer experience, and most problems surface at a location other than the one that caused them.** Although most problems surface in the service area, most of them do not originate there. Someone with overarching responsibility for the customer experience can address and, through functional alignment, reduce or eliminate disparate sources of dissatisfaction.
3. **It is cheaper to deliver a great experience than to deliver a good or acceptable one.** Because management generally believes that better service will cost more, it is biased toward providing both less and reactive service. Yet, as shown in Chapter 4, an enhanced experience is not necessarily more expensive (because there are fewer callbacks and lower demands on more expensive personnel) and has positive revenue impacts.

Key Functions of the CCO

The most important functions of the CCO are to:

- Supervise the delineation and mapping of all customer-touching processes.
- Gather and distribute unified Voice of the Customer data and information.
- Identify problems to solve and opportunities to improve the customer experience, and create the economic imperative for action.
- Decide who should take the lead in addressing problems and opportunities.
- Act as the customers' advocate to senior management, including tracking progress.
- Advise management of the costs—as well as the revenues and profits—of doing what's best for the customer.

The CCO should *not* be responsible for achieving targeted satisfaction and loyalty measures or for fixing quality and service problems. Those remain the responsibilities of the relevant operating and line managers. In other words, the CCO acts as an internal consultant, facilitator, and senior point person regarding the customer experience, but does not assume the responsibilities of other managers. In that sense, the CCO's relationship to the customer experience and to other managers resembles that of the chief risk officer to risk and to the managers of the functions that incur those risks.

How to Make the Position of CCO Work

Three critical factors, applied in order, will almost guarantee the CCO's success: compelling data, management commitment, and facilitation skills to produce results quickly. As illustrated in Figure 12-1, these three elements operate in sequence. You need the data first, often just to get management's attention, let alone its commitment. The ensuing commitment then creates the needed support for efforts to improve service processes in order to capitalize on the opportunity identified by the data. And finally, achieving that improvement demands facilitation skills to gain rapid success. The resulting small success with a measureable payoff creates the mandate to collect additional data on the next opportunity and keeps improvement efforts rolling toward bigger successes. Even basic data on the payoff of improved service are so powerful that we have seen executives simply use TARP's industry survey data or assumptions estimating the payoff of certain improvement actions create commitment.

Figure 12-1. CCO Success Factors

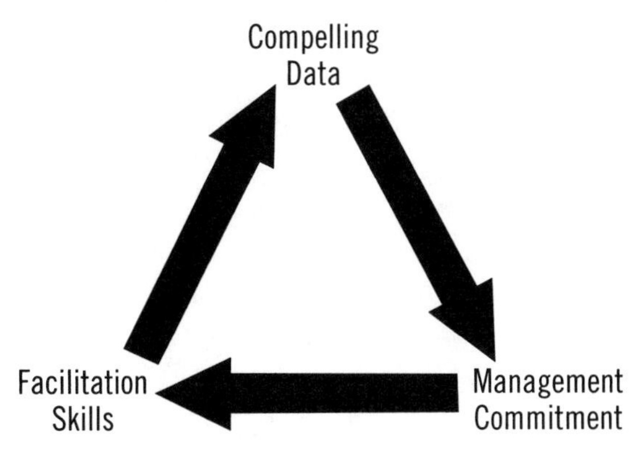

Compelling Data. TARP's review of the key factors in successful Voice of the Customer programs revealed that reliable data describing the *entire* customer experience will highlight the most lucrative improvements to make, and that such data almost always will compel management to take action. However, VOC is often fragmented, focused on a few interactions, and divorced from financial information.

This is why you must first map the process and all customer touches. For instance, based on the loudest complaints, a copier company focused on product quality and repairs; however, our research showed that the sales and installation phase caused four times as much revenue damage but was seldom the subject of complaints. Until we mapped the process and then got data on the relative number of problems and the amount of damage to loyalty resulting from each phase of the process, sales and installation had not received any scrutiny.

Compelling data include the top five reasons for attrition and the *one* that would be easiest to fix in the near term. They encompass reports from front-line employees and reveal the revenue lost through customer attrition. Every lost customer requires marketing to replace that customer with a new customer to keep the leaky bucket full, as noted in Figure 4-1.

Management Commitment. Senior managers must believe that the CCO can help them to achieve their goals, particularly their revenue goals. This requires buy-in from marketing and finance; if they buy in, everyone else will (including, usually, the CEO). Buy-in most often results from rigorous, conservative analysis of the revenue impacts. Line managers, provided with sound data outlining the payoff of improvements, will act on the basis of financial incentives and their self-interest.

Facilitation Skills Leading to Short-Term Success. The CCO must realize that she will get the most done by crediting others for successes. TARP has also found that positioning the first few customer initiatives as pilot projects will generate less resistance than proposals for massive change. Then, if you deliver measurably improved results, you have documented your success. With that record, you can repeat the cycle of identifying an aspect of the customer experience that, if fixed, will increase loyalty, revenue, and positive word of mouth. That, in turn, positions you to set another target, take action, and achieve another success. Only after several tactical successes should you introduce a broad strategy.

In plain English, the key to success as a CCO is using believable measures, picking your battles, and, like any good consultant, making your internal client look good.

FOCUSING ALL FUNCTIONS ON THE CUSTOMER EXPERIENCE

It's impossible for any one function within a business—even customer service—to deliver a superb customer experience. No single function can ensure that the company is doing it right the first time, nor can customer service by itself put things right in every case or ensure a satisfactory experience the next time. Every function has a role to play in creating the customer experience. Every function must understand its role, and how its decisions, activities, and actions affect the customer experience. And every function must understand the cause-and-effect links in the chain from itself to its upstream and downstream customers, including functions with only internal customers as well as those with both external and internal customers. The best way to gain this understanding is through process mapping.

A great customer experience is the result of a thousand things that were done right. Those thousand things are the sum total of the decisions, activities, and processes of every function in the organization. In most companies, many employees feel that they are not part of a business that serves customers with real wants and needs, but rather part of a bureaucracy that serves faceless stakeholders. The process map will support the notion of the customer experience and the role that each function—and each job—plays in delivering that experience.

Broadly, every function exists to take some sort of inputs and somehow add value to them, converting them into the output required by an external customer or by an internal customer who is serving an external, paying customer. Production takes raw materials and components and converts them into finished goods. Accounting takes data on financial transactions and converts them into financial reports. Human resources takes job candidates and converts them into well-trained, properly compensated employees who effectively interact with customers. Marketing and sales take prospects out in the marketplace and convert them into customers.

Map the Process to Define the Roles in the Customer Experience

It's essential that all functions understand their role in creating the customer experience. As noted earlier, while it is seldom used for services, process mapping can be a powerful tool for creating that understanding. Most organizations that are large enough to have significant customer service functions have long since mapped their production processes. Yet, when I've questioned executives as to whether they use maps for their service processes, it usually strikes them as a new idea. Process mapping helps people see everyone's role in producing the customer experience.

Although the role of each function depends on the industry, organization, value proposition, and customer, in general the roles might include the following:

- **Marketing** defines the customer experience (including items such as product features and advertising messages), sets customer expectations, and attracts prospects.
- **Sales and account management** communicates with prospects and persuades them to become customers and or manages channels that deliver the product. In many environments, such as private banking and business-to-business relationships, the account manager also tries to service the client—a key source of dissatisfaction.
- **Service** answers customers' questions, assists them with problems, and gathers information that will improve future customer experiences.
- **Production and operations** produces and delivers products and services to customers.
- **Billing and accounting** ensure that customers are billed the proper amounts and collect past due amounts.

Some organizational functions affect customers more directly than others. Any function that touches the customer, such as sales, customer service, field service, and billing, must obsessively consider the effects of its decisions and actions on the customer experience, as must all functions that produce and deliver the products and services that the customer purchases. However, it's worth it to create consciousness of the customer experience in such support functions as accounting, finance, human resources, and risk management, if for no other reason than to enable them to better serve the functions that affect customers more directly.

As an example of the challenges in aligning functions to deliver a great customer experience, I've chosen one of the thornier issues—the decision to move any or all service functions out of sales (when sales has been performing them) and into customer service. The rationale is that sales should be selling and service should be servicing, but in many companies salespeople also perform service functions, usually problem solving and troubleshooting. The next section highlights the issues and then discusses ways of handling the transition of all service functions out of sales.

Rationalize the Process: Clarifying the Roles of Sales and Customer Service

One of the most prevalent symptoms of the conflict that exists between sales and service is the perennial story I hear about every sales rep handing out his business card with the refrain, "Any time you have a question or problem, give me a call." You then call and hit the sales rep's voice mail, which does significant damage if you have a burning issue right then. That's one reason I believe that in most (but not all) environments, it is best for salespeople to focus on bringing in new customers and on developing business with existing ones, and to leave service issues to the service function. That is, when the organization fails to do it right the first time, the service function—or a unit of the service function—should be the touch point and have the responsibility and resources needed to fix the situation. Effecting this change in companies in which salespeople have been "doing it all" can present problems.

Problems with Shifting Service from Sales. The two most common problems in shifting service functions, such as problem solving, from sales to service are salespeople's resistance and difficulties in system design.

Some salespeople believe that they "own" their accounts and can be possessive about information and interactions. While it's great for salespeople to feel a sense of ownership and have a personal stake in their customers' well-being, it's dangerous to allow them to control accounts or customers. Doing so can undermine the customer experience, because salespeople may not be forthcoming about ways to improve that experience. Also, it encourages customers to identify with their salesperson rather than with the company or the brand. That exposes the company to potential loss of the account if the salesperson leaves and can limit the information the organization compiles on the customer. Salespeople must understand that their customers are the organization's customers and that the customer experience is too big for salespeople alone to design and deliver.

In situations involving ongoing relationships, it's best to have specific service representatives teamed with specific salespeople, at least in certain product categories and, at times, geographic areas. The team must establish a two-way flow of information. Salespeople want to know about inquiries and problems involving their accounts, and that's good. Without that information, they may look bad and may miss sales opportunities. Management must design efficient ways of handing customers from sales to service and from service to sales, and each function must be regularly updated on the status of problems. In other words, the system must enhance, rather than undermine, the customer experience and not simply offload problems from sales to service. Finally, the details of the system—whom customers should call in the future; how problems will be logged, tracked, and solved; and who will communicate about what with customers—must all be carefully thought out and properly implemented.

Benefits of Moving Service Out of Sales. Adopting a system in which sales sells and service services has two benefits that most salespeople find extremely attractive.

The first benefit is that the system reduces frantic phone calls and demands from existing customers and the accompanying aggravation for salespeople. If it does not do this, then the system is not working. While the transition from having salespeople handle service issues may take time, it shouldn't take more than two or three months to complete in most environments. When it's complete, salespeople should find that they've had bricks removed from their wheelbarrows and that they actually like the system.

The second benefit is that while this system will standardize the customer experience at a higher level of quality, make service available over broader hours, and enrich the flow of customer data, it will also free up salespeople's time and energy for selling (and making more money). Every problem that a salesperson must address shifts her attention from selling to problem solving. Most salespeople would rather be selling. Of course, if the solution involves cross-selling or up-selling, then the salesperson should get some of the credit even if service handles it.

The critical requirements for getting sales to relinquish service are to assure sales that their customers will get stellar service and that sales will still get credit for all sales. After that they will gladly allow service to handle problems. Locating problem solving in the service function supports both strategic and tactical customer service. It supports strategic customer service by completing the feedback loop that directs information about problems to the area of the organization that can prevent those problems in the future. It supports tactical customer service by giving customers dedicated problem-solving resources when their experience did not go as expected. With this arrangement, everyone wins: the company, the sales function, the service function, and the customer.

LINKING INCENTIVES TO THE RIGHT METRICS

As noted, the key to improved performance is incentives that are properly linked to measures of the customer experience. In many companies, this link is so flawed that incentives do more harm than good.

Twelve Guidelines for Linking Incentives to the Right Metrics

What follows are guidelines for effectively linking incentives to metrics.

Measure Loyalty, Not Just Satisfaction. Satisfaction does not indicate the customer's next action vis-à-vis the company, and can't be converted into revenue impact. Thus, the best metric is a market action, such as willingness to recommend or to buy again. This does not mean that satisfaction isn't worth measuring or using as a metric, only that a market action-oriented metric is preferable.

Use Simple Incentive Formulas Tied to Outcome Metrics. Many companies try to be too precise in linking incentives to factors that employees directly control. For instance, they'll survey customers about—and provide incentives for employees regarding—multiple tactical factors (like cleanliness of the rental car and courtesy on the telephone), but they'll leave critical factors (such as willingness to recommend) out of the incentive formula. Pay incentives on the recommend question and educate employees on how the tactical drivers affect the willingness to recommend. Your message is then clear and simple.

Tie at Least 20 Percent of Incentive Compensation to the Metric. TARP has found that major automotive, home service, financial, and telecom companies tie at least 20 percent of incentive compensation to the satisfaction target, and some as much as 30 percent. Employees tend to ignore anything less than 20 percent.

Set Rational Improvement Targets. Most companies set improvement targets arbitrarily, for instance, "We're at 81 percent satisfied, so let's shoot for 85 percent." It's far better to identify causes of dissatisfaction to address over the next year, and to calculate the improvement that addressing them is likely to generate. You can then say, "If we address issues A, D, and F, we can boost overall loyalty by 0.5, 1.5, and 1.0 percent, respectively and achieve a 3-point increase to an 84." Then people know their goals *and* how to achieve them.

Reward Improvement as Well as Hitting Targets. An "all or nothing" approach to incentives can create apathy among those for whom the targets are impossible. Instead, provide incentives for units that improve even when the corporate target is out of their reach. For example, if the target is 85, a unit might be given a third of the incentive compensation if it moves from a 65 to a 75 percent recommend rating.

Make Metrics Actionable. Employees must see how their performance affects satisfaction and loyalty. For instance, they should know that a second contact for the same issue lowers satisfaction by 10 percent, while a third contact lowers it another 20 percent. This clearly makes the case for first-call resolution.

Report Intermediate Progress Using Process Metrics. Annual surveys are too infrequent to allow course correction and maintenance of enthusiasm. For many U.S. companies, especially in the auto industry, the annual J.D. Power and University of Michigan Customer Satisfaction Index scores create just this problem. Organizations need quarterly, monthly, or ongoing surveys or process metrics. Ideally, you don't need to keep doing surveys; you may be able to get process metrics that describe the customer experience adequately. For example, at a delivery company, correct invoices and reduced damage to packages were key drivers of improved service. The company used the monthly number of calls on these two problems to measure progress and then confirmed the results with a quarterly survey.

Implement Incentives Gradually. Do not tell employees, "Starting tomorrow, X percent of your pay depends on this metric"; if you do, they will complain about the structure and measure of the metric instead of focusing on improving the customer experience. Instead, use the metric for six months *before* formally tying it to any of their compensation.

Use Multiple Metrics. Satisfaction and loyalty should be balanced with goals such as productivity, profits, employee satisfaction, and cost control. The satisfaction or loyalty metric works best when it constitutes between 20 and 33 percent of the overall incentive.

Discourage Gaming the System. Create both carrots and sticks for those who would play games like those seen with auto sales surveys. For carrots, communicate that everyone who does the right thing for the customer will win. You are not "grading on a curve"; everyone can make his numbers and be rewarded. For sticks, use survey questions such as, "Were you pressured to give a positive rating?" to detect manipulation of the system and assess penalities.

Reinforce Incentives with Continual Training. One-shot training doesn't work. Reps must be fluent in the response rules, aware of current problems, and always improving their people skills. This requires at least monthly reinforcement by front line managers. Best-practice companies devote at least two hours per month to revisiting basic skills and response rules.

Focus on the Long Term. Stable, cumulative incentives will promote a long-term focus, yet many companies revamp their incentives annually. While they may be trying to keep things fresh, the result is often confusion and diffused efforts. The auto company unit with the industry's best scores assures executives that satisfaction incentives will be in place for at least three years and increases the rewards as higher metrics are achieved. This approach assures people that "the rules won't change next quarter and this is not the flavor of the month."

Bonus Guideline: Be Careful with Net Promoter Scores. Many executives are now using the Net Promoter (NP) Score as a major metric. (The Net Promoter Score, developed by Fred Reichheld, is a measure of customers' willingness to recommend, that is, to spread positive word of mouth.) One well-known article refers to "the only question you need to ask—would you recommend us?" It's not a bad question, but the NP Score is calculated by subtracting "detractors" (respondents who give you a 6 or below on the 10-point response scale) from "advocates" (those who give you a 9 or a 10).

There are three difficulties in using the NP Score. First, it assumes that customers who give you a 7 or an 8 are "benign." This is not true, as they are probably spreading mediocre word of mouth and are not loyal. Second, the NP Score provides no diagnostics. Third, different situations can generate the same score. For example, most customers (say, 65 percent) could be in the middle, 30 percent could be advocates, and 15 percent could be detractors. Your NP Score would be 15 (30 − 15 = 15). Alternatively, you could have a highly polarized market in which 55 percent are advocates and 40 percent are detractors, and your NP Score would again be 15 (55 − 40 = 15).

Clearly, you must understand the diagnostics and distributions behind these scores and estimate the revenue at risk for each month that the status quo continues.

Use Incentives in Specific Environments

Linking incentives to metrics always presents challenges. Here are specific issues to address in specific environments.

Satisfaction Incentives for Contact Centers. Linking satisfaction metrics to incentives is both easier and harder in contact centers than in the rest of the organization. It's easier because of the link between employees' actions and customer satisfaction and loyalty. It's harder because the dissatisfaction with the CSR might actually be caused by a poor response rule or from emphasizing minimal talk time, which leads to truncated calls and short explanations. These also lead to increased callbacks and encourage callers to shop the system. Table 12-2 shows the types of data typically used for linking incentives to metrics and the strength of their correlation with actual loyalty.

An appropriate balance for reps tends to be one-third operational metrics (such as adherence to procedures), one-third impact and outcome metrics (first-contact resolution; recommend overall and by issue), and one-third team behavior, attendance, and input into problem prevention. When present, cross-selling should have a separate incentive.

Call monitoring and satisfaction surveys should generate similar outcome results. If, for example, the rep scores 95 on internal call monitoring, but customers rate the rep at 65, there's a lack of alignment. You may be requiring and measuring behaviors that customers see as unimportant, and neglecting behaviors that would boost loyalty. It's often useful to ask the person doing the monitoring, "How would you rate the caller's satisfaction at the end of the call?" and use the scale used in the customer survey. The two scores should be reasonably close.

Table 12-2. Correlation Between Various Metrics and Loyalty

Type of Metric	*Basic Operations Metrics*	*Operations Audit Metrics*	*Operations Impact Metrics*	*Outcome Metrics*
Content	Call-center performance ASA, talk time, abandonment, time in queue	Call quality monitoring, e-mail audit	Calls closed on first contact data by issue, calls transferred, multiple calls, fulfillment, timeliness	Outcome data (satisfaction and loyalty attribute ratings and escalations)
Strength of relationship of metrics to actual loyalty	Low	Moderate	Strong	Congruent

Satisfaction Incentives for Operating Units and Varying Locations. For an entire company or a subsidiary, use operations impact metrics and overall satisfaction and loyalty, for instance with products and services, along with willingness to buy again or recommend. Many companies use an index of two or three such metrics. Some leading companies simply focus on the "recommend" metric, assuming that all the others are generally collinear with it. Either approach works.

In different regions within the United States or across countries, TARP has found that people rate satisfaction differently. For example, we've found that residents in the northeastern United States usually give lower ratings for identical levels of service than those in the South (except Florida). Worldwide, satisfaction and loyalty ratings differed in several studies using identical service metrics. For instance, customers living in France tend to rate their satisfaction lower than customers of the same companies living in the United Kingdom. And Japanese tend to give fewer top ratings than Americans.

On the other hand, market action questions, such as willingness to purchase again or to recommend, are answered much more consistently around the world. So while it's not possible to have a comparable worldwide satisfaction index, it is possible to have a comparable loyalty index.

Satisfaction Metrics and Incentives for Dealers and Field Units. When customers are served by dealers and field units, the dealer's or unit's actions carry over to the company's rating. Customers see the company as being responsible for the service provided by dealers and field units. But TARP has also found that customers will, to a degree, differentiate between the two entities and give ratings that can vary by as much as 30 percent for actions taken by a dealer and by a company or headquarters. Still, there is significant spillover. Even when headquarters handles a call perfectly, if the dealer fails to follow through on headquarters' promises, headquarters will be partly blamed for the failure, as well it should be.

TARP has found that the best way to motivate a dealer, field unit, or channel is to show that poor service hurts it as well as the company in terms of eroded loyalty and bad word of mouth. Such economic modeling has proved very effective in motivating dealers to focus on satisfaction in the automotive, motorcycle, insurance, and franchising industries.

Satisfaction Incentives for Internal Customer Service. Most of the metrics for external customers also work for internal customers. There are two exceptions: complaint behavior and loyalty. Internal customers tend not to complain because of fear of retribution and a belief that nothing will change. TARP has seen noncomplaint rates as high as 93 percent in internal IT, HR, and government settings. Thus, it's best to collect data on trouble reports and then ask the customers how much time they waste each time the problem occurs.

As to loyalty, internal customers often perceive no ability to switch providers because they're required to use the internal service or the designated contractor. Yet TARP has seen many creative ways to switch providers, such as giving small contracts to local IT-support companies or simply using nonsanctioned providers, both of which create extra costs. The question to ask is, "If you could get this service from someone else at the same price, how likely would you be to continue to use our internal service?" TARP has found that customers take the hypothetical question seriously even in monopolistic situations. The other key questions are how often do these problems occur and how much time do you waste each time that they occur.

DELIVERING A GREAT EXPERIENCE THROUGH CHANNEL PARTNERS

If aligning functions to deliver the intended customer experience is difficult when these functions are within the company, consider the challenges when they're not. This occurs when your customers are primarily the customers of your distributors, retailers, agents, brokers, or other sellers or resellers. This also occurs when your products or services are used in other products or services or when you enter into licensing agreements. (I'll refer to all of these as situations involving channels and channel partners.)

In all of these cases, you automatically lose substantial control over the customer experience. How much you lose depends on the type of channel partner and the nature of your arrangement. The more formal agreements, such as marketing alliances, joint ventures, and licensing agreements, can allow you to establish more control over the customer experience, yet difficulties arise even then. For instance, even major brands such as Calvin Klein and Martha Stewart have learned that retailers and distributors can place their reputations and their revenues at risk.

Many arrangements tend to favor the channel over the provider of the product. That's because the provider of the product often needs the channel (say, Wal-Mart) more than the channel needs any single provider. The provider usually has limited access to the channel's customers and to information on those customers. Providers generally compete fiercely for the best channels, and anyone that such a channel views as troublesome may see other providers treated more favorably.

Channels in most categories vary wildly in the customer experiences they deliver. TARP's research has found that in durable goods and technology, a bad channel experience can reduce loyalty to the brand by at least 20 percent and as much as 80 percent—a veritable disaster for the brand. Yet the manufacturer or brand manager can do little about it, given that customers do not want a relationship with every provider they buy from indirectly. They want their grocery store to rectify problems with their Swanson frozen dinner and their men's shop to fix their Hickey Freeman suit.

What's a provider to do? There's no easy solution. Clearly, you must do business with the most reputable channels available to you, given business realities. Those realities include the ways in which your products, prices, profit requirements, and customer experience match those of the available channels. So the first goal would be to create a customer experience that's compatible with those of the channel partners you want to cultivate. This means setting the bar high relative to your competitors and finding like-minded channel partners.

Five other ways to create and deliver a good customer experience when dealing with and through channels are to:

1. **Obtain good information on customers.** Share your customer data and research with channel partners to encourage them to improve your customers' experience.
2. **Communicate with your customers.** Provide useful premiums to prompt customers to register at your web site, and then keep in touch with them.
3. **Make it easy to complain.** Make it easy for customers to complain via a toll-free "support" number and your web site; genuinely welcome complaints and news of problems.
4. **Design promotions carefully.** For packaged goods, promotions

are as large a source of complaints as quality issues; given the number of activities and functions involved, promotions must always be simple and well executed.

5. **Partner with your channels.** Use the contracting process with channels to set expectations regarding the customer experience and service levels. Also, provide your channels with incentives to report problems in enough detail that they can be prioritized.

It's worth taking the time to clearly formulate your views of the customer experience and to communicate them to your channel partners. In a sense, you can think of your channels as customers themselves, and compile useful information on them and on their experience with you—and then set expectations that can be met or exceeded.

NEVER DECLARE VICTORY; FOREVER STAY THE COURSE

We have worked with almost half of the Fortune 100, as well as with many other extremely successful companies. One of the most disturbing and disappointing occurrences I've seen is a really successful company with stellar customer experience that eventually stumbles. I've seen this happen in the auto, computer, food retailing, insurance, and pharmaceutical industries, among others.

I attribute this to two major issues. First, the company makes a major non-service-related mistake, such as a bad product decision followed by ignoring signals from the Voice of the Customer. The outcome prompts an unenlightened senior executive or financial manager to "slash and burn," shortchanging service to reduce costs. I have actually seen two companies decide to ship defective products to make their sales numbers, knowing that warranty complaints would skyrocket, *and* then reduce the warranty period, leaving customers without reasonable recourse and service without reasonable solutions. Both companies deservedly fell on very hard times.

Second, I've seen companies "declare victory" and even become arrogant, thinking that they can do no wrong. They believed their own hype and the satisfaction awards they had received. A great experience and continued loyalty was assumed, and attention and support went elsewhere in the company. Then new managers with new priorities came into critical functions. They sought to make a name for themselves and service was wonderful, so they cut costs and corners. Inevitably, service started to decline, often imperceptibly at first, then more markedly, usually taking about seven years to hit bottom. In a half-dozen companies, we've had to revisit the company in five to seven years to remind it why and how it used to deliver great customer experiences.

Creating great customer experiences—the key to continued loyalty and growth in revenue and profits—demands constant, diligent emphasis on and execution of the basics. You need ongoing Voice of the Customer information, well-designed systems and dedicated people, and financially justified policies and problem-solving procedures. You also need to understand the truly important strategic and tactical roles that customer service plays in creating the customer experience. Those roles have been so underplayed or poorly played in so many organizations that investing in customer service is one of the highest return opportunities in business today. Invariably, the data, the survey findings, and the experiences of companies that take a strategic approach to service bear this out, and I invite you to help your organization to realize those returns.

KEY TAKEAWAYS

1. You must have a detailed process map of all the touches your organization has with the customer.
2. Marketing, sales, and operations must agree to shift problems and tasks to service when service can handle them better; in most cases, sales should *not* be involved in solving routine problems and delivering routine service.
3. You must have at least 20 percent of incentive compensation tied to customer experience metrics or the program won't work.
4. A chief customer officer can facilitate alignment among the functions delivering the customer experience by using persuasive data to gain management commitment and achieving small successes followed by larger ones.
5. Complaints to your channel partners usually cause a 20 percent decrease in loyalty to your brand. Your channel service reflects on you; you have to be certain that channels understand the

value of a great customer experience to both of you and that they deliver it.

6. Once you're consistently delivering great customer experiences, the gravest danger is that you cut corners and shift your attention elsewhere; you can never declare victory.

POSTSCRIPT

What I've covered in this book is truly the tip of the iceberg of TARP's 38 years of experience. TARP has papers and data from literally every industry in existence. If you have issues that I have not addressed, please contact me at jgoodman@tarp.com and I'll be happy to share our experience.

Index